D0688801

WITHDRAWN

ART OF THE WORLD

NON-EUROPEAN CULTURES

THE HISTORICAL, SOCIOLOGICAL

AND RELIGIOUS BACKGROUNDS

THE ART OF THE SOUTH SEA ISLANDS

INCLUDING
AUSTRALIA AND NEW ZEALAND

BY ALFRED BUEHLER ·
TERRY BARROW · CHARLES P. MOUNTFORD

CROWN PUBLISHERS, INC., NEW YORK

The section on OCEANIA was translated by Ann E. Keep, who is grateful to Mr. B. A. L. Cranston, M.A., Assistant Keeper of the Department of Ethnology, British Museum, for reading the text and making many valuable sugestions.

Frontispiece: Marine animals on the sea-bed. Melville Island, northern Australia. *South Australian Museum, Adelaide. 35½ in. x 24½ in.*

FIRST PUBLISHED IN 1962

PRINTED IN HOLLAND
LIBRARY OF CONGRESS CATALOGUE CARD NUMBER: 62-11806

LIST OF PLATES

OCEANIA

Korwar figures. North-western New Guinea 36
Cult figures. Lake Sentani, northern New Guinea 41
Wall drapery. Humboldt Bay 44
Head-rest. Coast of Sepik River area 49
Spirit figure. Mbranda, Sepik River area 52
Painting from a cult-house. Kambrambo, lower Sepik 56
Shield on house. Tambunum, middle Sepik 58
Helmet-like mask. Tambunum, middle Sepik 64
Clan mask. Kararau, middle Sepik 68
Detail of two crocodile spirits. Ambanoli, middle Sepik lowlands 75
Painting from a cult-house. Slei, middle Sepik 78
Wooden board serving as door and part of door made of sheaths of palm-leaves. Upper Sepik 81
Cult figures. Southern border area of Sepik lowland 84
Cult figure. Djiginabu, northern Maprik territory 87
Painting from a cult-house. Ulupu, northern Maprik territory 90
Basketry mask. Numbungai, southern Maprik territory 93
Cult figures from a men's house. Jerik, Umboi I. 98
Dance shield. Trobriand Is. 101
Ancestor figure. Lorentz river, south-western New Guinea 102
Ceremonial poles. Coastal area of Asmat district, south-western New Guinea 107
Canoe ornament. Eilanden river, Asmat district, south-western New Guinea 110
Battle shields. Asmat district, south-western New Guinea 113
Shield mask. Wapo district, Gulf of Papua 116
Head mask. Purari district, Gulf of Papua 118
Door-jambs. Pitiliu I., Admiralty Is. 121
Cult-house with *malanggans*. Medina, north-western New Ireland 122/123
Head of a *malanggan* doll-like figure. Burra, north-western New Ireland 126
Malanggan frieze. Fessoa, north-western New Ireland 129
Mask belonging to a secret society. Gazelle peninsula, New Britain 130
Battle and dance shields. New Britain 133
Funerary figure. Bougainville, western Solomons 135
Fish figure. Wango, San Cristoval I., eastern Solomons 136
Mask belonging to a secret society. Southern Malekula, New Hebrides 138
Paintings from a cult-house. Gaua, Banks Is. 141
Door-jamb. Ouebia, New Caledonia 143
Dance mask. Bopope, New Caledonia 144
Striking part of club. Tonga Is. 147
Handle of fly-whisk. Tahiti 148
Image of a deity. Rurutu, Austral Is. 151
Image of a deity (Tiki). Marquesas Is. 154
Temple figure. Kailua, Hawaiian Is. 156
God of war. Hawaiian Is. 158
Feather cape. Hawaiian Is. 161
Detail of *tapa*. Hawaiian Is. 164
Ancestor figure. Easter I. 167
Plank of gable. Palau Is. 169
Detail of beam of house. Yap 171
Idol. Nukuoro, central Carolines 174
Face mask. Mortlock, central Carolines 177
Canoe ornament. Truk, central Carolines 182

NEW ZEALAND

Weapon (*patu paraoa*) 190
Border of flax cloak 192
Ancestral pendant (*hei tiki*) 195
Finial mask. East Coast district 198
Detail from facade of food store. Waerenga Village 201
Image on a godstick. Wanganui district 203
Ancestral images. Maketu, Bay of Plenty 205

AUSTRALIA

Marine animals. Melville I. 3
Head of Bainatja. North-eastern Arnhem Land 211
Bark painting: aboriginal spearing wallaby. Oenpelli, Northern Australia 214
Freshwater fish. Groote Eylandt 219
Shield. Northern Queensland 222
Carving of human head. North-western Australia 224

LIST OF MAPS AND TABLES

Australia and Oceania 24, 25
Table: Origin of local cultures in Australia and Oceania 30
New Guinea and Bismarck Archipelago 104, 105
Lower and Middle Sepik Area 189
Australia 206

LIST OF FIGURES

OCEANIA

1 — Round adze
2 — Rectangular adze
3 — Shouldered adzes and tanged adze
4 — Roof-top ornament. Aibom, L. Chambri, middle Sepik
5 — Idol. Choiseul I., Solomons
6 — Penis decoration. Admiralty Is.
7 — Dance and battle ornament. Ulupu, northern Maprik
8 — *Kapkap* breast-plates. Melanesia
9 — Ancestor skull. Central New Ireland
10 — Lime jar. Kilimbit, middle Sepik
11 — Lime container. Mussau I., St. Matthias Group
12 — Water-bowl. Umboi I.
13 — Adze. Central Carolines
14 — Decorative object from small house containing skulls. Choiseul I., Solomons
15 — Food-bowl. L. Sentani
16 — Head-rest. Geelvink Bay, north-western New Guinea
17 — Food-bowl. L. Sentani
18 — Ancestor figure. Awar, Hansa Bay, northern New Guinea
19 — Face masks. Lower Sepik
20 — Face masks. Yuat river area
21 — Masks. Middle Sepik
22 — Post from cult-house. Masanei, middle Korewori
23 — Bamboo lime container. Aibom, middle Sepik
24 — Prow of canoe. Kupkei, upper Sepik lowlands
25 — Ancestor figure. Astrolabe Bay. *Ethnographical Museum, Budapest*
26 — Cult figure. Finschhafen, Huon Gulf
27 — Cult figure. Umboi I.
28 — Food-bowl. Tami
29 — Face mask. Umboi I.
30 — Ornamentation on a wooden bowl. Tami
31 — Top of a wooden dance staff. Kiriwina, Trobriand Is.
32 — Wooden lime spatulae. Eastern tip of New Guinea and Kiriwina, Trobriand Is.
33 — Skull idol. Wapo-Gope area, west of Purari, Gulf of Papua
34 — Shield representing creative power. Ukurawi, Purari area, Gulf of Papua
35 — Detail of bark belt. Kerewa area, Gulf of Papua
36 — Decorative combs. Manus I., Admiralty Is.
37 — Figures on handles of wooden lime spatulae. Bipi I., Admiralty Is.
38 — Wooden lime spatula and spearhead. South coast of Manus I., Admiralty Is.
39 — Food-bowl. Iru, Manus I., Admiralty Is.
40 — Top of woman's dance staff. Mussau I., St. Matthias Group
41 — Striking part of club. Mussau I., St. Matthias Group
42 — Decorative comb. Mussau I., St. Matthias Group
43 — Middle piece of dance hood. Lelet plateau, central New Ireland

44 — Face mask. Omo, north-western New Ireland
45 — Head mask. Nemassalang, north-western New Ireland
46 — Cult figure. Konos, central New Ireland
47 — Ancestor figure. South central New Ireland
48 — Skull mask. Gazelle peninsula, New Britain
49 — Dance mask. Baining, Gazelle peninsula, New Britain
50 — Paddle. Buka I., Solomons
51 — Idol from a war canoe. Maravo Lagoon, New Georgia, Solomons
52 — Gable figure. Guadalcanal, Solomons
53 — Sarcophagus. Choiseul I., Solomons
54 — Food-bowl. San Cristoval, Solomons
55 — Dance club. Nitendi, Santa Cruz Is.
56 — Ancestor statue. Ambrym, New Hebrides
57 — Stone amulet. Ambrym, New Hebrides
58 — Roof-top ornament. Hienghene, New Caledonia
59 — Engraved bamboo. Oubatche, New Caledonia
60 — War club. New Caledonia
61 — Handles of lime spatulae. Kaniet, Para-Micronesia
62 — Oil-lamp. Fiji Is.
63 — War club. Fiji Is.
64 — Throwing-club. Fiji Is.
65 — War club. Tonga
66 — War club. Samoa
67 — Ornamentation on a ceremonial adze. Hervey I., Cook Is.
68 — Top of shaft of ceremonial paddle. Mangaia or Hervey I., Cook Is.
69 — Bottom of food-bowl. Nuku Hiva, Marquesas Is.
70 — Bread-fruit pounder. Tahiti and Marquesas Is.
71 — Belt. Oleai, Caroline Is.
72 — Foot-support on stilt. Marquesas Is.
73 — Architectural part from a men's house. Palau Is. *Museum für Völkerkunde, Hamburg*

The objects illustrated in Figs. 1—24 and 26—72 are in the Museum für Völkerkunde, Basle.

NEW ZEALAND

74 — God image. Okia Flat, Wickliffe Bay, Otago. *Otago Museum, Dunedin, N.Z.*
75 — *Manaia* creature. *K. A. Webster Collection, Dominion Museum, Wellington, N.Z.*
76 — *Marakihau.* Whakatane district. *B. P. Bishop Museum, Honolulu, Hawaiian Is.*
77 — Crayon impression from lid of feather-box. *Ipswich Museum, Suffolk*

AUSTRALIA

78 — Ground painting. Kalaia, northern Central Australia. *After photo by Charles P. Mountford*
79 — Petroglyph (the snake Yarapi). Nama, Central Australia. *After photo by Charles P. Mountford*
80 — Cave painting: running spearman. Inagurdurwil, Arnhem Land.
After photo by Charles P. Mountford
81 — Opossum-skin rug. Victoria. *National Museum of Victoria*
82 — Bark shields. South-eastern and South Australia.
Museum of Archaeology and Ethnology, Cambridge and British Museum
83 — Spear-throwers. South-eastern and north-western Australia.
British Museum and Museum of Archaeology and Ethnology, Cambridge
84 — Sacred object. Port Keats, Northern Australia. *Museum of Ethnography, Oslo*
85 — Smoking-pipe. North-eastern Arnhem Land. *South Australian Museum, Adelaide*
86 — Smoking-pipe. Milingimbi, Northern Australia. *Museum für Völkerkunde, Basle*
87 — Smoking-pipes. Milingimbi, Northern Australia. *Charles P. Mountford Collection*

88 — Sacred object. Northern Australia. *Museum of Ethnography, Göteborg*
89 — Ceremonial object. Western Australia. *British Museum*
90 — Ceremonial object. Central Australia. *Charles P. Mountford Collection*
91 — Smoking-pipe. Milingimbi, Northern Australia. *Museum für Völkerkunde, Basle*
92 — Ceremonial object. Central Australia. *Charles P. Mountford Collection*
93 — Sacred object. Port Keats, Northern Australia. *Museum of Ethnography, Oslo*
94 — Sacred object. North-western Australia. *British Museum*

Figures 1—73 were drawn by Valery Heussler, Basle, Figs. 74—77 by T. Barrow, Wellington, Figs. 78—80 by Hannes Pixa, Baden-Baden, and Figs. 81—94 by Charles P. Mountford, St. Peters, South Australia. The maps are the work of Hannes Pixa, using data supplied by Prof. A. Bühler.

ACKNOWLEDGMENTS

We take this opportunity of expressing our sincere thanks to all the private individuals, museums and institutions listed for their kindness in allowing reproduction of the plates on the following pages:

National Gallery of South Australia, Adelaide 211
South Australian Museum, Adelaide 3, 222
Koninklijk Instituut voor de Tropen, Amsterdam 107
Auckland Museum, Auckland 201, 205
Museum für Völkerkunde, Basle 41, 52, 56, 58, 64, 68, 75, 78, 81, 84, 87, 90, 93, 98, 102, 110, 113, 116, 118, 121, 122-23, 126, 129, 130, 133, 135, 136, 138, 141, 143, 144
Volkenkundig Museum 'Justinus van Nassau', Breda 44
University Museum of Archaeology and Ethnology, Cambridge 203
Ethnographische Sammlung der Universität Göttingen 147, 158, 164
Hamburgisches Museum für Völkerkunde und Vorgeschichte, Hamburg 169, 171, 174, 177, 182
Rautenstrauch-Joest Museum, Cologne (P. Lucken Collection) 49
Prof. Helmut Petri Collection, Cologne 224
Rijksmuseum voor Volkenkunde, Leyden 36
British Museum, London 101, 151, 156, 161, 167
Charles P. Mountford Collection 214, 219
Museum of Primitive Art, New York 148
Musée de l'Homme, Paris 154
Dominion Museum, Wellington 192, 198
Dominion Museum, Wellington (Oldman Collection) 190, 195

The coloured illustrations on the pages below were kindly supplied by:

T. Barrow 190, 192, 195, 198, 201, 203, 205
R. Kleinhempel, Hamburg 169, 171, 174, 177, 182
Ch. P. Mountford 3, 211, 214, 219, 222, 224
R. L. Mellema, Amsterdam 107
Fotowerkstätten H. Schmitz, Cologne 49
Schwitzer AG, Basle 41, 52, 56, 58, 64, 68, 75, 78, 81, 84, 87, 90, 93, 98, 102, 110, 113, 116, 118, 121, 122-23, 126, 129, 130, 132, 135, 136, 138, 141, 143, 144
J. Skeel, Orpington 101, 151, 156, 161, 167
Ch. Uht, New York 148
G. Vinaver, Paris 154
Fa. Foto Wollscheid, Göttingen 147, 158, 164

CONTENTS

List of plates and maps (5-6). List of figures (6).

INTRODUCTION 13–14

I. GEOGRAPHICAL SETTING, PEOPLES AND CIVILIZATIONS . . 15–36

Geographical setting (15): *area, physical structure* (15); *climate* (15); *vegetation* (16); *fauna* (16); process of settlement (17): *Asian origin of population* (17); *methods of research* (17); *successive waves of migrants* (18); *races* (19); *languages* (19); *cultures* (19): *Australians and Tasmanians* (19); *Papuans* (21); *round adze culture* (21); *Pre-Austronesian cultures* (22); *Austronesians* (22); *Southern Austronesians* (22); *Austromelanids* (23); *northern Austronesians and Polynesians* (23); *Micronesians* (26); *Indonesians* (26); *links with ancient Eurasiatic and Asiatic cultures* (26); *Dongson* (27); *Megalithic cultures* (27); *causes of the migrations* (28); *local cultures* (28). Modern Oceania: its peoples and their cultures (29): *Melanesia* (31); *Polynesia* (31); *Micronesia* (31); *common characteristics* (32); *technique* (32); *economic life* (33); *social structures* (34); *religious beliefs* (35).

II. PRINCIPLES OF OCEANIC ART 37–54

Culture and art (37): *nature of art* (37); *decoration* (40); *content* (40); *function* (42); *nature of primitive art* (43); *conventional art* (45); *'message'* (45); *arts and crafts: 'independent' and 'bound' art* (45); *art and environment* (48); *raw materials* (51); *art and technique* (51).

III. RELIGIOUS, SOCIAL AND TECHNOLOGICAL BASIS OF OCEANIC ART 55–96

Religious beliefs and social organization (55): *dynamism* (57); *mana* (59); *taboo* (59); *magic* (59); *animism* (60); *animatism* (60); *manism* (60); *totemism* (60); *polytheism* (61); *culture heroes and 'donors of salvation'* (61); *Supreme Being* (61); *mentality of primitive peoples* (62); *inner insecurity* (63); *order and orientation* (65); *religious experience* (66); *manifestations of divine power* (67); *passage and fertility rites* (70); *secret societies* (70); *signs of degeneration* (71); *ancestor worship* (71); *Melanesia* (72); *myths* (72); *Papuan culture* (72); *round adze culture* (73); *cannibalism* (76); *Austronesian culture* (76); *Polynesian culture* (77); *theological doctrines* (79); *mana* (79); *Micronesian culture* (80); *ancestor worship* (82). Social structures (82): *social func-*

tion of works of art (85). Technology (86): *raw materials: mineral* (86); *animal and human* (88); *vegetable* (89); *colouring* (91); *tools* (91); *art forms* (94). The artist's social status (94); *artistic sense* (96).

97–180 IV. STYLE PROVINCES AND STYLES

Melanesia (97); New Guinea (97): *north-western New Guinea* (99); *Humboldt Bay and Lake Sentani* (100); *Sepik district* (103); *coastal area* (108); *Lower Sepik* (109); *Yuat* (109); *Middle Sepik* (109); *Washkuk, Yeshan* (109); *Korewori* (110); *Upper Sepik* (111); *southern border areas* (112); *Maprik* (114); *Astrolabe Bay* (115); *Huon Gulf, Tami* (117); *Massim area* (120); *southern New Guinea* (124); *south-western New Guinea* (124); *Mimika* (125); *Asmat* (127); *Marind-anim* (128); *Gulf of Papua* (131); *Torres Straits islands* (134). Other parts of Melanesia (137): *Admiralty Is.* (137); *St. Matthias group* (140); *New Ireland* (140); *north-western New Ireland, Tabar Is.* (142); *central New Ireland* (146); *Namatanai* (146); *New Britain* (149); *Baining* (149); *south coast, Gazelle peninsula* (150); *Solomon Is.* (152); *western Solomons* (153); *central Solomons* (153); *eastern Solomons* (155); *Santa Cruz* (157); *Banks Is., New Hebrides* (157); *New Caledonia, Loyalty Is.* (160); *Para-Micronesia (outlying islands of north-western Polynesia)* (163). Polynesia (164): *Fiji* (165); *Tonga, Samoa* (166); *Society Is. (Tahiti)* (169); *Cook and Austral Is.* (169); *Marquesas Is.* (172); *Sandwich Is. (Hawaii)* (173); *Easter I.* (176). Micronesia (179): *Palau Is.* (179); *Carolines* (180).

181–189 V. THE ART STYLES OF OCEANIA AND THEIR HISTORICAL SIGNIFICANCE

Melanesia (181); *Papuans* (183); *round adze culture* (183); *Southern Austronesians* (183); *Austromelanids* (183); *Indonesians* (184); *Polynesia* (184); *Micronesia* (185). General characteristics of Oceanic art (185): *art of early planters* (186); *Oceanic styles* (187).

191–206 ART OF THE NEW ZEALAND MAORI

Adaptation to environment (191). Settlement of New Zealand (191): *seafaring tradition* (193); *media of the Maori craftsmen* (193). Classification of arts (194): *craftsmen-priests* (194). *Garment manufacture* (194); *rafter painting* (194); *decorated lattice-work* (196); *rock paintings, petroglyphs* (196); *jade ornaments* (196); *tattoo* (197). *Origin of wood-carving* (197); *symbols of wood-carving* (199); *ancestral and god images* (199); *ceremonial house carvings* (200); *foodstore carvings* (202); *the manaia* (202). *Avian hypothesis* (202); *the lizard symbol* (204); *the marakihau* (204). *Surface decorations* (204). Concluding remarks (204): *Maori art today* (206).

THE ABORIGINAL ART OF AUSTRALIA . . . . 207—225

Introduction (207). *Climate* (207); *techniques and materials* (209). Painting (209). Rock markings (212): *engraving* (212). Sculpture (213). Cave paintings (213): *hand silhouettes* (213). North-western Australia (214): *wandjinas* (214); *giro-giro (215); X-ray style* (216); *mimis* (217); Rock markings (217): *pocked markings* (217); *outline rock engravings* (218)); *rock poundings* (219); *ground paintings* (220); *ground carvings* (220). *Initiation and burial trees* (220); *burial trees and coffins* (220). Bark paintings (221). Movable art (221): *tools and weapons* (222); *sacred objects* (222); *pearl-shell ornaments* (223); *sculpture of the human figure* (223). Place of the artist in the tribe (223).

APPENDICES . . . . 227—250

Bibliography (235). Glossary (228). Index (241).

OCEANIA

BY

ALFRED BÜHLER

INTRODUCTION

The art of the South Seas has acquired a great vogue during the past few years. The first to experience its fascination were painters and sculptors, some of whom came to admire it with an enthusiasm that found reflection in their works. Subsequently its appeal spread ever wider among the general public. Today carvings and paintings from Oceania are no longer merely curiosities displayed in museums of ethnology, but important documents that help us to understand and appreciate the art of mankind as a whole. The effort to comprehend and interpret the art of exotic peoples is characteristic of our own age, when new conceptions of art have obtained an established foothold alongside the old humanistic ideals, strong though the latter still may be.

At the same time, however, it must be borne in mind that we cannot understand exotic art completely unless we are familiar with its postulates and fundamental principles, which are not to be found – or at least not exclusively – in the urge to artistic creation itself. Art is a human activity, and as such is closely connected with the culture that gives rise to it. This applies with particular force to primitive peoples. For this reason, when studying the arts of Oceania, we must proceed from the people themselves and the character and history of their civilization if we are to understand their art in its essentials, and not simply take a superficial emotional view of it. This is why in this volume a good deal of space has been given to the study of environmental factors and the general principles involved. It seems to me that these are more important than detailed descriptions, which can after all never be absolutely comprehensive.

Even when one has become reasonably familiar with the general principles underlying Oceanic art, it is still quite a difficult matter to interpret such works of art correctly, and there are still many questions on which it is impossible for us to come to definite conclusions. Generally speaking, we have to rely upon collections in museums. But these are necessarily somewhat 'lifeless', or at least seem to give the works of art they contain an entirely alien character. Far removed from their natural location, and divorced from their original context, they stand there in total isolation, without any relationship to the community from which they sprang. Often their original significance is hardly known, or can only with difficulty be made apparent to the viewer. Moreover, in many instances their outward appearance has also changed considerably: thus it is not uncommon to find that the painted decoration characteristic of many works from the South Seas has disappeared, or has

been preserved only in part. The objects we see in collections and museums thus have only a remote connection with real life. The disadvantages of housing art collections in museums are particularly apparent in this field.
With few exceptions it is unfortunately no longer possible to study the arts of the South Seas *in situ*. This is not so with regard to certain parts of Australia, New Guinea, and some small areas in Melanesia, but elsewhere this art disappeared or degenerated long ago. Oceania came within the orbit of our own civilization at a relatively late date, but the shock that resulted from this contact had particularly disastrous effects in this area. Although the remarks made in the following pages are usually phrased in the present tense, in almost every instance they refer to things as they were before the arrival of the white man, or at least before the encroachment of European civilization took place on a large scale.
Australia, New Zealand and other parts of Oceania are here treated separately by different authors. This is entirely justified so far as Australia is concerned, since the cultures and art of this continent were isolated from other parts of the world, and the connections that existed with Oceania were insignificant. New Zealand, however, was linked much more closely to the other islands and ought really to be treated as one of the regions of Polynesia both from the cultural and artistic point of view. But at the same time it is one of the largest and most important regions, with a style of its own, and this makes it legitimate to consider it separately.
The scope of this book is limited in the main to phenomena that can be regarded as belonging to art in the narrow sense of the term, although from time to time mention is made of implements, weapons and other objects of everyday use. In such cases we are usually referring to the decoration on such objects rather than to the objects themselves. Little attention has been paid to clothing and ornaments.
Of the three main regions into which Oceania is divided, we have concentrated primarily on Melanesia, so that Polynesia and Micronesia have received less detailed treatment. This is not accidental. Polynesia and Micronesia are far from possessing such an abundance of artistic treasures as Melanesia can boast of, and furthermore the latter region contains some areas, such as New Guinea in particular, about which little has so far been written in studies of Oceanic art.
No mention has been made of the rock paintings of Oceania, some of which are truly magnificent works of art. Little is known about their origin, and lack of space makes it impossible to discuss them here.
Our thanks are due to the authorities of all the museums who kindly allowed us to reproduce works of art in their possession and supplied information, and especially to Dr. C. A. Schmitz, who frequently gave valuable advice and criticism with regard to the section on Oceania.

I. GEOGRAPHICAL SETTING, PEOPLES AND CIVILIZATIONS

GEOGRAPHICAL SETTING

The Pacific Ocean extends over more than one third of the earth's surface. Apart from the northernmost part, it is only in the tropical regions and the south-west of this limitless watery waste that land is to be found. Within the tropical zone lie many thousands of islands, scattered across an area eight times larger than Europe. This is often referred to as the South Seas, and these island groups are nowadays commonly known as Oceania.

Size, physical structure

The total land area of Oceania covers approximately 463,000 square miles, which is a little more than one-eighth the size of Europe. New Guinea and New Zealand alone, the two largest islands, comprise more than 386,000 square miles in area. Both they and other large islands are situated in the western part of Oceania, and form the so-called inner island belt, the remains of a former continent that included Australia. They consist of ancient folded mountains, crystalline massifs and volcanoes, some of which are still active. Considered from a geographical point of view, the inner island belt, apart from New Zealand, forms part of Melanesia. As one goes further eastwards the islands in the outer belt generally speaking become smaller, until one reaches the far-flung outpost of Easter Island, which, however, is still more than 2500 miles distant from the coast of America. Some islands are mountainous ('high islands'), consisting of deposits of recent volcanic rock, including a few volcanoes that are active, and often with coral reefs. But most of them are low coral islands built upon submarine banks or volcanic massifs; these are not by any means absent in the west, but occur there far less frequently. Geographers divide the outer island belt into Polynesia in the east and Micronesia in the north. The total land area of Polynesia comprises an area somewhat greater than that of Switzerland, and extends over about 17,750 square miles, whereas the area of Micronesia is only 1042 square miles.

Climate

The term Oceania itself indicates the dominant role played by the ocean in this area. With its reef-building corals it helped to form the land. Above all, to a considerable extent it determines the climate of these islands. In spite of the predominantly tropical latitudes temperatures are seldom extremely high, even on the large islands. The masses of water have a compensating effect, so that the daily and annual variations in temperature are minimal. This fact, combined with the generally heavy precipitation, results in a hot and humid climate that remains even throughout the year. Local variations are evident only on the larger islands. Thus it can be very cold in the mountainous areas of New Guinea, and the glaciers of the South Island of New Zealand are one of its best-known features; but since this island lies in a high southerly latitude special conditions prevail here. On the larger islands precipitation is not always distributed evenly throughout the year. Alternating wind systems and the existence of mountain ranges which cause the rain to fall on the windward side may together lead to alternating rainy and dry seasons, but these are, however, only seldom very marked.

Vegetation

The hot-house climate of Oceania produces a luxuriance of plant life wherever the soil is sufficiently fertile. For this reason the mountainous islands in the west and all volcanic land formations where the rainfall is particularly heavy owing to the high relief are covered with almost impenetrable jungle, with swamps of palm-trees, reeds and rushes in the lowlands. Man has been unable to make any great modification of his natural environment in this region. It is true that grassy downland has been formed in areas that were once arable land, but one also comes across natural grasslands, particularly in the highlands of New Guinea; elsewhere the jungle soon reconquers plantations and gardens as soon as they are left untended. These green islands often give the impression of being dismal, monotonous and oppressive, despite their incredible luxuriance of vegetation. The flora is extraordinarily varied, although the variety of species diminishes the further east one goes. The vegetation is in general scanty on the low coral islands, with their barren and porous calcareous soil, where conditions are far from favourable for plant life. For this reason these islands, with their sparse undergrowth and ever-present palms, their dazzling white sandy beaches and foaming breakers, with the sea changing in colour from a brilliant green or deep blue to black, and the bright blue sky almost invariably dotted with clouds in fantastic shapes, present a sharp and pleasing contrast, both scenically and aesthetically, to those islands that are mountainous and heavily wooded, which are often enshrouded in mist all day long, and give the impression of fearsome and inhospitable places.

The flora of Oceania provides man with numerous kinds of foodstuffs, of which the most important are bread-fruit, the produce of the various sorts of palm that grow over the greater part of the area, and in swampy regions sago, obtained from the pith of one particular species of palm. Wood, bast and fibres, the leaves and buds of many plants, and the skin of various kinds of fruit all play an important part throughout the whole region in the fashioning of implements, weapons and ornaments.

Fauna

The fauna in Oceania lacks variety. Only in the west are large animals to be found in a wild state, among them marsupials (in New Guinea, in particular) and pigs, which were originally introduced as domesticated animals but then ran wild. There is, however, great diversity so far as bird life is concerned. The largest bird is the cassowary, found in New Guinea and some of the islands in the Bismarck Archipelago. As is also the case with the other fauna, the number of different species diminishes as one proceeds further eastwards. The sea and rivers abound in fish, crabs and shell-fish, as well as other kinds of edible animals and plants. Throughout the area the bones and teeth of various animals, and also the shells of turtles and molluscs, are an important source of raw material for making implements, weapons and ornaments. Finally, in many parts feathers are highly prized for various decorative purposes.

THE PROCESS OF SETTLEMENT

Oceania stretches far out into the Pacific, but the largest land masses lie close to south-east Asia, the Malay Archipelago and Australia, whereas in the easternmost parts one finds only very small islands, the furthest of which are still some thousands of miles distant from the South American continent. Thus for geographical reasons alone it seems clear that Oceania was settled from the west – i.e., from Asia, for Australia, lying as it does on the margin of the earth's populated areas, must be ruled out as a possible source. The theory that immigration may have taken place from America was advanced in earlier times, but was later discarded; it is only in recent years that it has again been put forward by Th. Heyerdahl, the Norwegian explorer whose voyage on the *Kon-Tiki* brought him great fame. But his hypothesis that Polynesia, and lands still further west, were settled by people coming from north-western and South America has been rejected by the majority of scholars. We may be almost certain that the peoples of Oceania and their civilizations originated in the Old World. There is indeed important evidence to show that migration took place eastwards across the Pacific to America, where the immigrants exercised an astonishingly potent cultural influence. On the other hand, we have only a few traces of such influences in the reverse direction. By far the most important of these is the South American batata (sweet potato), which was introduced to Oceania not by seafarers from America but by Polynesians who succeeded in reaching that continent. From Oceania the sweet potato eventually spread westwards as far as New Guinea. Other evidence that Asia was the cradle of the peoples of Oceania is provided by the fact that, apart from the indigenous sago palm, all the most important cultivated plants came from the west. This is also the case with regard to domesticated animals such as dogs, pigs and fowl.

Asian origin of population

Although it is now more or less generally accepted that Oceania was settled from the west, it has by no means been fully established which parts of Asia these peoples came from, when they came, or which route they took. On these points opinions are still divided, the reason being that written records exist only for the last few centuries of the history of the South Seas, from the time of the first European voyages of discovery onwards, and these naturally contain only a very small amount of reliable historical evidence. The Oceanic peoples themselves have no script, except the inhabitants of Easter Island, whose tablets merely contain ritual instructions, chants and genealogies and may in fact be something in the nature of mnemonic tables rather than inscriptions in the proper sense of the word. Nor are the oral traditions of the Polynesians, although often surprisingly exact, really reliable for the early period of settlement; and in any case these cover only part of the area.

Methods of research

For purpose of historical research we thus have to rely mainly on the racial, linguistic and cultural characteristics of the Oceanic peoples. But under the pressure of modern civilization many of the South Seas cultures disappeared or degenerated before they could be investigated properly, while in other areas such studies have yet to be carried out. Especially in New Guinea, one of the key areas in the history of Oceanic settlement, there are still districts that have not yet been fully explored, let alone studied. These gaps constitute in themselves a serious impediment to historical research. Still more serious, however, are the questions of principle that have to be solved when utilizing anthropological, ethnological and linguistic data to establish the record of the past. At first sight it might be thought a straightforward matter, when faced with affinities in race, language or culture, to infer that some contact existed in the past between the peoples concerned. But in reality such methods, particularly in the field of ethnology, are complicated and unreliable. For example, cultural affinities do not necessarily have historical causes, but may also occur for other reasons. It is quite feasible for peoples at the same simple level of technical development, and living in more or less the same geographical environment, to arrive at the same or similar cultural attainments independently of one another under the pressure of external circumstance. In the same way such coincidences may occur as a result of the existence of certain intellectual characteristics that are common to all human beings. Cultural affinities may thus be the product of history, but they can also be due to quite different causes. Unfortunately no fool-proof method exists whereby one can decide with complete certainty in each case whether the occurrence of similar cultural phenomena should be regarded simply as a coincidence or whether it should be seen as the result of particular historical events. In most instances we still lack sufficient data to come to firm conclusions. Students of the history of culture in the South Seas have no alternative but to attempt to gain as complete an understanding as possible of individual cultural phenomena (e.g., agriculture and the aids employed in farming, shapes of tools and weapons, methods of fishing and hunting, social structures, beliefs and rites, artistic forms and styles) and to compare them with each other in the various cultures where they occur. Where striking affinities or even coincidences are to be found, one may infer the existence of historical links, which may have been either strong or weak in each individual case; and by pursuing this method consistently one can make progress towards an understanding of the history of culture. But owing to the difficulties mentioned above, we have to remember that we are dealing only with hypotheses and not with authentic evidence. It is precisely the absence of objective criteria that is responsible for the astonishingly wide divergences often met with in studies of the subject. There would be no point in mentioning these divergences here and attempting to weigh one against the other. The object of the remarks that ensue is merely to give a general outline of the process whereby the islands of Oceania came to be settled, following the views of the most reliable modern authorities.

Successive waves of immigrants

The racial, linguistic and cultural evidence all point to the fact that Oceania was peopled by settlers who arrived in successive waves at different times.

One of the most striking features is that Polynesia and Micronesia give the impression of far greater homogeneity than Melanesia. The history of migration in the western parts of Oceania is apparently more complex than that of the migrations in the east and north.

Races

Turning first of all to the ethnic data, we observe a preponderance of dark-skinned people in the western parts of Oceania, whereas Polynesia and Micronesia are in the main inhabited by men whose skin is lighter in colour. Generally speaking, the former live predominantly in New Guinea (we are not concerned here with Australia), while parts of northern New Guinea and the other Melanesian islands form a hybrid zone where intermingling has taken place with men whose skin colour is lighter. But except perhaps in some parts of Australia groups of people of pure stock are nowhere to be found, whereas mixed groups exist everywhere. The ethnic composition is most variegated in the west, particularly in the Melanesian hybrid zone.

Languages

The linguistic picture in Oceania corresponds to the ethnic one, in so far as here, too, we can distinguish between two main groups. Those belonging to the light-skinned group speak Malayo-Polynesian or Austronesian languages, characterized by an astonishing uniformity of grammar and vocabulary; these are sub-divided into Polynesian, Micronesian and Melanesian dialects. In the area inhabited by dark-skinned races the main languages spoken are very different from one another, and so far it has not been established how they are related, if indeed they are related at all. They were formerly called Papuan languages (except for the Australian group). Nowadays the term generally used is non-Austronesian or pre-Austronesian. As in the case of ethnic composition, so also here Melanesia is a zone of contact and fusion between the two groups of languages. Austronesian idioms have, however, frequently found their way far into the area inhabited by dark-skinned peoples, where they have ousted the pre-Austronesian languages. Today the latter are still to be found only in New Guinea (particularly in the interior and south of the island), as well as in the Louisiade Archipelago and parts of the Admiralty Islands, New Britain, New Ireland and the Solomons. In other places fusion with Austronesian has occurred. For the history of Oceanic migrations it is not unimportant that vestiges of pre-Austronesian languages have also been noted in Micronesian and Polynesian idioms and that Micronesian has to a considerable extent been split up and interspersed with Indonesian elements.

Cultures

Similarly, cultural conditions also show a contrast between Melanesia and the other parts of Oceania. Polynesia and Micronesia are again relatively homogeneous, whereas Melanesia is split up into numerous diverse local cultures. This fact, as well as the anthropological and linguistic picture, indicates that settlement occurred at an early date and that its history is complex.

Australians and Tasmanians

On the basis of our present knowledge we have to assume that towards the close of the great Ice Age and pluvial period (Pleistocene) dark-skinned people, some of whom were actually Negroid, arrived in New Guinea and from there moved on to Australia and Tasmania. These were Palaeolithic and Mesolithic hunters and food-gatherers – nomadic people with a primitive level of technology. As they possessed no seaworthy boats they must have reached the new areas in which they settled mainly on foot. This was possible because during the Pleistocene the sea-level was about 330 feet lower than it is today. Between Asia, New Guinea, Australia and Tasmania there existed many isthmuses of land, and the narrow straits could be crossed by means of primitive rafts and canoes.

The Tasmanians were the first people to arrive during this early period. It is not certain where they came from, but bones and stone implements of Tasmanian type found in Thailand, Indochina and the eastern islands of Indonesia suggest that they originated in south-east Asia. Radio-carbon datings indicate that people of Tasmanian culture lived in southern Australia already during the eleventh millennium B.C. The Tasmanians must therefore have reached New Guinea earlier still. The Australians, who are also dark-skinned but have no Negroid traits, also arrived in their present home from south-east Asia by way of New Guinea. One radio-carbon dating shows that they were living in southern Australia as early as the fifth millennium B.C. They did not penetrate as far as Tasmania. These two groups of immigrants, the first to arrive in the area, had a decisive influence upon the cultural picture. In Tasmania there was only a single basic culture right up to the 19th century, when the aboriginal population was exterminated. In the case of some of the local cultures in Australia that are still extant we may assume the existence of a Tasmanian lower stratum; in the north there were important influences in more recent times from Indonesia and New Guinea.

Much less clear is the significance of the Tasmanian and Australian basic culture in New Guinea and other parts of Melanesia. Both Tasmanians and Australians probably migrated along the coasts of New Guinea, mainly following the southern shore of the island. But they did not penetrate into the interior, except possibly in the region of the large rivers, for as nomadic hunters completely ignorant of plant cultivation they found the most favourable conditions in the low-lying areas. The large number of sago-palms found there today were already then an inexhaustible source of edible plants; in addition there was doubtless enough game available for the relatively thin

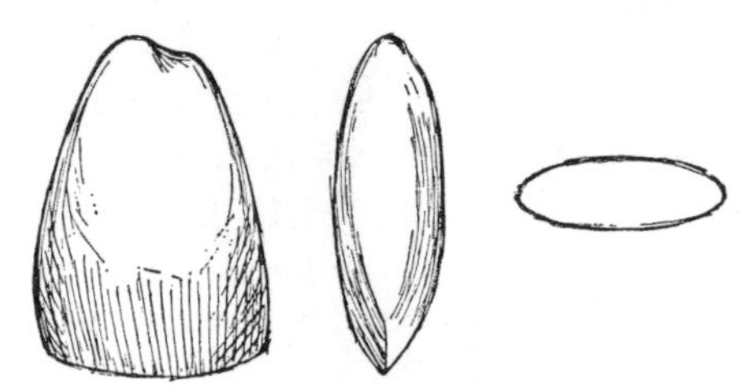

FIG. 1 – *Round adze, with* (extreme right) *cross-section.* *Cf. p. 21.*

population, and an abundance of fish that could be caught even with their very primitive equipment. People supporting themselves in this way are still to be found today on the south coast of western New Guinea, and less frequently in the interior of the island and in the north. It is thought that these cultures originated with the Tasmanian and Australian migrants. One common view is that in New Guinea the Tasmanians and Australians fused to form a hybrid race and culture known as Papuan. Other ethnologists, however, regard the Papuans as yet another group of dark-skinned immigrants, who also came to New Guinea by the land route and who, because of their Negroid traits, were more closely related to the Tasmanians than to the Australians; they may perhaps derive from the same root. However this may be, at first the Papuans were certainly only nomadic hunters, whose technical attainments were modest. They then proceeded to spread, mainly in the lowlands of New Guinea, but subsequently, under the pressure of later immigrants, were driven back into areas in the interior. The different conditions they met with here may have led them to develop a primitive type of agriculture by their own independent efforts.

Papuans

Papuan culture is almost exclusive to New Guinea and has survived chiefly in the western areas along the south coast and in the interior, as for instance in the hilly and swampy areas on the upper reaches of the river Sepik, where semi-nomadic tribes still live today. Outside New Guinea conclusive evidence has not yet been found of the existence of Papuan culture, although traces of it are said to have survived in New Britain.

Round adze people

The last major immigration of dark-skinned Negroid peoples took place after the end of the Pleistocene, mainly by sea. With them there found its way into Oceania the so-called round adze culture, named after the characteristic stone adzes, the blades of which are polished on both sides and have an oval form in cross-section. These people seem to have originated in southern Asia, but on their migration to Oceania they set out from China or Japan. In most cases they came by way of Formosa, the Philippines, Celebes and the Moluccas, until they reached the coastal lands of New Guinea and finally came to other parts of Melanesia, where round adze cultures still exist in their characteristic form. The beginning of these migrations has been assigned to a date between 3500 and 2000 B.C. Radio-carbon tests carried out on archaeological finds from this culture on Saipan (one of the Marianas, off the main route of their migration) have yielded the date of 1527 B.C., and others on New Caledonia the year 847 B.C. These settlers did not reach Australia, or, if they did, only in insignificant numbers. From an economic point of view the round adze culture is characterized by extensive development of agriculture, based upon cultivation of tuberous plants (taro) and the raising of pigs, and in the technical field by pottery and the polishing of stone. They may already have had outrigger canoes as well as primitive boats.

In parts of New Guinea the round adze people ousted the earlier immigrants, but in many cases they intermingled with them. For this reason it is hardly possible to distinguish between the different strata in the local cultures of the present day. These cultures are therefore often referred to simply as pre-Austronesian, by which is meant the hybrid culture that may have existed before the arrival of the Austronesians.

Pre-Austronesian cultures

In these pre-Austronesian cultures the influence of the round adze culture was decisive in the eastern parts of the island and on the northern slopes of the central mountain range (except for isolated areas in the interior, and those regions, particularly in the north-east, where more recent influences have made themselves felt). The round adze culture is also much in evidence in the Louisiade Archipelago, in parts of the Admiralty Islands, in New Ireland, the northern Solomons and in the mountainous areas of other Melanesian islands, but is met with less frequently the further one goes towards the south-east. Here too it has been overlaid or ousted by more recent cultures. Vestiges of it are also to be seen in Micronesia and Polynesia. But it has not yet been established whether these are due to round adze immigrants or are related to the Melanesian hybrid cultures which will be dealt with below.

Austronesians

The most important of the light-skinned immigrants who settled in Oceania are the Austronesians, a mixed race composed of Caucasoid and Mongoloid elements. They originated from eastern or north-eastern Asia, whence they spread over a vast area – or at least made their influence felt there; the area in which Austronesian languages are to be found extends from Madagascar (with off-shoots on the east coast of Africa) as far as Easter Island. They reached Oceania in two main streams, which most probably already developed independent cultures of their own after they left the area whence they both originated. Probably between 1500 and 700 B.C. (according to some authorities, much later) the various waves of the first (southern) group reached the northern coast of New Guinea and the other Melanesian islands by way of the Philippines, Indochina, Malacca and Indonesia; they did not penetrate as far as Australia. The second (northern) wave came much later, perhaps after the beginning of the Christian era; these immigrants began their journeyings in China and travelled via Formosa, the Philippines and Moluccas to Micronesia and Polynesia.

FIG. 2

The Austronesian immigrants, too, were Neolithic cultivators, but they were also excellent fishermen. They had quadrangular adzes, the blades of which are rectangular in cross-section. Their well-designed outrigger canoes were excellently suited for voyages across the high seas, and for this reason we may assume that they also reached the remoter parts of Oceania. Mention has already been made of the theory that pre-Austronesian round adze people made their way from Melanesia far to the east. If this is correct, then the second wave of Austronesian immigrants must have encountered a dark-skinned population with a culture of their own. But on the other hand there is a good deal of weighty evidence that supports the view that the earlier (southern) Austronesian immigrants, who came from Indonesia, fused with

FIG. 2 — Centre: *rectangular adze.* Left: *cross-section.* Right: *longitudinal section. Cf. p. 22.*

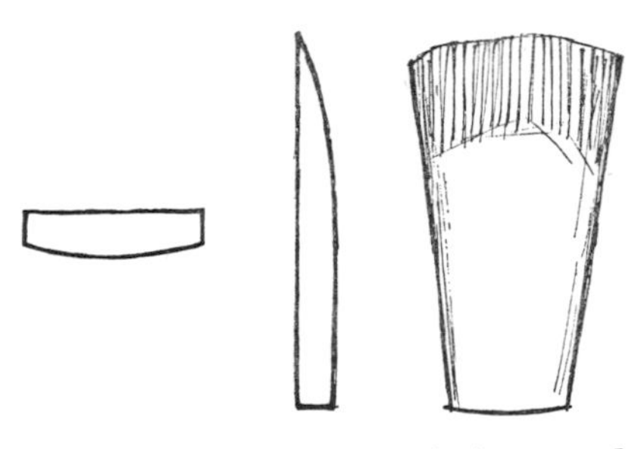

the pre-Austronesian population on the northern coast of New Guinea and on other Melanesian islands; and this is held to have produced the Austromelanid hybrid culture with its numerous local variants. According to this theory it was these peoples, who were of mixed race and culture, who then undertook further journeys to Polynesia and parts of Micronesia. It was thus from them, and not from early immigrants, that the Negroid traits and pre-Austronesian cultural phenomena found in Polynesia are derived. In any case it is beyond doubt that parts of Polynesia must have been settled already in early times. In Samoa, for example, this has been confirmed by radio-carbon tests that yielded dates in the first century A.D. In New Guinea the Austromelanid hybrid culture has survived, especially on the north coast, but also on the eastern part of the south coast, whence it spread into the interior as well. In addition it is to be found on all the other Melanesian islands (together with remnants of the pre-Austronesian influences mentioned earlier, such as the round adze culture).

Austromelanids

The second major immigration of Austronesians from the north, which also no doubt occurred in several waves, followed the route through Formosa and the Moluccas, as has already been stated. It must have begun at a fairly late date, and did not reach Oceania until the period 500 B.C. – 300 A.D. In contrast to the first main stream, their route led through Micronesia, where the Carolines presumably formed a base for voyages further afield. These voyages were probably carried out by small groups who first of all reached the Society Islands and the Samoa-Tonga group by way of the Gilbert, Ellice and Phoenix Islands. It was from these two centres that the other islands were peopled, although in the case of Hawaii (Sandwich Is.) it is arguable that this archipelago may have first been reached directly from the Marshall Islands. The 7th century saw a climax in Polynesian voyages of discovery. These were clearly not undertaken merely from a spirit of adventure but because they were essential in order to find new lands for the support of the increasing population. After the year 700 Polynesians advanced as far as the Marquesas, Hawaii, the Tuamotu Archipelago and Easter Island; some even reached the western coast of South America. New Zealand was also discovered and settled as early as the 10th century. It was reached a second time in approximately 1350 by the 'Great Fleet' from the Society Islands, the arrival of which is recorded in myth and legend.

Northern Austronesians, Polynesians

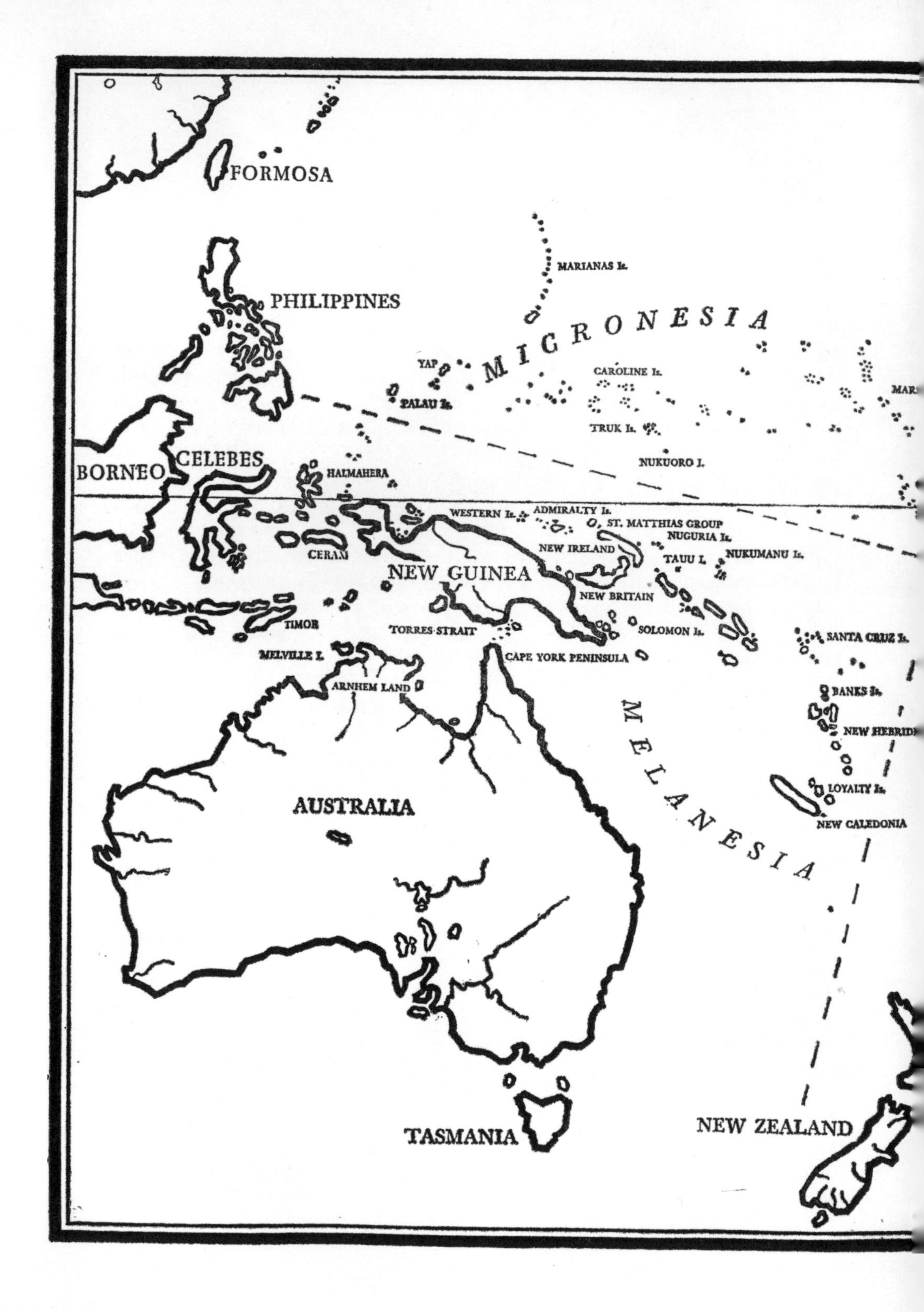
FORMOSA
MARIANAS Is.
PHILIPPINES
MICRONESIA
YAP
CAROLINE Is.
PALAU Is.
TRUK Is.
NUKUORO I.
BORNEO
CELEBES
HALMAHERA
WESTERN Is.
ADMIRALTY Is.
ST. MATTHIAS GROUP
NUGURIA Is.
NEW IRELAND
CERAM
TAUU I.
NUKUMANU Is.
NEW GUINEA
NEW BRITAIN
TIMOR
TORRES STRAIT
SOLOMON Is.
SANTA CRUZ Is.
MELVILLE I.
CAPE YORK PENINSULA
ARNHEM LAND
BANKS Is.
MELANESIA
LOYALTY Is.
AUSTRALIA
NEW CALEDONIA
TASMANIA
NEW ZEALAND

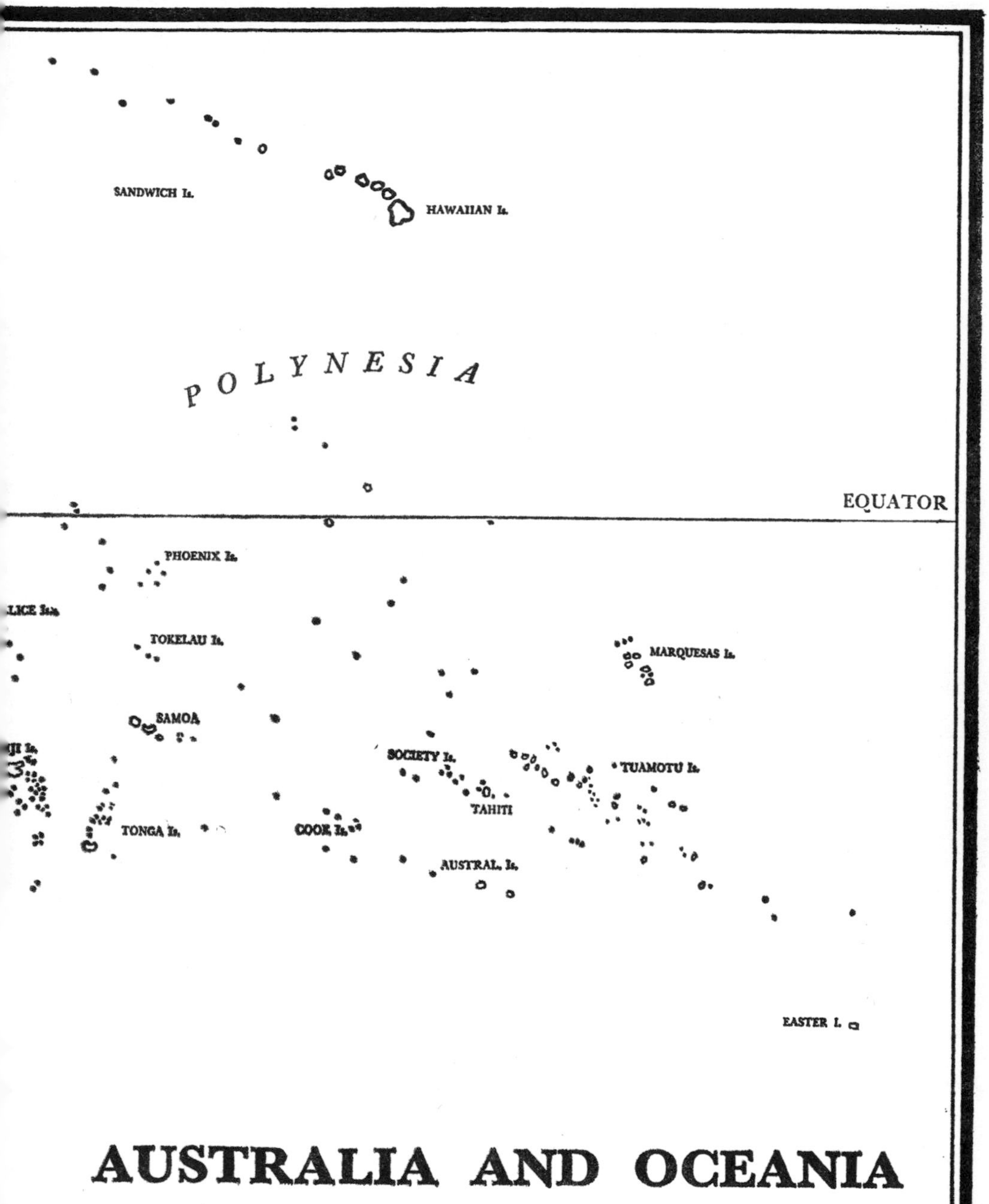

SANDWICH Is.

HAWAIIAN Is.

POLYNESIA

EQUATOR

PHOENIX Is.

LICE Is.

TOKELAU Is.

MARQUESAS Is.

SAMOA

JI Is.

SOCIETY Is.

TUAMOTU Is.

TAHITI

TONGA Is.

COOK Is.

AUSTRAL Is.

EASTER I.

AUSTRALIA AND OCEANIA

0 500 1000 1500 2000 2500 miles

AVERAGE SCALE

The Polynesian immigrants must have found many places in Polynesia already inhabited, particularly the fertile mountainous islands. It has been mentioned above that pre-Austronesian migrants may have advanced at least as far as central Polynesia, or alternatively that the Austromelanid hybrid culture spread thus far and further still. These peoples were either annihilated or absorbed; no doubt extensive intermingling also took place. A later wave of Polynesian immigrants was primarily responsible for the astonishingly advanced social and political structure to be found in many parts of Polynesia. In general the evolution of Polynesian culture owed much to the exhaustion of supplies of edible plants and animals and the decline of handicrafts, which resulted from the long voyages and the shortage of raw materials in many parts of the newly-settled areas. Thus the arts of pottery and (probably) weaving fell into oblivion; the same may possibly even be true of metal-working – at any rate the Polynesians used stone adzes exclusively. In addition to quadrangular adzes and derivations of this form they had so-called tanged adzes, and in some parts also shouldered adzes.

FIG. 3

Micronesians

During their migrations groups of the original Polynesians probably remained behind in Micronesia, especially in the eastern parts of this area. (There was also some migration in a reverse direction back to Micronesia, especially from the Samoa-Tonga group, just as some outlying islands in Melanesia were also reached in the course of such voyages.) With some justification Micronesia and Polynesia may therefore be regarded as one single vast cultural entity. But in Micronesia, especially in the west, one finds, in addition to Austromelanid elements, cultural phenomena which are absent from Polynesia, such as rice cultivation and weaving. This must be the result of influences exerted later from eastern Asia, Japan, Formosa, and in particular

Indonesians

Indonesia – influences which all made themselves felt after the Polynesian immigration, and in some instances much later. These influences were also responsible for the particularly pronounced Mongoloid features noticeable among the inhabitants of western Micronesia. Much has been made of the marked uniformity of Micronesian cultures, particularly in so far as certain material phenomena are concerned; but this is due less to these influences than to the very precarious conditions in which the population lived on their flat barren coral islands, most of which are lacking in raw materials. Regular contact between the various island groups was made possible by achievements in the development of navigation.

Links with ancient Eurasiatic and Asiatic cultures

Having outlined the history of Oceanic migrations, we may now go on to consider some detailed points, which do not greatly modify the general picture but have frequently been considered important for the light they throw upon the origin of the various art forms existing in Oceania. It should be emphasized in particular at this juncture that some at least of the Austronesian migrations began at a time when Bronze Age cultures were already flourishing in eastern Asia, whence these peoples came. This explains why links have been established between east Polynesian (Marquesan) and other styles and decorative motifs and those of ancient China; in addition astonishing affinities have been noted with northern Asiatic and ancient European styles. In the light of these similarities it has been suggested that these Polynesian forms are the last offshoots of an ancient north Eurasian culture. But such world-wide connections may possibly exist in another direction as well.

Dongson

Already during the earlier half of the first millennium B.C. the Dongson culture (so named after sites in Tongking where excavations have been carried out) spread to Indonesia. This was a Late Bronze Age culture, part of which belonged to the Iron Age, which also had its roots in the civilization of ancient China. From Indonesia it reached New Guinea; remains of a bronze kettle-drum have been found in the Vogelkop area (in western New Guinea), bronze axes and ornaments executed in typical Dongson style near Lake Sentani (in north-western New Guinea), and glass beads and rings, which presumably also belong to this culture, both here and in other more westerly parts of the island. More important still, however, is the fact that according to some authorities it is possible to trace back to Dongson influences certain ornamental styles, particularly those of the curvilinear type, found in Melanesia and above all in New Zealand. Although all these affinities are indeed astonishing, it is difficult to correlate them with the data mentioned above relating to the history of settlement. For this reason it must be assumed that at a comparatively late date further groups of immigrants, and with them further cultural influences, reached New Zealand and the Marquesas from China, and also reached Melanesia from Indonesia. But it is also possible that the wealth of styles referred to was the common heritage of an earlier phase of culture, which was already introduced to Oceania in its more primitive forms by earlier groups of immigrants, but on the other hand survived in India and China. There is, however, no evidence of very recent Indonesian cultural influence either in Melanesia or Polynesia, except in the coastal areas of western New Guinea.

In various parts of Oceania we come across Megalithic monuments – massive stone structures and stone terraces – and the characteristic features associated with this culture wherever it occurs. It is still vigorously alive in Assam and on certain islands in Indonesia, but remnants of it are to be found over the whole earth. This is frequently taken as evidence of a world-wide cultural movement, the roots of which are now generally thought to

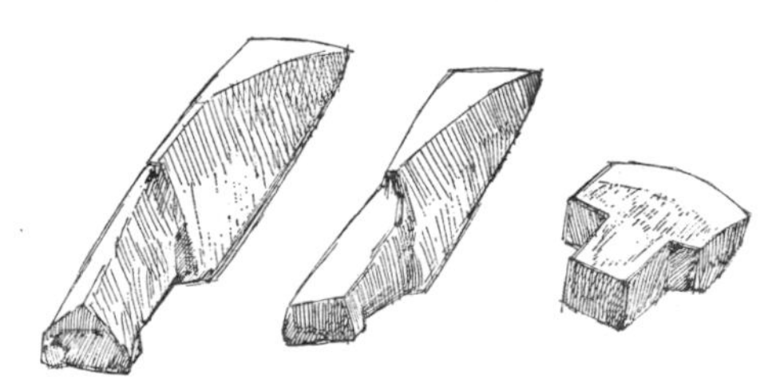

FIG. 3 – *Shouldered adzes and tanged adze.*

have lain in the eastern Mediterranean. According to some distinguished scholars it reached Oceania in two different ways: firstly, as an integral part of the southern branch of the Austronesian quadrangular adze culture, which spread over the whole of Oceania within the framework of the Austromelanid hybrid culture; and secondly, along with the Late Bronze Age and Iron Age Dongson culture, the influence of which was confined to Melanesia. The importance of Megalithic monuments in present-day civilizations has in many cases been greatly exaggerated, and doubts have also been raised about the theory just mentioned concerning the origin and antiquity of this culture. For instance, it has been argued that all Megalithic phenomena, in Melanesia at least, derive from an independent development of the round adze culture. To this culture, too, are assigned the mysterious stone mortars and pestles found here and there in New Guinea and some islands in north-western Melanesia, whose original significance the present inhabitants of these islands are unable to explain.

Causes of the migrations

It is impossible to say why the large-scale migrations from Asia to Australia and Oceania took place: whether they were undertaken voluntarily or under the pressure of other peoples. The earliest migrants, at least, had no specific destination in mind, and their voyages were in no way planned. With regard to later immigrations into Polynesia and Micronesia, on the other hand, opinions are divided. It has been held that the various island groups were settled as a result of people losing their way, or being banished, or emigrating owing to over-population at home. However, there are some important data that suggest that the Polynesian voyages of reconnaissance and discovery were in fact made deliberately. Last but not least, importance must be attached to oral traditions, which yield dates sometimes coinciding astonishingly closely with those obtained by different means, such as radio-carbon analysis. But even if these voyages and discoveries were mainly made by chance, this would not alter any of the main features in the picture of Oceanic population movements obtained from the comparison of anthropological, linguistic and cultural data. For according to this hypothesis, too, the peoples of Oceania and their cultures stem ultimately from Asia. There is no evidence whatsoever of any influences from America, and the possibility of influences from Australia must also be ruled out. The areas whence the migrations took place are located in eastern and south-eastern Asia (including Indonesia), areas that maintained links with the whole northern part of the Eurasian continent as well as the tropical regions of Asia.

Local cultures

From the outline given here of the history of the settlement of Oceania it is clear that the cultural scene is very variegated. It becomes even more confusing when one considers that the basic cultures and their hybrid forms so far mentioned do not exhaust the list. For everywhere they combined and developed independently, and in isolated areas forms often evolved that deviated very strikingly from the original model. And these local forms, too, were subject to external influences. Elements of culture were continually being transmitted from one area to another in New Guinea and the other islands, as well as between different archipelagoes, and migrations on a minor scale have taken place within the last few centuries. Contact between one culture and another, and fusion between them, were also fostered by sailors driven off course in a storm, or by people who went into exile voluntarily. There is a great deal of evidence in many parts of Oceania of such involuntary voyages, as a result of which even Indonesians were brought far into the South Seas. And finally there have even been authenticated cases of flotsam and jetsam washed up on the shore yielding implements of various kinds, and so giving an impetus to cultural change. All these eventualities have played a part in the formation of the local cultures existing at the present day, and taken together have often considerably modified their original character. In many cases this is particularly obvious with regard to artistic styles, and for this reason these local cultures may be set forth here in tabular form as follows:

Australian local cultures: Mainly fusions of Australian and Tasmanian basic types of culture. Influences of local cultures of New Guinea, felt primarily in the north, as well as recent influences from Indonesia.

New Guinea local cultures: In south-western New Guinea, probably remnants of Tasmanian and Australian basic types of culture. Fairly pure Papuan cultures, mainly in the south and in the interior. These derive either from some particular immigration or a fusion of the Tasmanian and Australian basic types of culture. Mainly a hybridization of Papuan and round adze culture. In the north and east, Austromelanid hybrid cultures, composed of elements of Papuan, round adze and southern quadrangular adze cultures. Recent influences from Indonesia.

Local cultures on other Melanesian islands: Predominantly Austromelanid hybrid cultures. Remnants of fairly pure round adze cultures. Contact and intermingling with local cultures of New Guinea and Polynesia. Recent influences from Indonesia.

Polynesian local cultures: Evolved from the northern quadrangular adze culture upon a substratum of round adze or Austromelanid hybrid culture. Recent influences from Indonesia.

Micronesian local cultures: Developed from the northern quadrangular adze culture and Indonesian influences, with stimuli from the Austromelanid hybrid culture.

MODERN OCEANIA: ITS PEOPLES AND THEIR CULTURES

On the basis of the findings arrived at in studies of population movements, Oceania may be divided into four regions, these ethnological areas largely coinciding with geographical ones. In this respect, too, Australia is a chapter unto itself. Melanesia includes the whole of the inner island belt except New Zealand, Fiji, and some minor islands in the centre and north, where the culture is related to that of Polynesia (or, in the north, to that of Micronesia). In addition Nukuoro in Micronesia has a Polynesian culture. All four

DEVELOPMENT OF LOCAL CULTURES IN AUSTRALIA AND OCEANIA

(after a sketch by C. A. Schmitz)

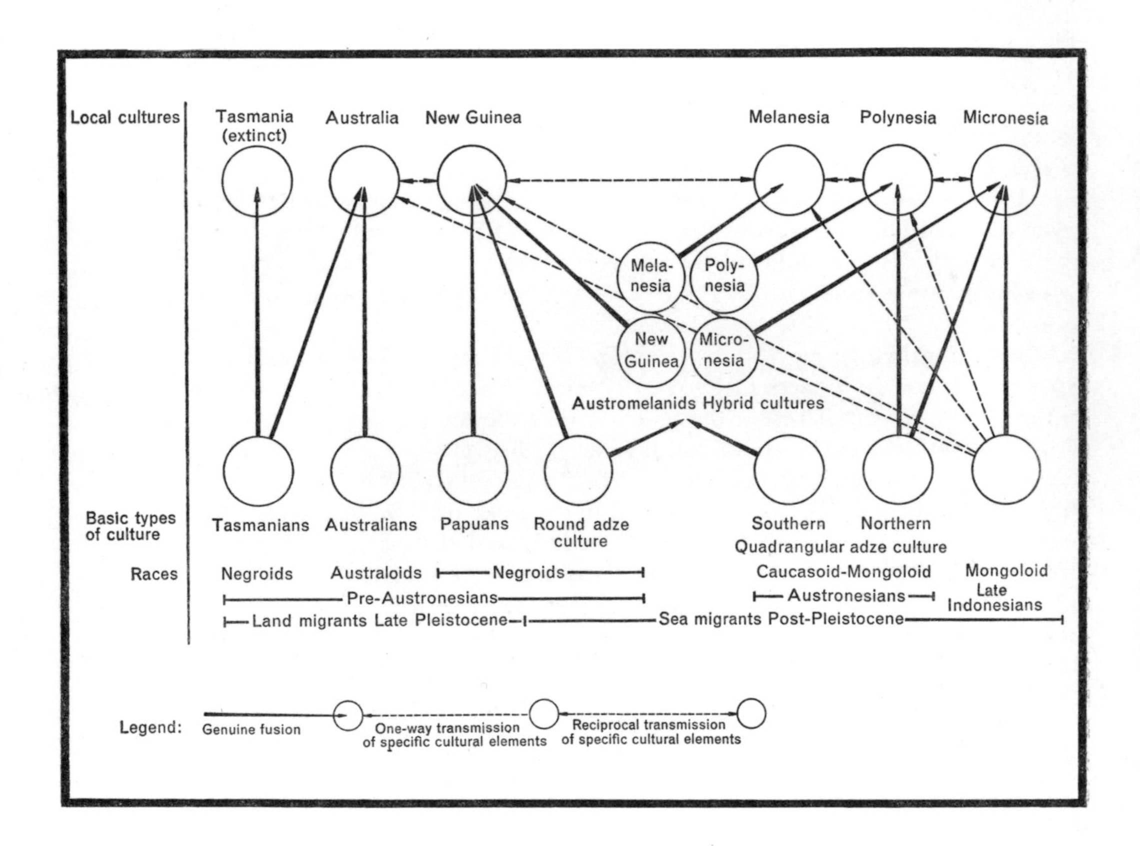

NOTES:

1. New Guinea and the other islands included in the designation Melanesia are distinguished here only for the sake of clarity. From an ethnological point of view they belong together.

2. The Papuans are referred to here as a separate group of immigrants. But according to the view held by some scholars these people and the culture which they developed in New Guinea evolved from the intermingling of Tasmanians and Australians.

3. In opposition to the view expressed here that Austromelanid hybrid cultures were the first to be disseminated in Polynesia and Micronesia, some authorities hold that they were preceded by the round adze culture.

principal regions have specific features of their own, yet taken together possess characteristics in common.
Australia, which will not be considered further here, is in itself extremely homogeneous, but differs very markedly from the other areas, as is evident already from the fact that the population is most emphatically nomadic.

Melanesia

The area with the most varied mosaic of peoples and cultures is Melanesia. The Negroid type, with dark skin, dark eyes, and dark frizzly hair predominates. They vary greatly in stature, and their hard facial features – large mouth, deep-set eyes, very broad nose, heavy jaws (often prominent) and receding chin – are by no means always so clearly marked. The intermingling of the dark-skinned races, referred to above, is very evident in this case; furthermore, the isolation of certain groups may have facilitated the development of special types. Thus, for example, those inhabitants of certain areas in New Guinea and the New Hebrides who are short in stature are frequently considered as variants of their taller neighbours, and not as belonging to races which immigrated independently. But Melanesia in particular has developed an unbelievable diversity of racial types, as a result of the overlaying of the dark-skinned groups by Austronesians whose skin is lighter in colour; these different types may vary from island to island as well as from tribe to tribe, and even appear side by side within individual groups. This is also the case with regard to the languages they speak. The pre-Austronesian languages are in themselves highly differentiated, and in addition to them there are Austronesian idioms which penetrated as far as New Guinea and blended with local idiosyncrasies, thus making the picture still more complex. In short, Melanesia is characterized by an unbelievable profusion of local cultures. They also derive from various immigrations, from mutual contact, and independent evolutionary trends which it is only in rare instances possible to trace today.

Polynesia

Polynesia seems to be more homogeneous in every respect. Although there are also vestiges of dark-skinned people in this region, it is predominantly inhabited by men whose skin is lighter in colour. As a rule they are handsome tall people with wavy dark hair, regular facial features and large dark eyes. It is usually assumed that they are related to the European races, but very often thick straight hair and slightly slanting eyes, as well as other features, betray Mongoloid influences. From a linguistic point of view the whole of Polynesia is markedly Austronesian, and there are only some traces of pre-Austronesian languages. The individual islands do indeed possess dialects of their own, but these are to a large extent similar to one another. Polynesian culture is also very homogeneous. There are many local variants, but these do not detract from its uniform character. A typical feature found throughout Polynesia is a low level of technological development, as evidenced by the absence of certain crafts – in striking contrast to the astonishingly high level of social and political organization.

Micronesia

From an anthropological point of view Micronesia is also a fairly homogeneous hybrid zone. The main traits are Polynesian – although, as a result of Indonesian influences, the Mongoloid element is very prominent in many areas; there are also some Negroid survivals. The Micronesians are in general of smaller stature than the Polynesians and have a darker skin. From a linguistic point of view they belong wholly to the Austronesian group, despite traces of pre-Austronesian idioms. Their dialects, however, are more highly differentiated than those in Polynesia. So far as their culture is concerned, there are fairly well-defined differences between the various groups, with more pronounced Polynesian substrata in the eastern archipelagoes, whereas the western islands, on the contrary, are characterized rather by Indonesian, and possibly also Melanesian, influences. To a greater extent than in other parts of Oceania the homogeneous character of Micronesian culture is due to the poverty of their resources, particularly on the numerous coral islands. As in Polynesia, this often led to technological impoverishment as well.

Common characteristics

This sketch of the three main ethnological groups shows that significant diversities exist which are without doubt important for the development of art, but on the other hand it should not be overlooked that there are certain basic cultural elements common to the whole of Oceania which are equally significant from the point of view of artistic trends. These, too, deserve to be mentioned in this context, although later we shall return to this point and shall have the opportunity to list other characteristic differences.

Technique

Before the arrival of the Europeans the use of metal in any form was unknown anywhere in the South Seas – an area nowadays inhabited by over two million people; the sole exceptions, of no real importance, were in western New Guinea, as a result of Indonesian influences. To use a generally accepted term, these were in all respects Stone Age cultures, in which tools, implements, weapons (spears, bows and arrows, clubs, slings, bone daggers, etc.), clothing and ornaments were made exclusively of stone and earth, and in particular of vegetable and animal materials.

For working wood the main implements used were stone adzes of various types and shapes. Stones and shells were not only polished but also perforated with the aid of arenaceous quartz. Pottery was for the most part produced with the most primitive devices, and at any rate without the aid of a potter's wheel. Incidentally, pottery is not known anywhere in Polynesia except in Fiji, and in Melanesia and Micronesia there are only some areas where this craft is practised. Among weaving techniques interlacing, knotting and plaiting were highly developed. Textiles, too, are mostly produced without any implements or devices. Weaving is confined to the Marianas, Carolines, some islands in northern Melanesia influenced by Micronesia, Santa Cruz and some places in the New Hebrides. Knotted bast fibres are used for this purpose everywhere. Spinning is completely unknown in Oceania. For clothing, ornaments, masks, etc., frequent use is made of bark-cloth (*tapa*). This is obtained from various kind of tree: the outer bark is scraped off;

the inner bark is soaked and then beaten out in strips on a log with a wooden or stone mallet, until a paper-like substance is obtained.

Economic life

The same homogeneity characterizes economic conditions in Oceania. The peoples of the region are all settled agriculturalists, except for a few little-known semi-nomadic tribes in New Guinea (e.g., on the upper Sepik, Digul and Mimika), who live off wild sago, fish, game and such edible plants and fruit as they can gather. Agriculture is carried on even in the swampy areas near the coast in New Guinea, where sago forms the main food staple, for palms are frequently planted and the cultivation of tuberous plants is also common. The most important of these plants are yam and taro, and in many areas also the sweet potatoes. Bananas are also important, and, especially on coral islands and in the coastal areas, the fruit of the bread-fruit tree, the pandanus- and coconut-palm. Rice is in general grown only in the Marianas. Tobacco is cultivated and used everywhere; in the western parts of Oceania (Melanesia and western Micronesia) it is supplemented by betel-pepper and the fruit of the areca palm, while in Polynesia and some parts of Melanesia the *kava* plant is grown, from the roots of which an intoxicating beverage is produced.

It is only in exceptional cases that the hoe is employed in cultivation; the main tool is the digging-stick. One comes across fields that have been carefully laid out, even terraced, as well as artifical irrigation and drainage works. In the Bismarck Archipelago, and particularly in Micronesia and Polynesia, certain kinds of taro are planted in natural swampy areas. In Micronesia artificial beds are dug for this purpose, in which a layer of humus is formed with the aid of sand and vegetable refuse. However, such exceptions apart, the fields often appear very unkempt: they are made by clearing the jungle with fire and are dotted with half-charred tree-trunks and stumps. Since they are not manured regularly, the soil becomes exhausted very quickly and for this reason the land has to be abandoned after it has yielded only a few crops. In many parts of Oceania, therefore, agriculture is only to a limited extent carried on by settled farmers; in Melanesia, in particular, the sites of villages often have to be moved whenever new land is cleared for cultivation in order to enable the inhabitants to live in the vicinity of their fields. Another typical feature of agricultural life is the fact that, while the menfolk perform such tasks as clearing the land and other laborious work (e.g., erecting protective fences), the womenfolk are responsible for planting, tending and harvesting the crops. Only in exceptional cases is it the men alone who perform the function of planting certain crops — for instance, yam in some parts of New Guinea.

In addition to agriculture in many areas the gathering of wild plants and fishing also play an important, and sometimes even a vital, role for settled tribes. Reference has already been made to the utilization of the vast numbers of wild sago-palms (in addition to those that are cultivated) in the swampy areas of New Guinea and several other Melanesian islands. Fish and small animals of every kind are essential to supplement the nourishment obtained from plants, especially in coastal areas and on low coral islands. The work is divided between the men and the women, with the former generally being responsible for the more difficult and dangerous tasks, while those that are simpler and lighter are carried out by the women. Hunting, too, is the province of the men, but it plays a secondary role nowadays owing to the scarcity of suitable game.

Over large areas pigs, dogs and fowl have been domesticated; all of these have been introduced to Oceania from Asia. As late as the 18th century the pig was still unknown in New Zealand, Tonga and on many coral islands, whereas dogs were to be found everywhere and fowl everywhere except in New Zealand. Dogs are bred as an article of food in Polynesia and Micronesia, but less frequently in Melanesia. Pigs are universally regarded as a costly delicacy, but they are too scarce to form part of the regular diet. Finally, there are fowl, very frequently kept rather for their feathers, which are popular as ornaments, than for their meat – let alone for the sake of their eggs.

As a rule there is little specialization in economic activity of any kind, either in agriculture, fishing, hunting or crafts. In the main the peoples of the South Seas live a self-sufficient existence, and in most cases village communities and other groups, and even individual families, live off their own produce. In reality, of course, there are many exceptions to this rule. Tribes who inhabit coastal and river areas often have at their disposal a bountiful supply of fish and other foodstuffs obtained from the water, including salt, but on the other hand are unable to cultivate enough edible plants, whereas with their neighbours who live far from the sea it is precisely the reverse: they have an abundance of plants but not enough animals. This results in the development of markets for the exchange of surplus products. A similar situation exists with regard to craftsmen and their wares. There are, for example, villages specializing in pottery, or in which rings are made from trochus shells, or where sea-shells are collected for use as ornaments; what is not needed in the village is then bartered for other commodities. But in such cases, in Melanesia at least, this work is never carried on by professional artisans who derive their living exclusively from the proceeds of their craft, as is the case with us. Apart from a very few exceptions, these craftsmen are always tillers of the soil who in case of emergency can produce at least part, but in most cases all they need in order to subsist.

Social structure

The social structure and political organization of the peoples of Oceania is less uniform, even in broad outline, than are their economic conditions. The only point common to the whole area is the exceptional social and political importance attached to kinship groups. In Melanesia the largest political unit is almost invariably the village community or group – although there are some relationships that extend further afield – and within these the kinship groups (clans) have all power in their hands. In some areas there are hereditary princes. But it is more usual for authority to be exercised by village elders, or all adult males. Some form of social stratification, with a class of nobles, is characteristic of Austronesian (and especially Polynesian) cultures; usually the nobility comprises, in addition to royalty and chiefs, priests and other persons particularly well qualified in some field or other. The same is true of the eastern areas of Micronesia, but the western islands have closer parallels with the complex social structures of Melanesia. Only in Polynesia do we find larger rigidly-controlled political organizations and states, whose rulers sometimes wield absolute power. Such phenomena indicate – as does the existence of social stratification – that the Polynesians have already progressed far beyond the primitive stage, and that in this respect they have approached close to the level attained by the archaic cultures in Asia and Europe. Such a comparison also holds good with regard to their cultural attainments. Only in their primitive level of technology are they on a par with the other peoples of Oceania.

Religious beliefs

In the realm of religion, too, similar differences occur between Melanesia and the other areas of Oceania. Belief in the power of supernatural beings, spirits, deceased persons and ancestors is met with everywhere, but there are very pronounced local variations. In Micronesia, and more especially in Polynesia, religion takes the form of a veritable cult of gods and heroes. All these types of religious belief, together with the social life, are so important as the foundation on which the whole of Oceanic art is based that they will be considered in another chapter in greater detail.

As a result of the coming of the Europeans the aboriginal cultures of Oceania have been greatly modified, and in large part completely destroyed, by the impact of modern civilization. This applies mainly to Polynesia and Micronesia, but the Melanesian cultures, too, have been unable to avoid the consequences of this confrontation between different cultures, and although here the process began later its results were no less disastrous. Apart from some small areas in the New Hebrides and western New Britain, it is only in the interior and south-west of New Guinea that one can still find cultures that have not been influenced at all – or at least only slightly – by the white man.

Korwar figures from north-western New Guinea. Containers and figures of this kind are made to provide an abode for spirits of the departed, and often also to safeguard the vital force believed to be contained within the skull of the deceased. *Left:* wooden figure with skull. Biak, Geelvink Bay. *Right:* wooden figure with glass beads for eyes and neckband of bark-cloth. Saukorem, northern coast of Vogelkop peninsula. *Rijksmuseum voor Volkenkunde, Leyden. Height of figure on left 15¾ in., of figure on right 13 in.* *Cf. p. 99.*

II. PRINCIPLES OF OCEANIC ART

CULTURE AND ART

The large number of cultures that exist in Oceania, particularly in Melanesia, and the astonishing differences that are to be found between them, should not lead us to think that we are dealing with isolated phenomena which developed entirely independently of one another. On the contrary, the historical survey above has shown that in many instances there were historical connections between these cultures, and that they had an impact upon one another even where great distances were involved. For this reason the local cultures of Oceania can only be understood properly if these relationships are given due consideration. To take one example, we have to bear in mind that a culture in Polynesia may be based in part upon postulates that are otherwise characteristic of Melanesia, and likewise that aspects of Melanesian culture may only be fully comprehensible if one proceeds from fundamental principles relevant to Polynesia. Only a broad study of this kind can do justice both to past and present-day conditions. And we have also to remember that, in spite of all their diversities, the cultures of the South Seas nevertheless do have important features in common which enable them in the final instance to be seen as a single large unit – albeit one whose limits cannot be defined precisely. An attempt to demonstrate this has already been made above, in the survey of present-day cultures.

What has been said here about culture as a whole applies equally to individual cultural phenomena. They, too, are unique, but at the same time can only be understood within the framework of the basic principles common to all the cultures of Oceania and the facts of their history. This is also true of art, as one of the aspects of culture. In order to study art we have to consider, not only the character and history of civilization in the South Seas, but also other significant factors, some of which are relevant to areas far beyond the borders of Oceania, and even to cultures that are not primitive at all. It is nevertheless essential for us to acquaint ourselves with these factors if we are to understand the nature of Oceanic art. First of all we shall have to consider certain general points, then the basic principles governing Oceanic art, and finally the specific characteristics of the art produced in various parts of Oceania.

Nature of art

Art, in the most general sense of the word, as a phenomenon that attempts to reach beyond the everyday world and at first sight pursues no readily apparent or understandable purpose, is something that is found in all human communities. It would be impossible to imagine the existence of man without art in some form or another: music, dancing, poetry, painting or sculpture. Art is something characteristically human, and only human at that. It is as much a part of culture as the use of fire, as crafts, economic life, social organization or religious beliefs. Together with these phenomena it makes its appearance at the dawn of man's history. It, too, is one of the signs of his spiritual freedom, of his capacity to attach value to his possessions, needs and emotions. It has been asserted that tools, crafts and other so-called material aspects of culture came first, and that spiritual achievements, art included, only appeared later. But this is more than doubtful. Even among the most primitive peoples of today we find none lacking art, and prehistoric man in Europe, whose technology was doubtless very far from advanced, has acquired well-deserved fame through his art. But there are also objections of principle to this hypothesis that people can exist without art. For to antedate the beginning of crafts to the development of art is to mistake its very essence. All cultural phenomena, including art, are in equal measure responses to the needs of life. This applies both to technical and to social or spiritual achievements. One of these may be of lesser importance than others in a certain culture, but none of them is ever completely absent. If this were not so, culture could not fulfil its task as a response to all human needs, including spiritual ones, and human communities would in the long run be unable to survive. Even expressly warrior or merchant peoples, or cultures in which material, political or social needs take pride of place, are not entirely lacking in artistic accomplishments. Precisely when dealing with primitive peoples, whose way of life is determined above all by the difficulties they have in satisfying their vital needs, and where this fact is the one that strikes an observer most immediately, it is easy to forget that here, too, art meets a deep inner need and is therefore just as essential as social institutions for the maintenance of order within the community or of its religious beliefs. Moreover, the existence of spiritual phenomena in life is particularly characteristic as an indication of complete emancipation from a life governed wholly by instinct. They represent a means of solving the problems raised by the loss of the security formerly provided by instinct — problems that do not arise where instinct remains supreme — and culminate in endeavours to create

FIG. 4 — *Roof-top ornament of fired clay, parts of which are painted white. Human face (with cowrie-shells for eyes) and cock. Aibom on L. Chambri, middle Sepik area, northern New Guinea. Height 23¾ in. Cf. pp. 86, 111.*

values which are not necessary where conduct is governed by instinct. There can be no doubt that art is one of these spiritual phenomena.
Thus artistic creation clearly satisfies a need that is deeply rooted in mankind. It may perhaps be the product of an attempt to resolve inner tensions. Spiritual conflict, profound distress or insecurity, or unsettling experiences of various kinds can lead to artistic creation: to an attempt by the artist to express feelings that are vital to him and bring him relief from tension, but which at the same time can evoke corresponding reactions on the part of a spectator who is faced with a similar situation. The fact that not every man is an artist, but only a few, and that not everyone is capable of comprehending or appreciating a work of art, is not a valid argument against the importance of art in people's lives. Inclinations vary from one individual to another. Every community has members with a particular bent for technology or organization, as well as men of action, thinkers — and artists. Each of these individuals brings his own gifts to bear in creating and upholding a culture that is meaningful to the entire community.
In plastic art especially the drive for artistic expression has often been termed 'aesthetic'. If this were so, one would have to regard as a work of art every object whose form gives the artist and his public satisfaction. According to this definition any product that is perfect in form and has an appealing decoration would have to be labelled a work of art. But in this connection one has to bear in mind that one can expect 'perfect' forms, i.e. those that answer to one's desire for beauty, to be produced wherever the material is worked in a manner true to its properties and with consummate mastery of technique. But this would involve stretching the concept of art much too far. From a purely aesthetic point of view articles of clothing and ornaments would also have to be included in the category of works of art, although this (sometimes unjustly, perhaps) is not usually done. For it is precisely in clothing and ornaments that an additional motive comes into play which has nothing to do with the desire for beauty. Striking and sumptuous articles of this nature are appreciated as a means of emphasizing social differences *vis-à-vis* other members of the community, in much the same way as the possession of particularly 'fine' implements, weapons, etc. With primitive peoples the individual's desire for prestige is particularly frequently expressed in such articles of adornment. They often also serve as insignia of some kind, or as emblems of tribal allegiance, age, social status and rank, or to denote particular accomplishments. Thus 'art' of this type serves many functions not primarily related to the satisfaction of aesthetic needs. But even where this is so, a certain shape devoid of content suffices to make the object a work of art. We are therefore dealing here at best with ornamenta-

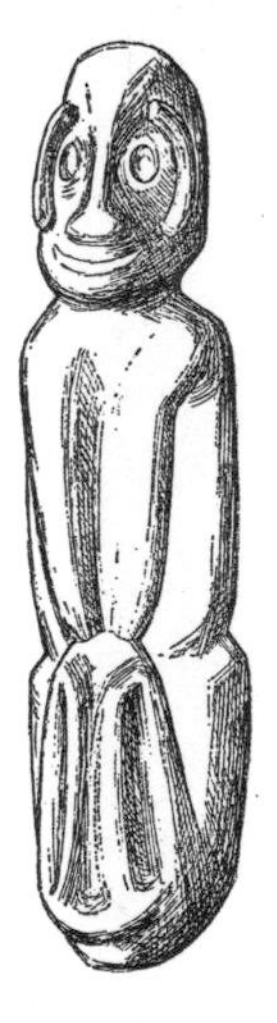

FIG. 5 — *Idol of hard volcanic rock. Choiseul I., Solomons. Height 18¾ in. Cf. p. 86.*

tion, or decorative art. Only in this case – and only subject to certain provisoes at that – is it possible to rely exclusively upon aesthetic criteria; and only in such cases is it legitimate to demand first and foremost that a work of art should be 'beautiful'. But in this connection it must be borne in mind that aesthetic ideals are not based upon universal norms but vary from one people to another and from one age to another. If, for example, we Europeans were to interpret works of art from a purely aesthetic point of view, we would have to rule out in advance a considerable part of primitive art simply because it does not correspond to our own ideals, limited as they are by the civilization in which they have developed.

Decorative art

This proviso should in no wise be taken to mean that the aesthetic point of view is not legitimate when evaluating a work of art. Decoration, too, has its place and purpose in the community; indeed, it performs an indispensable function. It could even be argued that perfection of form and consummate technique are the purest form of art, *l'art pour l'art,* since in this case the work in question is entirely divorced from everything human and only follows the rules and norms of form – exhausts itself in form, so to speak. But it is a known fact that masterpieces in particular often deviate very markedly from the aesthetic norms accepted in the community in which they are produced. Thus form alone is clearly not decisive in defining what is true art. In fact works of art that meet formal requirements often evoke a sense of emptiness and meaninglessness. This clearly shows that the pursuit of form based on purely aesthetic considerations cannot suffice to create a true work of art. This must express something more: in addition to form it must have content.

Content

The content of a true work of art is determined by the mind and personality of the artist. For every artist his product is an expression of his deepest emotions, whether these relate to inner conflicts that he seeks to master, or experiences and impressions he needs to communicate, or the urge to engage in creative activity. Every work of art stems from the artist; it is a part of him and thus has an individual character. This is also the case with regard to the style of a work. Even where existing styles are closely followed, each work is nevertheless a new creation that originates in the artist's mind. In it he comes to terms with himself and his environment, or acts as the medium for impressions of which he may perhaps not even be aware, but which nevertheless bear his own personal imprint.

However far one goes in recognizing that great accomplishments in science

Wooden figures from Lake Sentani. Their significance is unknown. They differ from one another in style, e.g., in the manner of rendering eyes, nose, mouth and ears. Particularly striking in the figure on the left are the posture of the arms, the hands resting upon the hips, broad shoulders, gradated hips and block-shaped feet. The double figure on the right is distinguished by bent limbs and more rounded forms. *Left:* male figure, top of a wooden house-post. Ayajo. *Right:* ritual female figure, in seated posture with a child standing on the knees. Ifar. *Museum für Völkerkunde, Basle. Height of figure on left 41¼ in., of figure on right 36¼ in. Cf. p. 100.*

and the arts may be the result of unique genius, one has to admit that they never develop independently of the cultural milieu. It is true that works of art, like all other cultural phenomena, both material and spiritual, are created by individuals. But these individuals – and this applies also to artists – do not live in isolation. They belong to a community that is oriented in a particular direction; they share in a culture that has a certain profile and abides by certain rules. For this reason their works derive from this culture and are connected with it, even if they are thought to be revolutionary innovations, or even attacks on that society and culture. Each work of art is therefore the expression not merely of individual experiences, sensations and values, but also of the influences and attitudes of the culture concerned. The message of a work thus expresses cultural as well as personal attributes. What is true of the artist is also true of the viewer. He, too, can comprehend a work of art in an individualistic way, and appreciate or re-live whatever emotions may be expressed in it. He can also reject it, or remain unmoved by it, if it has no 'appeal' for him. But just as strong as his individual reactions, or even stronger, are the bonds imposed upon him by the culture to which he belongs. In extreme instances – where the viewer's approach is clearly not artistic at all – this factor may be so important that the work is interpreted exclusively from a conventional point of view. Nor is this necessarily a pointless way of looking at a work. It is of particular importance where cultural aspects or values find expression in a work of art. For in this case they are just as significant as the artist's individual message, and often even more significant, for its proper appreciation. Such works acquire a certain symbolic value – as, for example, in our own religious art. As a result of this relationship between art and human society, a work has, in addition to content and form, a certain function. This function is a dual one. For the artist his work is both a personal expression of his own feelings and at the same time an indication of his attitude to his own society and culture. For the viewer both these functions are important if he is also to orientate himself in this society and culture.

Function

Art has often been described as a means whereby man gives expression to his natural need for play. This view may be valid if play is considered as directly related to the urge for spiritual freedom. Furthermore, art, like games, has its own rules which in some way do not come within the framework of normal activities; and again neither art nor play has any readily understandable practical purpose. Nevertheless art is more than play. It has a deeper meaning; it is not simply purposeless. It gives the mind and the heart an opportunity for expression such as is not possible in any other way. It is for this reason that it has to exist in every culture, and for this reason that it is so important as one of the functions of culture.

This function is of course also significant in decorative art. It has already been noted above that certain decorative objects have a clear-cut purpose to fulfil as insignia or marks of distinction, where they also serve to satisfy

FIG. 6 — *Penis decoration made of univalve shells, with chipped-out involute lines and engraved ornamentation. Worn on the penis as a decoration when performing a dance or in battle. Admiralty Is. Length 2¾ in., 3 in. Cf. p. 88.*

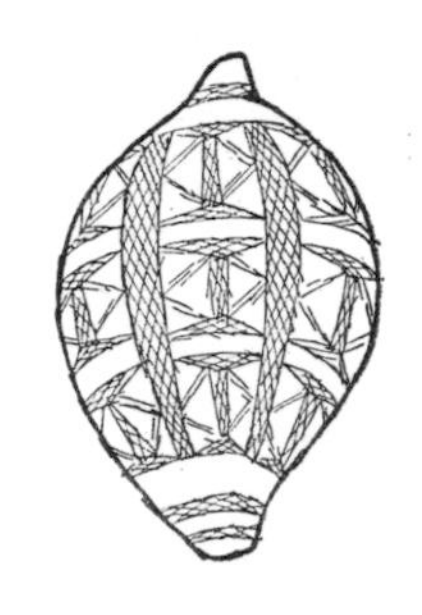

the wearer's or owner's need for prestige. But the man who designs such a decoration is likewise desirous of recognition, just as is the artist who is driven by a deep inner impulse to create. At least, we can hardly imagine an artist without his public, although in art that is not purely formal content and function play a much greater role both for the artist and for the viewer.

Nature of primitive art

What has been said above with regard to the nature of art in general holds true by and large for primitive art as well. But in comparison with the art of advanced civilizations this has various idiosyncrasies. We shall now proceed to examine these, and shall henceforward be concerned only with setting down the essential facts about the fine arts (i.e., the plastic art and painting) of the primitive peoples.

The most characteristic point to note about primitive art is the striking extent to which content, form and function are closely bound up with the culture as a whole, and particularly with individual aspects of that culture. For this reason it expresses in a much more intelligible manner the generally accepted norms, values and ideas, as well as the customs and habits, of that particular culture. Primitive art is, so to speak, wholly conventional. The reason for this stems primarily from the external isolation and inner harmony of primitive cultures. They seem to us to be organic entities, in contrast to our own civilization, which the individual perceives as an aggregate or accumulation of disparate phenomena. Since primitive cultures are 'simpler', i.e., less comprehensive, it is much easier for those who belong to them to understand them and 'fulfil' them; or if they cannot do so entirely, then at least this is easier for them than it is for us. One of the most important points about such cultures is that all the aspects that comprise them, and all the individual phenomena that they contain, stand in a vital relationship to one another and have a fixed place in the culture as a whole. They are governed by values and norms which are understood and accepted by everyone. Primitive culture and society thus gives the impression of being a collective entity, and this is also evident in its art. Our civilization, on the other hand, is so vast and complex, even in its external features, that it is impossible for an individual to comprehend it in all its material aspects, let alone in all its spiritual aspects. It is upheld by the work of men who are professedly specialists; but they can only be familiar with a certain part of the culture as a whole. Its collective character has to a large extent disappeared, and

Wall drapery from Humboldt Bay area. Bark-cloth painted with earth pigments. The animals depicted are emblems of clans. Wall draperies of this kind served to decorate men's houses. *Volkenkundig Museum 'Justinus von Nassau', Breda. 51¼ x 31½ in. Cf. p. 103.*

frequently the individual experiences great difficulty in trying to orientate himself in it. In addition to this our civilization is fragmented by a wide variety of intellectual trends. This does not mean that it is devoid of any characteristic features — for its complex nature is in itself one such feature. But it should be obvious how easy it is under such circumstances for art to develop along independent lines, and thus to bear a much more individualistic imprint than is the case with primitive peoples. In modern works of art we therefore always have to look for the inner motive. If we succeed in finding it, then the work has an 'appeal' for us. But frequently, due precisely to the complex character of our culture, the majority of viewers are unfamiliar with the motive, and for this reason the work can be 'understood' only by individuals or small groups of people.

Conventional art

Such fragmentation is impossible among primitive peoples. Here both the artist and the public share common cultural standards. The culture as a whole is accepted as a given fact. This has a decisive effect upon the artist's work, and his products are in general understood without any difficulty. It is true that under these circumstances, too, the artist has a certain freedom as regards content and form. It is, however, difficult for him to avail himself of this freedom, and it is therefore exercised only seldom and to a limited extent. Normally the artist lives completely under the influence of prevailing convention, and this is even more the case with society as a whole. If therefore an artist were to endeavour to break through the limits of conventionalism he would most probably find his work rejected. But in such highly collective cultures rejection by the community generally leads to capitulation on the part of the artist.

'Message'

In primitive cultures a work of art obtains particular significance as a 'message' or communication that finds general acceptance among those to whom it is addressed. In this respect it is of much greater importance for the community than it is for us. In the first instance, works of art in any case play a much greater role with peoples that have no written script. Secondly, and this is the main point, in such cultures they can perform this function of communication fully, since this is what they are conventionally expected to do. In most cases they are a means of representing, sustaining and reinforcing concepts of various kinds. They are the most important medium through which the basic values of a culture can be illustrated, propagated, taught and firmly implanted in men's minds. That certain motifs and symbols play a very great part in this is obvious. As a result of the immense significance which it possesses, primitive art is very firmly linked to tradition and can only follow an independent line to a very modest extent.

Art and crafts: 'independent' and 'bound' art

In view of all the bonds to which primitive art is subject, one may ask whether it can really be called art at all; for it seems as though the artist's freedom and creative volition are too strictly inhibited, and that a work of art is evaluated to an excessive extent according to the possibility of its being put to use within the compass of existing conventions. To put this point in a different way: one has to ask oneself whether, in view of these binding ties and restrictions, primitive art is in fact no more than a craft, which produces objects for certain utilitarian purposes – products which are more highly appreciated the better they are adapted to the purpose they serve. In order to clarify this problem we have to look at it in greater detail.

All objects and values, whether material or spiritual, are invariably the work of individuals. They become cultural phenomena only once they are accepted and adopted by a community. To take an example: time and time again individuals of a religious disposition have, as a result of their spiritual experiences, come to hold religious beliefs which have been granted recognition by society and have acquired the form of a 'church'. In this form they have become an aspect of the culture of that community, and so have gained general validity. But it will be conceded that not all members of a church are invariably men and women of religious disposition. There are some believers who do indeed frequently experience an inner relationship with the divinity within the framework of the church that has become an institution in their culture; but there are also others who are only members of the church because this is the accepted thing in their society, because the church fulfils certain functions of importance for each individual in it. With such people the insight afforded into cultural values is apparently the primary consideration, and the importance of the church as a religious institution takes second place. But from this it by no means follows that either religion itself or the church as an institution are superfluous. The same is true with regard to the role of art in primitive culture. Here, too, the artist may have been motivated by a deeply-felt inner experience to create a work recognized and accepted by the entire community. Even a carver or a painter who copies such a work may experience the same emotions as the original artist through the medium of the concepts embodied in the work. Other copyists, however, may perform their task mechanically and lifelessly, and thus be no more than craftsmen devoid of any creative experiencc. The same situation may arise in regard to the viewer. A work that is completely bound up with certain cultural phenomena and is entirely conventional in form, but which nevertheless is still a work of art, can be appreciated as such only by those capable of the appropriate emotional experience. Others will only be able to appreciate it from the standpoint of its symbolic significance or the function it fulfils. So long as it is in accordance with the given norms relating to content, form and function, and corresponds to the postulates laid down, it is accepted by the vast majority of those who behold it or make use of it. But with primitive peoples art has an important function to fulfil even in the case of those 'philistines' incapable of experiencing the feeling of joyous satisfaction that inspired the artist. Owing to the universally valid conceptions associated with it, art does not lead an independent existence, as is frequently the case with us, but forms an essential aspect of the culture of the community. It rests upon a totally different and much broader basis; and

FIG. 7 — *Ornament worn when performing a dance or in war. Stylized human figure of midribs of palm-leaves, cordage, univalve shells, boar's tusks and feathers, painted black and red. Held by the teeth on a flap or worn round the neck on a cord. Ulupu, northern Maprik territory, northern New Guinea. Length 12¼ in. Cf. p. 88.*

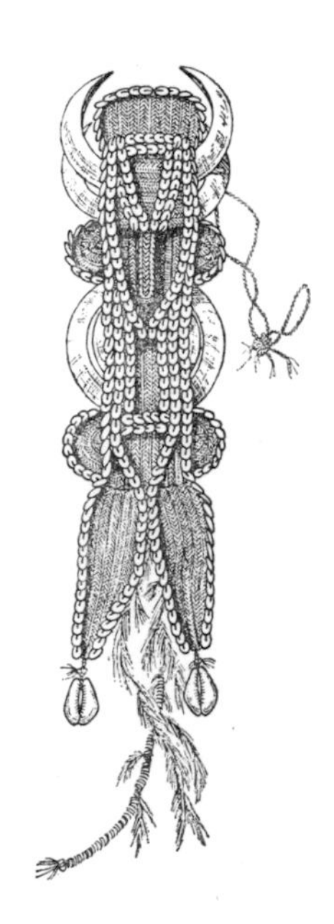

this very fact often makes it extremely difficult to distinguish between an artist and a craftsman, between a genuine work of art and a run-of-the-mill product. The inherent value of the work must necessarily take second place and be only partially related to its artistic qualities. The way in which it is fashioned is decided in most cases not by the artist himself but by the prevailing custom. The artist has to abide strictly by certain traditions with regard to the material he uses, the technique he adopts, and also his motif and style. The emotional quality of the work thus undergoes a certain modification. The viewer is moved less by its artistic quality than by its symbolic function. In communities bound by convention a common or garden work may thus fulfil certain functions just as well as a masterpiece. A 'bad' figure of a saint may be just as significant as a 'good' one. Symbols are important not primarily because of their artistic form but because of the values they express.

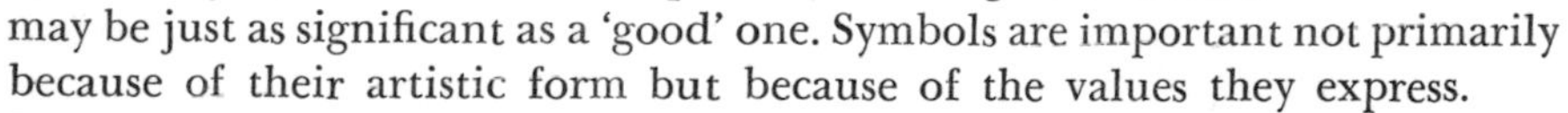

Thus it is understandable that primitive peoples often do not regard carvings and paintings as works of art at all, and that they do not even possess a term corresponding to our word 'art'. Such works are held in high esteem rather as a means of expressing certain ideas in conventional form. Unfortunately few reliable data are available, but we may nevertheless take it for granted that most viewers are only concerned with the question whether a work conforms to existing norms with regard to its content (i.e., its motif) and form, and whether it fulfils its traditional function. Artistic considerations are by comparison less important.

As a result of these rigid demands imposed upon their art, the primitive peoples find it very difficult to make revolutionary innovations in their art, or (generally speaking, at least) to adopt unfamiliar styles which fulfil some new function. For this reason sudden and radical changes in motifs and styles are extremely rare, and the tendency is rather towards gradual and continuous modification. Even artistic products of high quality are found objectionable and are rejected if they do not fit into the place allotted them in the culture concerned. Even in very recent times, under the influence of modern civilization, the fetters of tradition have only in very rare cases been shaken off. Wherever carvings and paintings are produced nowadays for the commercial market, detached from their traditional function, we find that the ancient motifs and styles are almost invariably presented in a degenerate form; we have only empty shells devoid of content.

The views advanced above — that true artists do appear from time to time, and are appreciated as such, in spite of the fact that art is so rigidly bound by tradition — are borne out by an examination of some of the exquisite works that exist. But other considerations also lead to the same conclusion. Let us recall how completely medieval European art was dominated by religious tradition. In spite of this the masterpieces of this era are appreciated still today, and rightly so. This is also the case with regard to the masterpieces of so-called folk art, which likewise is bound by tradition. Thus great artists can apparently perform outstanding feats even when subject to intense pressure from the culture to which they belong. This is no doubt also the case with primitive peoples. Although they appreciate great works of art primarily for their traditional significance, and there are 'craftsmen' among them as well as true artists, the situation is nevertheless not radically different from that existing in our own civilization; it is merely that with them the situation is more striking, and even in a sense more favourable. For primitive peoples at least appreciate art as an aspect of culture, whereas this approach is denied to most peoples in the modern civilized world. It is, however, something that helps to keep true art alive — so long, at least, as the basic principles of the culture concerned remain alive as well.

The very significant part played by primitive art as a function of culture, and the fact that it is so narrowly confined within the limits of tradition, naturally result in these functions also becoming standardized. This is why, within a certain culture, art displays an astonishing homogeneity as regards content and form, as well as motifs and style. Of course these cultural standards or characteristics vary from one primitive people to another. Apart from a few common features, far greater variations are to be found than, for example, in countries that belong to our own European culture. Thus in primitive art uniformity within a certain culture stands in contrast to the diversity that exists between the art of one people and that of another.

Art and environment

It has been argued that such differences, and especially the actual development of art and the level of artistic achievement reached, are conditioned by the economic circumstances of the people concerned and by their physical environment: e.g., a people who had little to boast of in the way of technology and lived under difficult conditions would not be able to achieve much in the way of art. But such environmental theories must be rejected. Influences of this kind are never decisive. In Oceania especially, technology is nowhere at a high level, and life is often very precarious indeed. In the swampy areas of New Guinea or on the very inhospitable coral islands, for example, the utmost effort is necessary to satisfy the most essential material requirements. In spite of this fact these areas in particular have yielded some of the finest works in the whole of primitive art.

We could at most consider as an environmental influence the fact that hunter

Wooden head-rest, painted with earth pigments and decorated with cords and cowrie-shells, from the coast of the Sepik district. Head-rests of this kind were used to support the head when sleeping. Typical beak style. *Rautenstrauch-Joest Museum für Völkerkunde, Cologne. Height 5½ in.* *Cf. p. 108.*

peoples take animals of thc chase as a motif in art, (one thinks in this connection of the Palaeolithic cave paintings in Western Europe or the African rock drawings), or pastoral peoples depict their cattle — although the latter occurs less frequently. But then we should be surprised to find peoples that are most emphatically cultivators also taking animals, rather than plants, as their principal subjects. Evidently the choice of motifs is in each case determined by the basic character of the culture and its spiritual profile, the form of religion and society, and only through the medium of these factors by physical environment.

It is much easier to conceive of a direct relationship between the milieu and the preference shown for certain forms of art, *viz.* poetry, music, dancing or plastic art. For example, the desert peoples of Asia Minor and North Africa are renowned for the unparalleled depth and beauty of their poetry, whereas so far as the plastic arts are concerned they lag far behind. In Oceania, too, similar differences have been noted. It has been held that in Polynesia the myths and other poetic works are superior to the sculpture, whereas Melanesia, on the other hand, is considered to excel in plastic art and painting. If one accepts this view, it could certainly be explained by the fact that the limitless wastes of the ocean, as of the desert, have a different effect from the stifling luxuriance of dense tropical jungle. But even here such influence is possible only through the medium of culture; this is the really decisive factor. If this were not so, one would find identical forms of

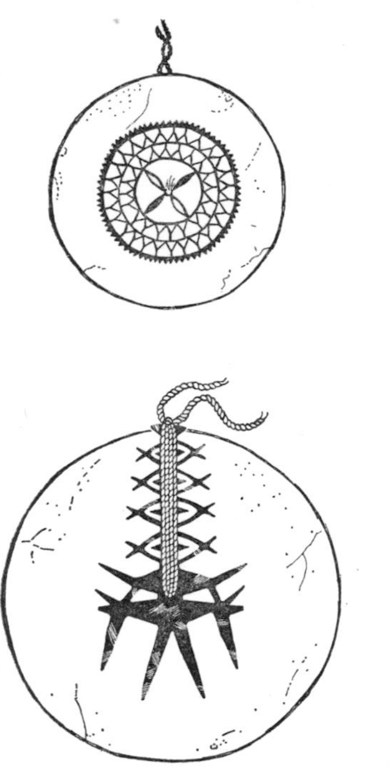

FIG. 8 — Kapkap *breast-plates from Melanesia. Discs made of flat polished pieces of giant clam-shells. Decorative layer of turtle-shell.* Top left: *Medina, north-western New Ireland; diameter 3½ in.* Top right: *Kanabu, north-western New Ireland: diameter 6¼ in.* Below: *Nitendi, Santa Cruz Is.; diameter 6¼ in. Cf. pp. 88, 157.*

FIG. 9 — *Ancestor skull, modelled over with resin and lime. Flap over the hair of lime; cords on the sides; opercula of snails for eyes; painted red and yellow. Central New Ireland. Height 7 in. Cf. p. 88.*

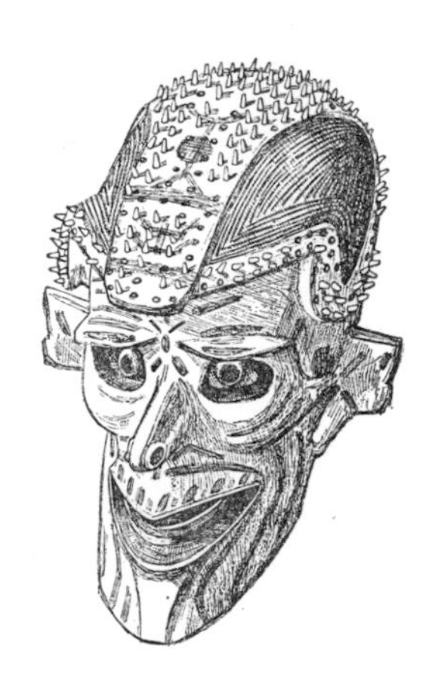

art wherever the milieu was the same, but this is manifestly not the case.

The existence or non-existence of certain raw materials may with a high degree of probability be considered a potent factor determining the different ways in which art developed and the various forms it took. One should, however, avoid drawing exaggerated conclusions. If one may explain the great scarcity of stone sculptures in the Sepik area of New Guinea by the shortage of suitable material in this swampy country, one has also to bear in mind that there is a complete absence of stone carving in other parts of the island where such material does exist. There is more to be said for the view that the shortage of wood in many parts of Micronesia, and particularly on Easter Island, accounts for the fact that large wooden sculptures are either totally lacking or very scarce, and for the absence of 'superfluous' decoration on implements of every kind, and (on Easter Island) the development of distorted figures: these have been attributed to the desire to utilize every inch of the wood available. But on the other hand one does find entirely 'practical' forms of utensils on St. Matthias (Mussau) Island, Fiji and in many parts of Polynesia, where the conditions mentioned above by no means apply.

Art and technology

Technology is only of limited importance in determining the trend of artistic development, as has been pointed out above. This is shown most clearly by the degeneration of aboriginal art in all parts of Oceania after contact with modern civilization. Decadence set in despite the fact that the islanders now came into possession of tools made of iron. With the exception of the Sepik district, where this resulted in at least a temporary refinement, the improvement in tools did not bring about any progress. It is thus only in individual instances that technology can exert any influence upon the course of artistic development. Here too it is the character of the culture that is of decisive importance, whether in a positive or a negative sense. From a technological point of view the Palaeolithic cave-dwellers in France and Spain would probably have been less capable of creating their masterpieces than some peoples in East Africa or the East Indies, whose art is far less outstanding although they were much more advanced technologically. It thus becomes ever clearer that art, as one aspect of culture, is bound up with all the phenomena in that culture and its general character. There is no need to stress further the fact that it also forms a part of that culture when seen from a historical point of view.

Wooden male spirit figure from Mbranda, middle Yuat, Sepik district, painted with earth pigment and decorated with human hair, univalve shells, rings of clam-shell and boar's tusks. Woman's kilt of strips of bast; headband of rattan; knee- and ankle-bands of cords. Figures of this kind were in the possession of individual families. They most probably represent mythological figures, perhaps a cannibalistic primeval

FIG. 10 — *Lime jar with blackened engravings (fish motifs). Kilimbit, middle Sepik district, northern New Guinea. Height 6 in. Cf. pp. 89, 111.*

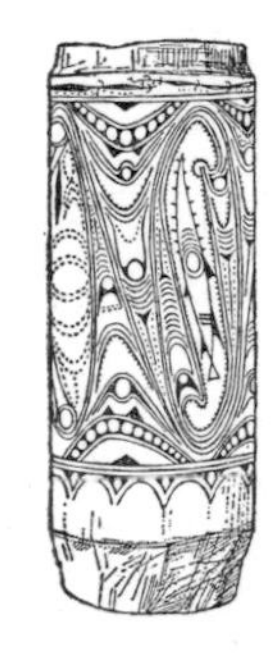

When considering and trying to understand primitive art we have to see it in the cultural setting and bear in mind the consequences of this all-important fact. It is not enough to interpret primitive art from an 'aesthetic', or purely formal, point of view. People with artistic talents may be captivated by it, but nevertheless be led quite astray in their judgements upon it. Trends in modern art have often been compared to the art styles of primitive peoples and attributed to common postulates, although this is of course absolutely impermissible. On the other hand, people not artistically minded reject works of art that are completely alien to them or, still more frequently, label them as 'primitive' in the sense of crude and unfinished, immature, naive and childish. But this, of course, is also wrong. In evaluating a work of art inadequate media and even poorly-developed technical ability are not the main criteria. Moreover, these statements are also erroneous for the reason that 'primitive' artists very frequently manifest outstanding technical skill. It is true that primitive art is quite frequently naive. However, this is not a shortcoming but rather a positive feature, since this enhances its elemental artistic effect. In addition to this it should not be overlooked that frequently 'naiveté' of form is compatible with content of the greatest profundity. For this reason alone such works can neither be called immature nor childish. This is also ruled out by the fact that they give expression to the tradition of countless generations.

In the same way as attempts have been made to relate primitive art to the drawings and paintings made by children, so also it has been associated with works produced by people who are mentally unbalanced. This is of course also completely inapt, for the art of primitive peoples is in no way abnormal. It would, however, be useful to know more about its psychological background. Unfortunately very little work has as yet been done along these lines. It seems, however, as though a psychological approach could help to clarify a good deal that has so far remained something of a mystery.

The fact that primitive art is to such a great extent conditioned by culture also makes it very difficult for us to evaluate its quality. A sculpture from the South Seas, for example, is usually judged according to the degree to which it conforms to the particular norms of content and form in the culture from which it derives, and according to the degree of technical skill displayed

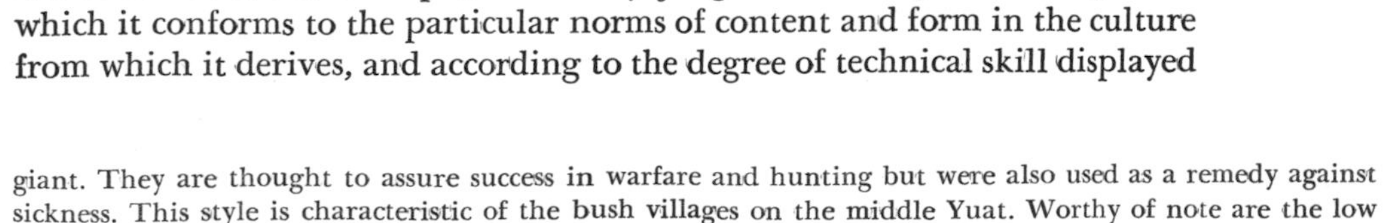

giant. They are thought to assure success in warfare and hunting but were also used as a remedy against sickness. This style is characteristic of the bush villages on the middle Yuat. Worthy of note are the low setting of the head, accentuated shoulders and hips, pendant arms and tapering face. *Museum für Völkerkunde, Basle. Height 81 in. Cf. p. 109.*

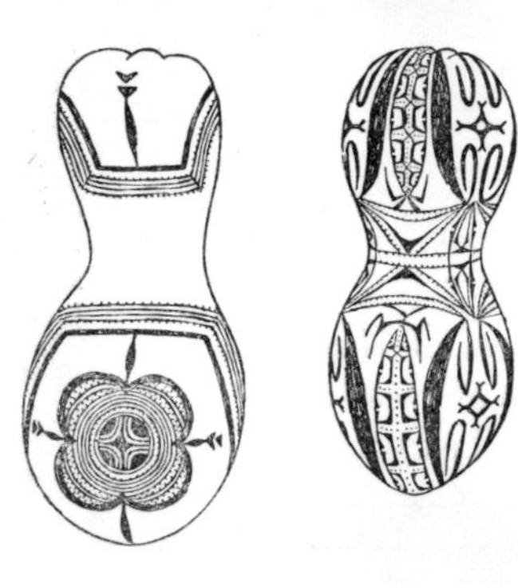

Fig. 11 — *Lime gourds. Artificially deformed calabashes with burnt-in ornamentation.* Left: *Mussau I., St. Matthias Group. Height 11½ in.* Right: *Sori, Manus I., Admiralty Is. Height 10 in. Cf. pp. 89, 139.*

in the workmanship. Frequently it is also more highly appreciated the older it is. Even among experts only a few particularly gifted men and women are capable of recognizing genuine works of art intuitively, since the objective criteria for this are lacking. And even these experts have to adopt the approach indispensable for a complete understanding of primitive art: they have to familiarize themselves with the culture of the peoples concerned. For it is in this that primitive art is rooted. It is bound up with it by the function it fulfils and by the fact that it has to comply to such a large extent with its norms. It is therefore now necessary for us to consider those basic aspects of culture in Oceania that are of particular significance for the art of this region.

III. RELIGIOUS, SOCIAL AND TECHNOLOGICAL BASIS OF OCEANIC ART

RELIGIOUS BELIEFS AND SOCIAL ORGANIZATION

It has been emphasized above that with primitive peoples all individual cultural phenomena are closely linked to the culture as a whole, as well as to each other. These close organic and functional interrelationships make systematic study very difficult. For this necessarily involves classifications that do violence to the self-contained nature of primitive culture. It means that one has to cut through too many of these interrelationships between various phenomena and give too little consideration to the typical features of a culture, to its predominant characteristics. Quite apart from this, it is a sheer impossibility to classify certain concepts held by primitive peoples into a logical system corresponding to our own way of thought. To take two examples: to call a mechanical process a 'technique', and to classify it accordingly, would give a totally incomplete picture; to understand and evaluate it fully one has also to consider its social significance and function, as well as the magic and religious ideas and rites connected with it, which we, however, would classify under entirely different headings. Besides, any object, whether natural or artificial, possesses not only external, material and functional aspects that are easy for us to recognize; it can also be something more, imbued with mysterious power and effect. This is only recognizable and comprehensible if we take as our starting-point the general homogeneity of primitive art, which makes it unsuited to systematic analysis. Art is also closely linked to, and dependent on, other aspects of culture. If, in spite of this, religious beliefs and social phenomena alone are to be examined here in detail as the basis of Oceanic art, this can be explained as follows. It is true that many works of art have an expressly ritualistic character, as has already been pointed out. But artistic intent may also be manifested in secular objects such as, for example, ornaments and clothing, cooking and eating utensils, household furniture, tools of all kinds, weapons, boats and houses. These are often decorated in a manner that seems to bear no relation to their function or purpose, and not infrequently with artistry of the highest quality. But these additions, superfluous though they are from a practical point of view, should in general not be seen simply as decoration. For very often motifs taken from cult objects are employed, which in many cases retain their religious character even when applied to a profane purpose. As symbols or representations of supernatural forces, they can enhance the effectiveness of the weapon, ornament or implement decorated in this way. Thus all these forms of artistic expression are in the last instance rooted in religious beliefs. This is no doubt by far the most important element underlying Oceanic art, and primitive art generally. Even works that appear

Painting from a cult-house at Kambrambo, lower Sepik. The earth pigments, soot and fired lime are applied on three pieces of leaf-sheaths of sago-palm, which are beaten out flat, scraped until thin, and sewn together. Paintings such as these have a religious significance and are related to ancestor worship or mythological tradition. The shape of the face and the curvilinear decoration (which is not particularly noticeable here) are typical of the style of painting found on the lower Sepik. *Museum für Völkerkunde, Basle. Height approx. 37½ in., width approx. 38½ in.* *Cf. p. 109.*

to fulfil a purely social function are frequently influenced by religion, since there is a particularly close tie between religion and social organization in the case of primitive peoples. For this reason, when considering the basis of Oceanic art, it is quite justifiable to treat religious beliefs first and then go on to deal in second place with sociological phenomena, neglecting other aspects of culture.

Religious beliefs

As in other spheres, so also in the study of religious concepts attempts have been made to proceed analytically and to draw a distinction between individual forms of belief. Sometimes these forms have even been considered as stages in religious development and, by analogy with other spheres of human activity, seen as evidence of a regular progress from lower to higher forms of culture. Today it is a known fact that it is impossible to speak of regular development in this way. In the case of religion in particular it has been shown that, although it is possible to distinguish between different forms of this kind, they are invariably only a part of the total conceptual vision, or a certain aspect of it, and are never identical with it. However, these hypotheses have to be considered briefly here, for they still play an important role in ethnological studies, and many of the findings obtained in this way can still be applied fruitfully today.

Dynamism

The theory of dynamism or psychic force stresses the fact that a central role in the beliefs of primitive man is often played by the concept that animate and inanimate objects and natural phenomena possess certain qualities and powers that are not perceptible to the senses. These phenomena are frequently not regarded as supernatural, superhuman or divine, nor as irrational, but simply as an established fact. In some cases they are thought to be manifestations of a higher and 'sacred' vital force. Certain human beings or other living organisms, man-made objects or natural phenomena may possess this force to a particularly high degree. They are then considered sacred and more than usually effective. In the long run such conceptions must lead to a belief in mysterious omnipresent forces, which determine the existence and development of the world and all life upon it. Especially in this point the theory of dynamism coincides to a consid-

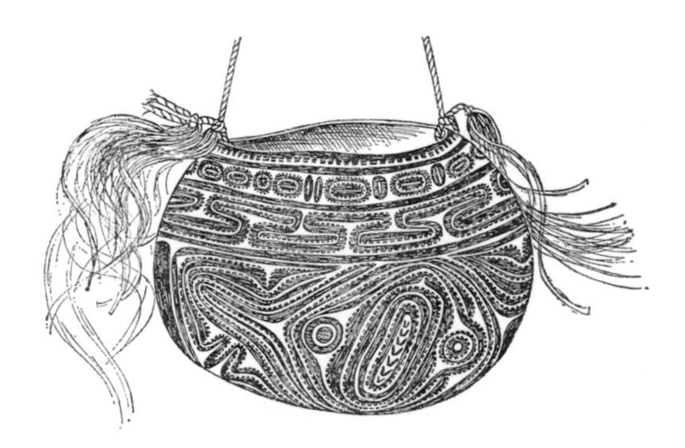

FIG. 12 — *Water-bowl with engraved ornaments. The depressions are painted red. Umboi I., to the west of New Britain. Diameter 6¼ in. Cf. pp. 91, 120.*

Wooden shield on house, painted with earth pigments, from Tambunum on the middle Sepik. In this area shields of this kind are affixed horizontally to both gable sides of dwelling-houses, on the ridge below semi-circular projecting parts of the roof, in such a way that the painted side faces downwards.

FIG. 13 – *Adze. Shaft of wood, blade of polished piece of giant clam-shell, bound on with cord. Central Carolines. Cf. p. 91.*

erable extent with other theories, of a comprehensive and integral nature, about the essence of primitive religion, which will be dealt with below. Within the compass of the belief in psychic forces, which exists throughout Oceania, many phenomena are included that are of the greatest importance for the peoples of the area. In Polynesia especially, there is a very widespread belief in a force that is generally regarded as supernatural. It is termed *mana,* and all special abilities and achievements that deviate from the normal are attributed to its influence. *Mana* in itself is neither good nor bad, but its effect may be either. Men who possess it only to a limited degree are highly exposed to the dangerous influences of those who possess a large quantity of *mana.* By taking appropriate steps it is possible to increase or strengthen one's *mana,* and similarly it is also possible to lose it if one neglects to take certain precautions. Such concepts are frequently attributed to those rules, prohibitions and prescriptions of abstinence that are included in the term taboo (*tapu*). They enable one to avoid contact with someone else's harmful *mana,* or to protect one's own *mana* from danger. They are also often designed to afford protection to the *mana* force that is of importance to the community as well as to the individual. Powerful persons who are particularly rich in *mana* are able to declare as taboo certain areas of the country, certain places in villages, houses or parts of houses, animals and objects, as well as various techniques. Any infringement of these prohibitions leads automatically to punishment by irrational forces, frequently in the form of illness or death. They thus afford a means of instituting and upholding law and order, and at the same time of making arbitrary changes in the law.

Taboo

Cult objects, and thus works of art as well, may be considered charged with *mana.* Typical examples of this are to be found with especial frequency in Polynesia, but also in New Guinea. Taboo concepts, too, can be expressed in works of art, as, for example, in signs denoting prohibition. Magic is likewise often regarded as an emanation of psychic force. The explanation given is that it is a technique by means of which the mysterious power can be harnessed for certain purposes. Thus magic acts can serve to enhance the fertility of human beings, animals and plants, to bring about rainfall, and to ensure success in hunting and warfare. Furthermore, these acts often play an important part as love-charms and as a means of destroying one's

Magic

They most probably take the place of the large gable masks common elsewhere in the middle Sepik area as a means of affording protection to houses. Pronounced curvilinear style, with the four faces reduced to essentials. *Museum für Völkerkunde, Basle. Max. diameters 42½ in. and 33 in. Cf. p. 109.*

enemies. Here, too, such acts can be performed with the aid of cult objects.

Animism

Like dynamism, what is termed animism (the belief in souls and spirits) is to be found in one form or another throughout Oceania, most frequently in Melanesia. This belief is based upon the idea that souls can leave the body either temporarily (e.g., while asleep or dreaming) or permanently (at death) and continue to exist independently, and that they can often enter a realm inhabited by other such departed souls, where they become spirits. They are thought capable of exerting an influence upon the affairs of the world and the lives of men, and as such are conceived of as supernatural forces.

Animatism

This belief occurs in another form known as animatism, where it is applied to the whole world of nature, to all animate and even inanimate things.

Manism

Manism, the belief in ancestral souls or spirits, is often regarded as a specific form of animism. But precisely in this instance we see very clearly how difficult it is to distinguish between dynamistic and animistic concepts. For the belief in vital forces can also result in the idea of a supernatural power derived from ancestors. Here we are dealing with a personification of vital force devoid of any apparent connection with the concept of a soul.

Where animistic beliefs are held, works of art, and especially human and animal figures, can be regarded as the abode of souls. This view is also often put forward in connection with ancestor worship, and it is frequently asserted as a matter of course that all human motifs in art are ancestor figures.

Totemism

It is even harder to distinguish clearly between the concepts involved in totemism than it is with animism. Totemism means belief in the existence of special relationships between man and certain species of animals and plants, inanimate objects of natural or artificial origin, and other natural phenomena. For this the term totem, as used in North America, has come to be accepted. But often these are not religious beliefs at all. A totem can also simply be an emblem, a heraldic device or even just the name of a community or particular groups within a community. The significance of these forms is above all social. Totemism only has a religious significance where a mystical relationship with the totem is claimed by certain individuals, the male or female sex, village communities, a sub-tribe, a whole tribe, or – and this is particularly frequent – kinship groups (clans). The totem is often regarded as the founder of the group concerned, or as a being closely associated with

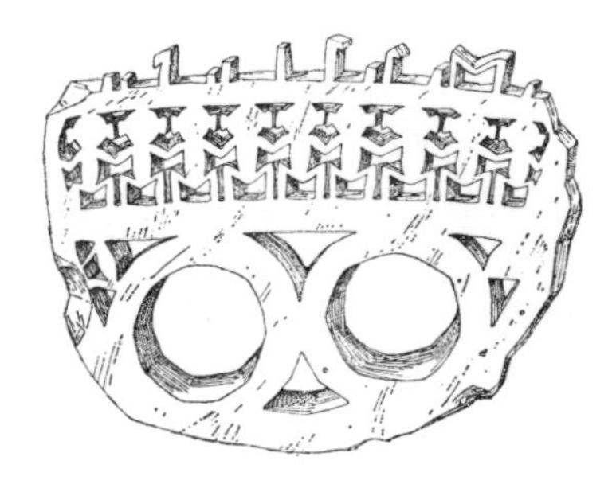

FIG. 14 – *Decorative object from a small house containing skulls. Polished and sawn-out piece of shell of a giant clam. Anthropomorphic motifs. Choiseul I., Solomons. Height 9 in., width 11¾ in. Cf. pp. 92, 155.*

FIG. 15 — *Food-bowl of fired clay, with incised faces and ornaments. The bowls are made by women, and the decorations applied before firing by men. Amanggabi, upper Korewori, Sepik district. Diameter of mouth of bowl 7 in. (The bowl is illustrated with the mouth downwards.)* *Cf. pp. 95, 111.*

the believers' earliest ancestors. Such views, particularly in the form of clan totemism, seem to be absent on the whole from Polynesia and Micronesia, but are to be found in many parts of Melanesia. No wonder that many Melanesian works, especially those featuring animal motifs, have been called totemistic.

Polytheism

The last form of religious belief to be considered here is polytheism (belief in more than one god). Gods are personified beings with supernatural attributes and powers. They have a realm of their own but in their general conduct are akin to human beings. In Polynesia they appear to differ from men only in the fact that they have a more plentiful supply of *mana*. Beliefs of this kind are often held to be a further development of belief in souls or spirits. Only in Polynesia do we find fully-fledged polytheism and works of art that can justly be called idols in the true sense of the word.

Culture heroes and 'donors of salvation'

Early studies of the so-called 'donors of salvation' and culture heroes were concerned with details rather than with the principal forms of these beliefs. Such figures are thought to be supernatural in origin and to possess superhuman powers. They are known in myths from all parts of Oceania. Among certain peoples in New Guinea that are still for the most part at the hunting and food-gathering stage they are often seen as 'the lords of animals', whereas cultivators regard them as the providers of plants and other cultural phenomena. They are believed to have created the world or to have brought man everything necessary for his subsistence. These concepts may perhaps be connected with the idea of a 'Supreme Being', which is also met with in the South Seas.

Supreme Being

This supernatural power or deity, often conceived of in a very vague manner, is generally identified with the Creator. But nowadays it is in most cases thought of as rather remote from the affairs of the world, and for this reason it plays only a minor role in ritual (apart from a few exceptions, to be mentioned later). In the theory of primitive monotheism, which was at one time very fashionable, this view was developed into a dogma, according to which all people originally believed in one god, a belief which degenerated in the course of time. But expressed in such an extreme form this theory is untenable.

Although sculptures of this supreme being seem to be unknown in Oceania, we do frequently find representations of culture heroes — although these are

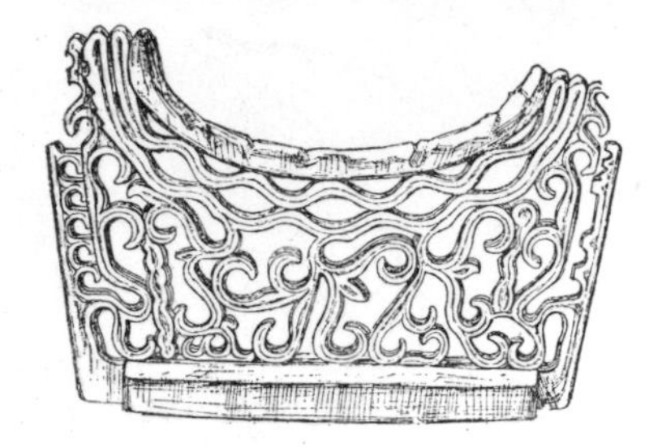

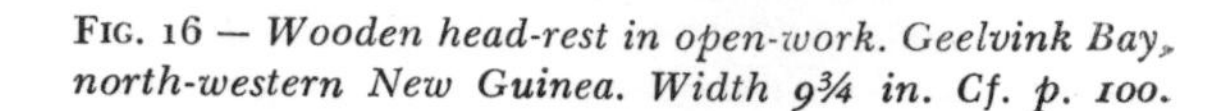

FIG. 16 — *Wooden head-rest in open-work. Geelvink Bay, north-western New Guinea. Width 9¾ in.* *Cf. p. 100.*

often wrongly referred to as ancestor figures, either because their original meaning has been forgotten or because the collectors were unable to identify them.

As has already been pointed out, none of the hypotheses mentioned can fully account for all the Oceanic religions. Each deals only with one group of them, and none does justice to them all. For this reason these religions can hardly be distinguished from one another. Quite often they are to be found 'fused' in the same culture, even in areas where this cannot be explained as the result of a sequence or hybridization of cultures.

All these difficulties stem from the fact that Oceanic religion has been approached from without, through our modern scientific eyes. By taking external characteristics we can understand only details, not the religion as a whole. Therefore to an increasing extent attempts have been undertaken in recent years to supplement and replace the old ideas, and particularly to comprehend the essence of primitive religion through the eyes of the people concerned.

Mentality of primitive peoples

Primitive thought has often been referred to as pre-logical or non-logical, in the sense that primitive man is said to be largely incapable of comprehending the connection between cause and effect, and to approach all things spiritual and material as a member of a community rather than as an individual. In such an extreme form these theories are unacceptable, but at the same time they should not be dismissed out of hand either. The ability to think rationally exists with primitive peoples to the same extent as it does with us. If this were not so, they would not have been able to create everything necessary for their subsistence. For the people of Oceania in particular have to struggle against the greatest natural difficulties in inhospitable areas such as jungles and coral reefs. They have nevertheless succeeded in subsisting, in providing themselves with food and shelter, and even with a certain modicum of prosperity. They can boast of knowledge and equipment that frequently fills us with the greatest astonishment. All these achievements, however impressive they may be, are based almost completely upon observation and experience, not upon conceptual abstractions and constructions, or upon an awareness of regular laws or broad parallels. The mode of thinking of primitive man is predominantly non-scientific or pre-scientific, in contrast

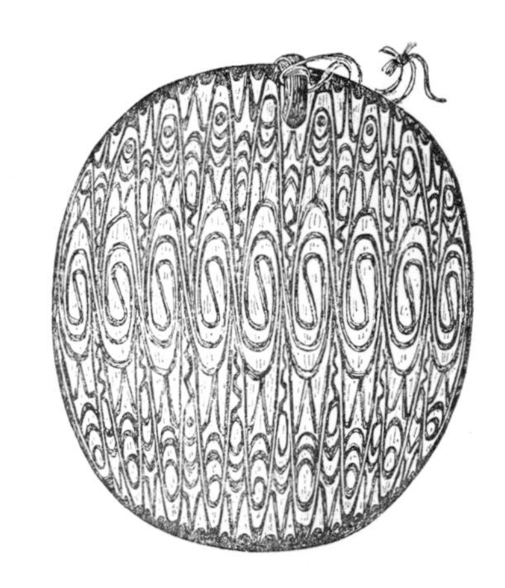

FIG. 17 — *Wooden food-bowl, almost flat but with raised rim. On the lower side are raised cut-out curvilinear ornaments; the depressions bear traces of white paint (lime). L. Sentani, northern New Guinea. Max. diameter 20 in. Cf. p. 103.*

to that of our own civilization, where this mode of thinking, though by no means extinct even now, has been forced far into the background. This, in my view, is why primitive people are unable to recognize even simple associations: bad weather, drought, crop failure, illness, epidemics and even death are events that they cannot explain or comprehend. This approach has further consequences. If man is unable to make conceptual classifications on the basis of objective characteristics with the aid of abstraction, generalization and synthesis, he may under certain circumstances establish associations between living creatures, objects, acts and phenomena where he feels a connection exists or ought to exist. He thus makes a different kind of classification, and in a sense attains a different kind of reality. Where we, for example, are unable to associate in our minds birds with human beings, this is quite possible for primitive peoples; their mode of thinking and their beliefs make such a correlation seem quite real, even though at the same time they are, of course, capable of distinguishing between birds and men. For them the rules of our logic have no validity. Thus there is only a minimum of rationality in the approach of pre-scientific man to happenings in his life or in his environment.

Inner insecurity

Furthermore, primitive peoples, not being very advanced in matters of technology, are much more dependent than we are upon their environment. Only to a limited extent can they harness the powers of nature to their own purposes, or modify their environment in any way. Thus nature must inevitably seem to them something mighty and mysterious. When confronted with it they have a feeling of impotence and helplessness which they must overcome if they are to survive. This is true even when seen merely from an external point of view; and such feelings are of still greater consequence for their inner attitudes. When man loses his instinct and acquires spiritual freedom, he at first experiences only a feeling of inner insecurity; he finds himself in a situation which he can change to the advantage of himself and his community only by means of the evaluations, orders and prohibitions which he himself has created, and above all by orientating himself positively towards his environment. This holds good for all mankind and all stages of cultural development. Even in our own day our scientific knowledge is insufficient to help us conquer our feelings of impotence and inner insecurity.

Helmet-like mask from Tambunum on the middle Sepik. Rattan, painted in parts with earth pigments and trimmed with human hair; the ears and nose are decorated with strips of leaves. Masks of this kind are in the possession of the clan and are shown publicly during initiation ceremonies. They represent clan

Even in our scientific world-outlook there are large gaps that make it impossible for the individual to orientate himself completely. This can only be done with the aid of beliefs. Thus without beliefs of some kind, without religion, even the most civilized people, with the most comprehensive scientific *Weltanschauung*, cannot exist for long. How much truer must this be in the case of primitive peoples who have no noteworthy scientific ideas at all. They have to orientate themselves entirely within the sphere of the irrational, so to speak – i.e., through religious beliefs. Their world-view is thus a religious one.

The problem now arises how these beliefs evolved and what they need to comprise in order to fulfil their function. Many of the views expressed on this matter differ widely, but on essentials there is a consensus of opinion. These differences relate especially to the way in which the problem is approached.

Order and orientation

It was stated above that the phenomena of nature must give primitive man the impression of the existence of tremendous power. It follows from this that he sees mysterious forces at work everywhere, to which he ascribes the creation, development and continued existence of the world in which he lives. Since he lacks the power of rational thought, it is only thus that he can orientate himself as he needs to do in order to survive. This is made easier for him by the fact that he sees a system in nature, for all its incomprehensibility. Even if he cannot see the connections between various phenomena, he must be conscious of the rhythm of life: the recurrence of birth and death in man, animals and plants, the continual succession of day and night, the phases of the moon and the seasons of the year, of the antithesis between male and female and between heaven and earth. He sees in them the dominion of forces that can be either propitious or unpropitious to him, and he relates all these effects to himself. Being in his very nature uncertain of his place in the world, he seeks to fit himself into this order, to participate in it, to identify himself with it or to subject himself to it. In accordance with the form these efforts take, various kinds of belief develop. Whatever course man adopts in his attempt to find his place in the world, his creed must provide a satisfactory explanation of the origin of the world, of man and of culture. Only then can it help him to orientate himself properly and to integrate himself into his environment, to form human communities based on systematic principles and to achieve a feeling of inner security. All these things are attributed to forces which we call irrational, but which prescientific man regards as reality. In this way he comes to believe in sacred

spirits or ancestors. From a stylistic point of view this piece recalls the wooden masks from the same style province. *Museum für Völkerkunde, Basle. Height 35½ in.* *Cf. p. 109.*

divine forces which are 'different' but yet operate in this world and in all its phenomena, and which he seeks to comprehend with all available means in order to partake of this force.

The second way in which the beliefs of primitive man may be understood also proceeds from his experience of the primeval force of nature, and leads to the same conclusions as the first way described above. Experiences of this sort can of themselves, and not through speculation, lead to the idea of the existence a general creative force in nature, to the 'concept of the sacred'. This idea results in particular from mystical experiences such as are often undergone by religiously-minded people, which may involve visions. It is, however, subsequently necessary to make representations of the images seen in this way if they are to be passed on to other members of the community, and be understood by those who have had no personal knowledge of the force concerned. Only if the general creative force is translated into some tangible form can the belief connected with it become a religion in the institutional sense and thus an important element of culture.

Religious experience

Today it is a well-established fact that many primitive myths contain such imagery, in the form of acts, of some personal experience of the general creative force. These traditional legends, which are moulded by the conceptual framework of the people concerned, present this force in a personified form, and serve to acquaint man with the creation of the world and the established order. They also help to demonstrate to non-believers the order that reigns in the world and enable them to participate in it. They thus form the basis of religion as a cultural institution. Here, too, supernatural, sacred and divine forces are seen as having created the world at the beginning of time and as having established the principles governing human society. Here, too, knowledge of these forces must lead to the desire to illustrate this order from time to time, so that other people may share in it and identify themselves with it. In Oceanic, and particularly in Melanesian, cults this is expressed in a very clear manner. Many religious ceremonies are nothing more than a re-enactment of the act of creation, a realization of religious experiences enshrined in myth. This is also the case in areas where myths are lacking or seem to be lacking, i.e., where they were

FIG. 18 — *Wooden ancestor figure, painted red. Typical beak style. Awar, Hansa Bay, northern New Guinea. Height 11¾ in. Cf. p. 108.*

FIG. 19 — *Face masks. Typical local styles of the lower Sepik area.* Top left: *wood decorated with feathers, human and animal hair, bast, univalve shells and boar's tusks: painted black, white and red. Kanduonum. Height 22½ in.* Top right: *wood painted red. Marienberg. Height 18½ in.* Below: *wood with traces of painting. Kerker. Height 18 in. Cf. p. 108.*

apparently forgotten, or where the original concept were stifled by new ideas, for reasons which will be considered below.

Manifestations of divine power

In all religions ritual ceremonies, and even sculptured figures and other images, serve somehow as manifestations of the power and deeds of the divinity. It is not accidental that even in the Christian church the central part of the service is formed by the holy communion: the participation in and union with this force. But in the case of primitive peoples the manifestations are much more tangible. The men engaged in a ritual dance *are* the mythical figures they represent; the act of creation reproduced in dramatic form *is* that event; the masks *are* supernatural beings, even when they are worn by men. Even the spectators find themselves at this moment not in the everyday world but in a sacred world — or better, one in which the divine and the profane have not as yet become distinct from one another. This results in an affirmation — indeed, a realization — of the sacred order.

These postulates provide the basis for an understanding of much of Oceanic art. It is not representational, but instead personifies what it portrays. It is a means of illustrating the sacred powers of creation and order so that everyone may share in them. Apart from purely decorative works, it is not envisaged as art but serves the purpose of revealing to man the forces that have the fate of the world in their hands. Such works of art affirm and reinforce the sacred order created by supernatural forces. Proximity to them evokes in the viewer the feeling that he forms part of this order himself. So overwhelming is this feeling that, as has already been pointed out, religious motifs are apparent not only in cult objects, but also in utensils of all kinds,

Clan mask from Kararau on the middle Sepik. The upper part is of basket-work, with two faces modelled in a mixture of red earth and coconut oil; it is trimmed with univalve shells, human hair, cassowary feathers and a skirt-like drapery of bark fibres. Only initiates were privileged to set eyes on this mask, which weapons, ornaments and the decoration on houses. It is very probable that they have not completely lost their religious meaning even here, in the realm of the profane. In cultures where the idea of the embodiment of supernatural forces in images has become highly developed, this can result in a vast abundance of carvings and paintings. The more of them there are, the greater is the guarantee that one will participate in the supernatural forces. Typical in this respect are large areas of Melanesia, and in particular certain districts of New Guinea (the Sepik lowlands, Maprik, areas on the south coast and elsewhere), as well as New Ireland and the New Hebrides. One finds supernatural forces embodied in this way in cult objects, decoration on houses, canoes, implements, weapons and ornaments of various kinds.

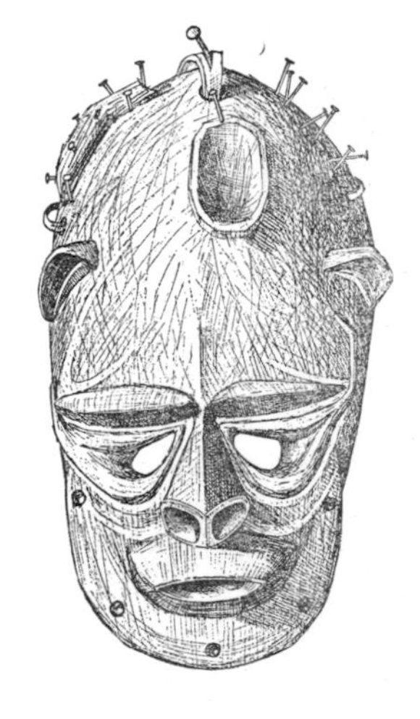

Supernatural forces are not exclusively embodied in works of art. Utensils, too, and in particular curious and unusual objects can become sacred, in which case they acquire basically the same significance as is possessed, for instance, by a cult figure. This is the meaning of the strikingly-shaped stones found in various parts of northern New Guinea, which are associated with mythological figures. This is also the case with the stone mortars and pestles found in New Guinea and the Bismarck Archipelago, and also with the stone club-heads sometimes encountered there by the present inhabitants when working in the fields, the original purpose of which is unfamiliar to them. As well as objects appertaining to nearby tribes, personal possessions such as utensils can also be sanctified, and accorded appropriate esteem, by means of special decorations and rites. Such 'symbols' are typical of many areas in Polynesia.

If one bears in mind that it is insufficient knowledge of the relationships existing in nature that leads to this idea of the world being ordered by supernatural forces, one can also readily understand that the re-enactment of the creation and the personification of those forces play a particularly important part on all occasions which, in the view of the aborigines themselves, are in some way out of the ordinary. For in such cases there is a danger that the existing order might be disrupted, and an attempt is therefore made to reinforce and sustain it by means of rites and cult objects. Such occasions transpire in the lives of individuals as well as of the community as a whole: e.g., birth, puberty, marriage, death. They are generally marked by passage

represented the spirit or founder of a clan and was shown at initiation ceremonies. This is a characteristic example of a type of mask commonly found on the middle Sepik: nose distinctly bent with flaring nostrils, corners of the mouth turned up, eyes tapering upwards with large round pupils (upper face), and curvilinear painting. *Museum für Völkerkunde, Basle. Overall height 70¾ in.* *Cf. p. 109.*

FIG. 20 — *Face masks. Typical local styles of the Yuat river area.* Left: *wood trimmed with univalve shells, cassowary feathers and cords. Anti-fuogo, middle Yuat area. Height 26 in.* On p. 69: *wood bearing traces of painting. Nails are used to fasten the hair and feather decoration. Lower Yuat area. Height 15¼ in. Cf. p. 109.*

rites (*rites de passage*). Particularly important are the puberty or initiation rites of young men and women, especially the former. From the point of view of the community they denote the moment when a child becomes an adult, with all the rights and responsibilities that this involves. It is only then that he becomes a full member of the community — a man such as was once created by the gods, so to speak. Frequently this proceeding, as it is described in myth, is then repeated in acts, which are usually very plain in their meaning, although they may be purely symbolic. On such occasions, especially in Melanesia, a large part is played by cult images, and more particularly by masks. This is also the case in death and burial rites, which are sometimes performed on an equally splendid scale. Sowing and harvesting of crops, too, are very frequently marked by appropriate rites to ensure fertility, and these again sometimes take the form of magnificent festivals. Finally, it is clear that in times of emergency and war the intervention of the supernatural forces of order is especially necessary. Incidentally, feuds are frequently carried on largely for the purpose of re-enacting and affirming some event celebrated in myth and legend. Head-hunting and cannibalism are no doubt also to a large extent rooted in such beliefs.

Passage and fertility rites

In general it is the men of the tribe who perform all the rites in which the act of creation is repeated or supernatural forces are personified. The part played by women is small: in most cases they form the audience, which has at the most a minor part; and frequently the cult acts are kept secret from them. But even among the men only those may participate in the rites who have been 'initiated', in whom the act of creation has been re-enacted in the initiation ceremony, and who are thereby qualified to share in the sacred power, and even to embody it. These functions, or at least the most important of them, are often entrusted to secret societies, which originally, no doubt, were in most cases purely cult organizations. It is true that we can also imagine other social and political reasons for the formation of such all-male societies, but it seems that the primary purpose of the secret societies was to maintain the traditional sacred order in the community and to inflict punishments upon transgressors. In most cases this was carried out with the

Secret societies

aid of masks and the presentation (i.e., the erection) of images which, together with the rites, personified the act of creation and the sacred forces, and thus also the established order. Only at a later stage, as these ideas degenerated, did these societies in many instances become terroristic organizations which exploited the population, or societies that engaged in black magic, and which used for this purpose figures that originally embodied mythological persons.

If we accept this view that Oceanic religion is based on belief in the existence of a general creative force, this indicates very clearly that the hypotheses mentioned above deal only with superficialities and a few aspects of the subject – indeed, even just later supplements to the previously-held beliefs. They do not touch upon essentials. They pick out arbitrarily striking phenomena from the same complex and take them as the *leitmotif* of various forms of religious belief. The theory of dynamism comes closest to the heart of Oceanic religion. It alone does justice (to some extent, at least) to the idea that force (creative power) is expressed in nature, in human beings and in their culture. But it does not penetrate to the core of this belief, to its essence as religious experience.

The idea of divine power and its realization in ritual must originally have sufficed to satisfy man's need for orientation, order and security. To put it differently: the beliefs and ritual actually contain within themselves salvation for mankind. But it is part of the nature of every human institution that it comes to be applied in 'humanized' form, i.e., for egoistic purposes and as 'profitably' as possible. This is also true of beliefs – particularly so, in fact – since there are no doubt many people who are incapable of experiencing profound religious sensations that could satisfy all their needs.

Signs of degeneration

Even if we leave obvious signs of degeneration out of account, religions that have become cultural institutions ('churches') and their cults serve in the main practical purposes. They are means of obtaining salvation and privileges of all kinds. This fact naturally finds expression in many varied ways: for example, in the idea of an omnipresent creative force, manifested in nature and in all natural phenomena. If one believes that particular objects, e.g., curiously shaped stones and roots, are especially endowed with this force, then clearly one can utilize them as an embodiment of this force, thereby participating in it by coming into its proximity. Since the creative and vital force is also manifest in man, it plays a particularly important part in the watering down of the original belief. This results in ancestor worship, of which many varied forms are encountered in different parts of Oceania. In many cases it has been superimposed on mythical ideas to such an extent that cult figures which doubtless once had a completely different significance are now termed personifications of ancestors.

Ancestor worship

It has already been pointed out that the manner in which the notion of an omnipresent creative force is represented in imagery or ritual, or is embodied in sacred objects, depends upon the religious outlook of the

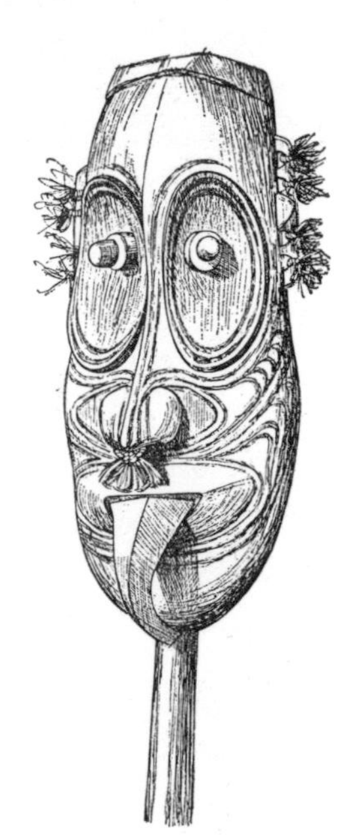

Fig. 21 — *Masks. Typical local forms of the middle Sepik area. The illustrations on pp. 71 and 72 (below) are of face masks; that on p. 72 (top) depicts a gable mask (decoration on a house).* P. 71: *wood trimmed with univalve shells, human hair and cassowary feathers, painted red and white. Cowrie-shells for eyes. Kararau. Height 23½ in.* P. 72 (top): *wood with tassels of bast, painted white, yellow and red. Torembi. Length of face 17 in.* P. 72 (below): *wood painted white and red. Rings of snail-shell for eyes. Korogo. Height 25½ in. Cf. p. 110.*

people concerned. Although it has now been proved that the character of religion is basically the same everywhere in Oceania, there are nevertheless differences between one culture and another. Here we can, however, only deal in outline with some points that are of general significance.

It is in Melanesia that one finds the ideas described above, and endeavours to portray supernatural forces, expressed most clearly. As an illustration of this we may consider some of the findings arrived at by Schmitz during investigations carried out recently in the Huon peninsula in New Guinea. These are of general significance for Oceanic religion and show very clearly how original beliefs can be identified in myths, which became fused and altered in the course of time, but which still provide the key to the understanding of many ritual acts and motifs in art.

Myths

Schmitz has identified three cultures on the Huon peninsula: (i) the original Papuan hunter and food-gatherer culture; this is the oldest, and only a few remnants of it are now extant; (ii) the planter culture of the round adze people, likewise pre-Austronesian, which is the intermediary culture; (iii) the latest culture, that of Austronesian planters and fishermen. Each of these has its own religious pattern and its own myths.

In all three groups the myths at first have certain common basic features, such as are frequently met with the whole world over in all mythological renderings of the act of creation: in the beginning there was a pre-human epoch in which supernatural powers, i.e., personifications of the creative force, held sway. Under their influence the world of humans was born. But its genesis could only take place after a catastrophe in the course of which the first men were created. In this human world the supernatural 'gods' as a rule become invisible, having assumed the guise of men, animals or plants. But their activity goes on, and in certain circumstances it is even possible to establish contact with them. The most important polarities in the human world — man and woman, father and mother — also play a very significant part in the story of the creation, in which there also figure other antithetical pairs such as above and below, heaven and earth, land and sea, and day and night. In myth either the male or the female principle predominates, according to the relative significance attached to the two sexes in economic life, and the cults and social structure follow the same principle.

Papuan culture

In the myths of the Papuan culture, in pre-human times heaven was below and the earth above. During a mighty thunderstorm the 'gods' turned the world over, so that it obtained the form it has today. The first men sprang from the blood of a dove (female principle) through the acts of an aged man (male principle) with the aid of fire and canes of bamboo. Heaven, the sun, light and fire are associated with the father figure, as are also animals of the chase. The existence of all these concepts indicates a culture of hunters and food-gatherers which has now largely disappeared, this being an economic structure in which the menfolk played a dominant part. It would be very difficult to relate present-day art forms with this mythological complex. This could at the most be possible in New Guinea and perhaps on some islands of the Bismarck Archipelago; for hunter and food-gatherer cultures are not to be found anywhere else in Oceania. The highly developed wood carvings in Melanesia can certainly not be attributed to them, although this is more likely in the case of the painted bark-cloth used for various purposes. The frequent appearance of the snake motif in ancient New Guinea cultures may possibly be related to the mythical concept that the father deity may assume the guise of a snake.

Round adze people

According to the myths of the round adze people, in pre-human times heaven and earth formed one entity; heaven was then much closer to earth than it is today. The genesis of the human world was only made possible by separating heaven from earth, an act performed by supernatural beings in various guises. The celestial powers are representative of the male principle. Related to them are lightning, thunder, light, fire, the sun and the moon. Water, the sea and the earth's surface owe their origin to the terrestrial, or female, principle.

The creation of man, too, is exclusively the work of representatives of the terrestrial deities. Twin sons of the Earth Mother kill a primeval monster who devours human flesh; their descendants, who are exclusively female, are the progenitors of modern man. Cultivated plants develop from the dead bodies of celestial primeval deities, which are male; cultural products are created by deities of the terrestrial (female) half. All these traditions stress the antithesis between female and male, and the triumph of the female side. Here, too, there is a striking connection between myth and economic and social conditions in the cultures concerned, where the women also play a very important part.

Since large areas of Melanesia, and New Guinea in particular, belong to this group of ancient planter cultures, it may be assumed from the outset that mythological motifs, some of which have been referred to above, have a very considerable influence upon the art of these areas. But this is also the case in Polynesia, where Melanesian influences in one form or another also penetrated. In Melanesia male and female figures are often apparently personifications of these pre-human beings. In particular the man-eating primeval giant in human guise seems to be a common motif. Furthermore, the frequent representations of double human beings or double-headed

FIG. 22 — *Wooden post from a cult-house. Local style of the middle Sepik area. Masanei, middle Korewori. Height 10 ft. Cf. p. 111.*

Detail of two crocodile spirits in wood, painted with red earth pigment, from Ambanoli in the Korewori river area, in the middle Sepik lowlands. In the middle Korewori area several villages possessed such crocodile spirits. They were clan property and were kept in cult-houses to which only initiates had access. They play a part in initiation ceremonies and in the preparation for warfare and hunting expeditions. The style is a local one. Of particular significance are the faces, framed by hooks, on the animals' backs, which call to mind the cult figures of the southern border area; another characteristic feature is the curvilinear decoration. *Museum für Völkerkunde, Basle. Overall length of the specimen at the rear 23 ft., and that in front 21 ft. 6 in.; length of details shown 12 ft. and 10 ft. 3 in.* *Cf. p. 110.*

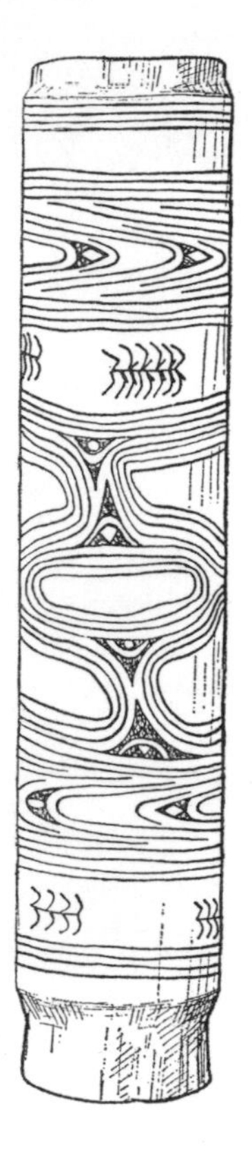

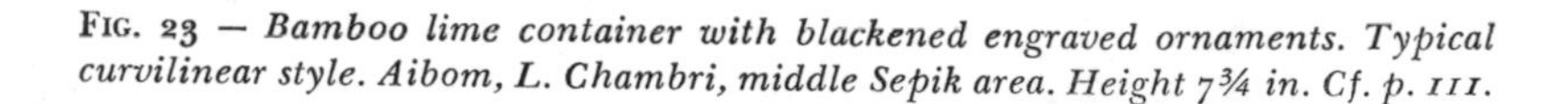

Fig. 23 — *Bamboo lime container with blackened engraved ornaments. Typical curvilinear style. Aibom, L. Chambri, middle Sepik area. Height 7¾ in.* *Cf. p. 111.*

Januses may be connected in part with the celestial twins who killed that giant. Animal motifs may also have their origin here. Often the primeval monster is visualized as a boar, eagle or crocodile. Finally, the celestial beings are also related to the snake and to animals of the chase.

In the beliefs of the round adze people cannibalistic practices are a re-enactment of the killing and devouring of the primitive giant; and from this, too, head-hunting and the pig-sacrificing cult are derived. All these are in the last instance episodes in creation, and they often constitute the central element in ritual. They are also of significance in the art of many districts, particularly in Melanesia. They are prevalent where they serve to accentuate the relationship with the supernatural. They are closely connected with the splendid artistic development that occurs, in Melanesia particularly, after one crop has been sown and before the new season begins (harvest and fertility ceremonies), at birth, name-giving, puberty, marriage or death (passage rites), when magnificent sculptures, paintings, masks and ornaments of all kinds are produced. On such occasions mythological figures are often represented either figuratively or with the aid of sound: originally slit-drums and trumpet-like instruments served to reproduce the voice of the man-eating primeval monster; in northern New Guinea the sacred flutes, played in pairs, represent the twins (the victors over the giant), while stamping or pounding drums from the same district represent the primeval mother. These instruments, too, are not infrequently fashioned with exquisite artistry.

Austronesian culture

The third mythological complex found on the Huon peninsula belongs to the maritime planter culture, originating with the southern branch of Austronesian immigrants; in this culture tilling of the soil and fishing are equally important. The creation is frequently represented as a splendid epic, and is related genealogically to the historical past, especially to the process of settlement. In the beginning was the creative force, which is rarely conceived of as impersonal, but more frequently as a 'tree of creation' (tree of life), or even as a personified supreme deity. The male principle, celestial power, is represented by two hostile brothers, one of whom, inventive and enterprising, creates the land from the sands of the primeval sea, while wandering about the face of the earth, either alone or with the help of companions. To him therefore belong the country folk, birds, quadrupeds and especially dogs; he may appear in the guise of a dog. He is also closely related to the sun, fire, boat-building, wood-carving and other cultural achievements. The elder brother, on the other hand, is typically conserv-

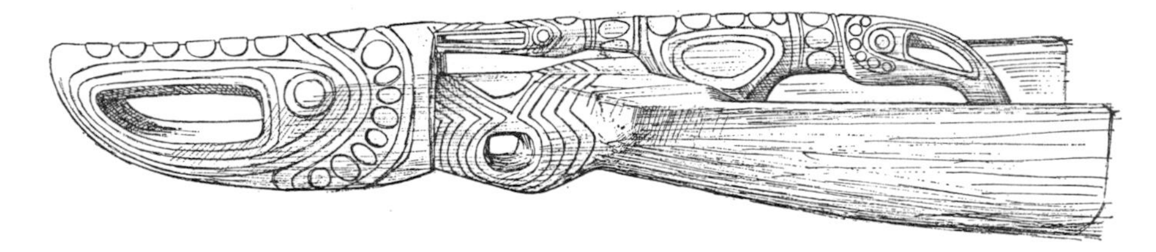

FIG. 24 — *Prow of a canoe with traces of painting (in white, red and black). Head of crocodile and birds. The style is typical of this region. Kupkei, upper Sepik lowlands. Length 7 ft. 6½ in. Cf. p. 111.*

ative. Both figures are complementary, polarities of the celestial male principle. Man issued forth from the union of the younger celestial brother with the terrestrial woman, and it is she who created the most important cultivated plants, especially yams. She is often represented as a turtle, and the elder brother as a fish. These myths, too, have been expressed in art, in the form of animal and human figures. With some of them new motifs (turtle, dog) were introduced, while others are identical with those of the round adze people. Especially closely associated with the Austronesian culture are the ceremonial buildings (cult-houses and men's houses) which are a very typical feature of many parts of New Guinea and are of architectural as well as of artistic significance. Probably they are in essence representations of the cosmic concepts of this culture. Also in this case some of the ritual consists of the re-enactment of various phases of the creation.

Cult-houses

On the basis of the facts relating to the history of settlement it must be assumed that in some parts of New Guinea the myths of the round adze culture and those of the Austronesian culture fused to a considerable extent. For this reason it is often hard to draw a clear dividing-line between the corresponding motifs in art. In a similar way this is of course also true of other Melanesian islands, indeed even of Polynesia, where we have to reckon with the existence everywhere of an Austromelanid lower stratum. This is evident here from the myths. But in the sacred traditions and religions of Polynesia pride of place is taken by concepts which exist in rudimentary form in those areas of New Guinea that are subject to Austronesian influences, as well as in other Melanesian islands. The creative forces have here developed into one magnificent pantheon. Ancestors are deified, and noble families trace their genealogical descent back to the gods. These are the predominant principles of Polynesian religion. This is a religion catering mainly for men, with a well-entrenched priesthood which in its social status belongs to the aristocracy. All these phenomena can be attributed to the more recent immigrants into Polynesia who, as has been mentioned above, came from lands that were in close contact with the ancient advanced cul-

Polynesian cultures

Painting from a cult-house at Slei, in the northern part of the middle Sepik area. Sheaths of palm-leaves are sewn together and tied to a bamboo frame, and are then painted with earth pigments. In cult- and dwelling-houses of this area ornaments such as these are frequently affixed to the two central posts of buildings. They probably serve a protective function. Pronounced curvilinear style with representations of faces, a typical feature of paintings in the middle Sepik district. *Museum für Völkerkunde, Basle. Height 44 in., width 61½ in.* *Cf. p. 111.*

tures of Asia. The Polynesians are the only people in Oceania who could boast of a theology in the proper sense of the term. Their doctrines were in the main disseminated outwards from Raiatea, one of the Society Islands, which for a long time was the spiritual centre of Polynesia. The oldest idea of all is the concept of personified cosmic deities representing natural phenomena and certain general cosmic principles; they are classed into a male (celestial) and a female (terrestrial) group. They are regarded as the fathers and mothers of the principal deities, and it is from them that the principal noble families derive their origin. They are the protectors and patrons of certain areas of the earth and of certain activities. Thus there are, for example, gods of the forest and of crafts, of war, peace and agriculture, the sea and fishing, and of thunder and rain. According to the earliest doctrine the god of crafts held pride of place. It was he who fashioned the first woman out of clay, and from a union with her gave birth to the first human beings. At a later stage the god of the sea and fishing was chosen as supreme being; he was then regarded as the creator of his fellow-deities and of the whole world as well. And finally, in the Society Islands at least, a son of the sea god presided over all the other deities. These doctrines have spread outwards from Raiatea throughout Polynesia, the most recent ones having penetrated less far than the others. But besides these deities there are also other local ones, who are greatly revered. Below the deities are demi-gods or culture heroes, to whom some acts of creation, particularly of cultural products, are in many cases ascribed. Next in order are legendary historical personalities, also frequently deified, the discoverers of various archipelagoes, and finally the direct ancestors of the present inhabitants.

Theological doctrines

There is a parallel to the development of these theological doctrines in the evolution of the concept of creative force as an abstract principle, i.e., in the concept of *mana*. This exerted a great influence upon Polynesian religion. The power of deities, culture heroes, ancestors and also living men is based upon their possession of *mana*, and therefore does not differ fundamentally between one individual group and another, but only in degree. A mighty chief can under certain circumstances possess more *mana* than an ancestor of lesser rank or even a deified human being.

In some places a great number of deities, especially the cosmic ones, were not worshipped, or at least were revered only within the framework of regular state religions. As a rule the divine patrons of individual professions or occupations are much more prominent, such as the god of the sea and fishing, the god of agriculture, of wood-carvers and (particularly in the

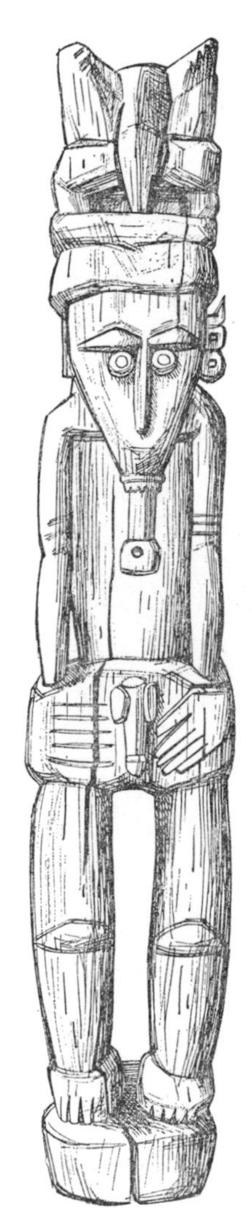

FIG. 25 — *Wooden ancestor figure with a bird figure on the head. Astrolabe Bay. Height 4 ft. 1¼ in.* *Cf. p. 115.*

FIG. 26 — *Wooden cult figure, painted white, red and black. Typical Tami style. Finschhafen, Huon Gulf province; presumably originating from Tami. Height 4 ft. 7 in.* *Cf. p. 119.*

east) of war. But ancestors of individual families in particular play a very important part in ritual. This is no doubt connected with the well-developed historical sense possessed by the Polynesians and their social system, with its class divisions; both these factors led to attempts by men to establish connections with the gods through their ancestors.

One would somehow expect the many variants of the more recent Austronesian religion and the remnants of pre-Austronesian beliefs already mentioned to find expression in a corresponding variant of Polynesian art as well. But so far as motifs are concerned this is only to a limited extent the case. In religious art deities, and to a much greater degree ancestors (according to the importance attached to ancestor worship), are often represented in human form; only in isolated instances do we find mythological motifs as well, such as lizards and fish as personifications of the sea god. But in the purest Polynesian cultures especially, symbolic objects were used almost universally in place of idols. Even ornaments can acquire divine significance. It is easier, as will be shown below, to trace stylistic influences of pre-Austronesian cultures in Polynesian art.

Beliefs similar to those found in Polynesia are also encountered in Micronesia, with the difference that on the whole ancestors and mythological culture heroes are more important than actual deities. Furthermore, especially in the west, there have been recent influences from Indonesia. In the art of Micronesia religious concepts have, so to speak, found no expression. If attempts are made in the ritual of the Oceanic peoples, and thus also in many of their works, to represent or personify the forces of creation and the act of creation itself, with the object of participating in the creative force so manifested, it is at the same time also possible for this force to be transmitted through men. According to the *mana* concept man owes his existence to the creative force, which is permanently present in him. The

Left: wooden board, painted with earth pigments, from the Green River area on the upper Sepik. Such boards were used as doors, but also as shields. Significant from the stylistic point of view are the black painted decorative parts which project in the form of raised fillets. The principal motif calls to mind two faces opposite one another. *Museum für Völkerkunde, Basle. Height 54 in., width 20 in.*

Right: part of door made of sheaths of palm-leaves, painted with earth pigments, from the May river, upper Sepik district. Stylistic affinities with the middle and lower Sepik area. Curvilinear ornaments and toothed design. *Museum für Völkerkunde, Basle. Height 48½ in., width 15¾ in.* *Cf. p. 112.*

more significant his achievements are, or the higher his rank in society, the greater must be his share of this force, and the more 'sacred' he becomes, with the power of doing either good or evil. This is also the case after his death, which does not lead to the extinction of his creative power. The ancestor cult, which has mostly overshadowed the older religious ideas, is rooted in these concepts; it is particularly widespread in Melanesia, while in Polynesia it has developed a stage further and leads on to the worship of deities. The reason for this is that man hopes to attain prosperity more easily through his ancestors, who are closer to him, than through deities. In Melanesia for this reason bones, hair and parts of the bodies of deceased persons are preserved in an attempt to safeguard the creative power they contain on behalf of the individual concerned or the community as a whole. An example of this may be seen in the skulls of deceased persons found in the Sepik valley and other parts of Melanesia, over which facial features are often modelled in an artistic manner. Furthermore, in many areas motifs that formerly appeared in myths serve today to represent ancestors. Other cult objects, too, have been divested of their mythological character and have likewise become associated with ancestral spirits. For these reasons the art of New Guinea in particular, as well as of certain other parts of Melanesia, has to be considered as closely related to ancestor worship.

Ancestor worship

Throughout Oceania there is an intimate connection between religion and social structure. The influence exerted by one upon the other is very definitely reciprocal. The way in which the community is organized is a manifestation of mythological events and of the world order and all the concepts associated with them. But on the other hand figurative representations of the creation must conform to the basic characteristics of the culture and society concerned. Even if the social structures of New Guinea and most other parts of Melanesia at the present day are of a very hybrid character, the connections that exist can still be recognized. Here, too, there are three kinds of social structure, which differ from one another in fundamentals, and which correspond to the three religious patterns mentioned above.

In the religion of the Papuan cultures of New Guinea, where the economic structure is generally still based upon hunting and food-gathering, or is derived from these modes of life, the chief role is played by a celestial father deity; the Earth Mother is by comparison much less important. Accordingly kinship groups are mostly patrilineal in structure; the succession occurs in the male line, and men enjoy privileges in other respects as well.

In the mythology of the pre-Austronesian round adze culture, which is basically

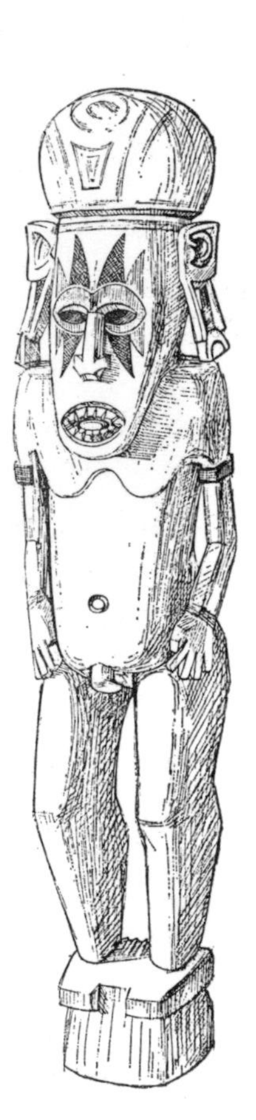

FIG. 27 — *Wooden cult figure, painted white, red and black. Tami style. Umboi I. Height 3 ft. 7¼ in. Cf. p. 119.*

a planter culture, particular value is attached to the polarity between the male and female principles, with the latter being predominant. This corresponds completely to the matrilineal clan structure, i.e., a kin relationship favouring the female line. The antagonism between the two sexes, the accentuation of polarities in mythology (culminating in the separation of heaven from earth), and the dualistic principle of world order, have a parallel in the dual structure within the clans, or in the existence of two classes, each with particular rights and duties, which are complementary to each other and ensure the orderly life of the community.

A patrilineal structure of society generally predominates in the Austronesian cultures of Melanesia (as well as Polynesia and Micronesia), which from an economic point of view are dependent as much upon fishing as upon agriculture, if not more so. But in Polynesia rights are inherited in equal measure by men and women. Here, too, dualistic organizations can appear, but in this case they are based rather upon the twin brothers, as the embodiment of the celestial powers, than upon the polarity between male and female.

Neither a well-developed chieftainship nor class distinctions are generally found in pure pre-Austronesian cultures, whereas in the Austronesian cultures of New Guinea social stratification does occur, with a class of slaves on one hand and of landowners, lords or nobles on the other. This class distinction is, however, much more pronounced in most areas of Polynesia and Micronesia. In Polynesia members of the most recent group of immigrants often form an aristocracy that holds the earlier inhabitants in subjection. The lower classes are composed of peasants who own their land, serfs who enjoy no rights, and prisoners of war. In the middle, and especially the upper, stratum families combine to form clans, which can trace their descent back to a common ancestor. Within the clan greatest respect is enjoyed by those families whose heads can trace their descent back in a direct line through a number of first-born sons (or, more rarely, first-born daughters) to an ancestor, and through him to a deity. These families are treated with the respect due to a god and are worshipped accordingly. The head of the family in particular, who may on occasion be a woman, is regarded as the embodiment of the creative power, or *mana*, of the clan concerned. For this reason such people often used to be regarded as sacred

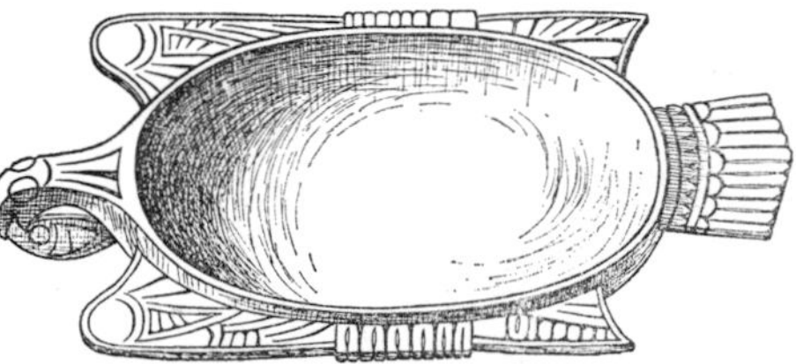

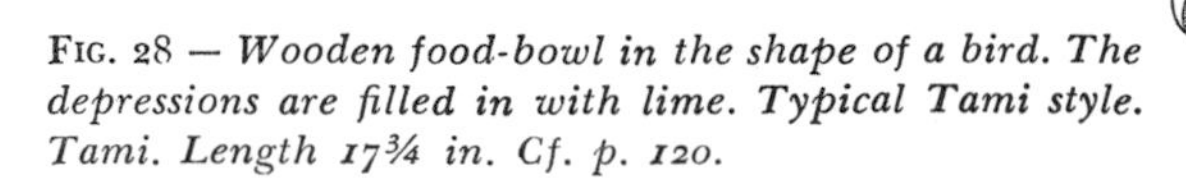

FIG. 28 — *Wooden food-bowl in the shape of a bird. The depressions are filled in with lime. Typical Tami style. Tami. Length 17¾ in. Cf. p. 120.*

Wooden board-like cult figures from the southern border area of the Sepik lowlands. The figure on the left, painted in a reddish colour and black, is from Amanggabi on the upper Korewori. The smaller figure, from Kapriman on the Blackwater river, is blackened and wears a headband made of the fur of an ar-

FIG. 29 — *Wooden face mask, painted white, red and black. Mask of the bull-roarer and circumcision spirit. Typical Tami style. Umboi I. Height 19¾ in. Cf. p. 120.*

symbols, who exercised no administrative functions; but sometimes, especially in the larger archipelagoes, they were rulers who exercised absolute power. Here mighty dynasties existed, which were able to found well-organized kingdoms and whose members ruled as autocrats for generations. The heads of other clans in the aristocracy were the chiefs of districts or villages, and their members also held positions of esteem as priests, speakers in assemblies, overseers and craftsmen (especially stone- and wood-carvers and boat-builders). Their entire social position is thus in the last instance based upon evidence of genealogical seniority, i.e., of their descent from the earliest ancestors and the gods. The closer a man is to the gods in this respect, the greater the esteem he enjoys. Furthermore, the fact that specialization may convey high status explains why gods or deified ancestors are the patrons of various crafts.

Social function of works of art

The mere fact that close links exist between religion and social structure throughout Oceania goes a long way to show why many works of art not only play a part in ritual but are also directly related to certain social groups, and that this function is often the more important one. It should also not be overlooked that rites of an expressly religious character can also have very great social significance. Such ceremonies, which often take years, and even decades, to prepare and perform, strengthen the ties within the community and afford those who take part increased prestige. Once again we see how close the relationship is between religious and social phenomena, and thus that religious works of art have an important role to fulfil within society. In this connection we may mention, for instance, the insignia of rank worn by Polynesian noblemen, the feather belts of Tahiti, or the famous feather capes and helmets of Hawaii. At the same time these are

borial marsupial; the eyes and ankle-band are of cowrie-shells. *Museum für Völkerkunde, Basle. Height of figure on left 71½ in., of figure on right 59½ in. Cf. p. 112.*

FIG. 30 — *Carved ornamentation on a wooden bowl, with lime rubbed in. Snake and fish motif. Typical Tami style. Tami. Length 6 in. Cf. p. 120.*

symbols of divine power. The colour red is considered especially sacred. In Melanesia, on the other hand, the most important shrines, figures, masks and paintings are very often in the possession of clans and other groups, i.e., they too are important both from the religious and the social point of view. The same is true of masks, which likewise very frequently have a particular function to fulfil in the ritual of these groups. Finally, the possession of various carvings and masks can also afford enhanced prestige, and (in the New Hebrides and the Banks Islands) can even be connected with the evolution of veritable rank systems within the male societies. These few points will have to suffice to illustrate the fact that the key to an understanding of the function of the arts in Oceania lies, not merely in religion and ritual, but also in social organization.

TECHNOLOGY

Mention has already been made of the low level of technical development generally prevailing among the Oceanic peoples. This point may now be developed with particular reference to art.

Firstly, so far as raw materials are concerned, these exist in astonishing abundance. Only the most important of them can be discussed here.

Raw materials: mineral

FIG. 5

In many parts of Oceania one encounters sculptures of hard volcanic rock. Worthy of note are: the bird figures (and also a human head) on prehistoric pestles from north-eastern New Guinea; statues and heads on net sinkers from the Solomons; the famous nephrite pendants of the New Zealand Maori; and above all the stone figures of eastern Polynesia, which often attain monumental proportions; in parts of the latter region stone utensils are decorated with figures. Figures and carvings in relief in soft limestone are authenticated from the Sepik district and elsewhere, objects of calcareous clay and brown coal from Astrolabe Bay in New Guinea, chalk carvings from southern central New Ireland, and marly clay statuettes from the Admiralty Islands.

FIG. 4

Oceanic pottery generally has little in the way of decoration. Vessels in complex shape (with a glaze-like film of resin) are produced on Fiji. Decoration of figures on bowls and jars, as well as roof ornaments, are a common feature in the middle reaches of the river Sepik; Aibom on Lake Chambri in particular has become well known as one of the places where they are produced. Different kinds of earth mixed with oil are also used to make modelled figures

Wooden cult figure, painted with earth pigments and soot, from Djiginabu, northern Maprik territory. This figure, which was shown only to initiates, represents a clan or ancestor spirit. Upon figures such as these depend the well-being of members of the clan and the crops of yam and other produce. Typical northern Maprik style, with a curious projection, said to represent the nose, which rarely occurs elsewhere in the Maprik district. The geometric ornaments, most of which are rectilinear, are a characteristic feature. *Museum für Völkerkunde, Basle. Height 58½ in.* *Cf. p. 114.*

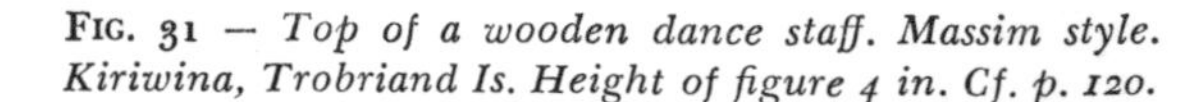

FIG. 31 — *Top of a wooden dance staff. Massim style. Kiriwina, Trobriand Is. Height of figure 4 in. Cf. p. 120.*

— as, for example, on the middle Sepik, where they are modelled over human skulls and wooden masks; but they are of course not fired.

The marine mollusc-shells which are popular as ornaments throughout Oceania also play a part in art. Figures made of this material are, however, rare. In Melanesia they occur on arm rings in the shape of birds' heads and with other motifs. Much more common are engraved and notched decorations on bivalve and univalve shells used as ornaments. Mother-of-pearl discs and shell plaques carved in open-work are to be found in the Solomons, in particularly fine forms. Throughout Oceania, but especially in New Guinea and northern Melanesia, mollusc-shells or parts of them are used, either in their natural state or worked, as a trimming on carvings and wooden masks, on corded and plaited figures, and as eyes on wooden figures, etc. Cuttle-fish bone (sepia) with incised figures are found at Astrolabe Bay (northern New Guinea) and especially at Santa Cruz.

Turtle-shell is very popular as an ornament in all areas of Oceania that are not too far distant from the sea. Among the finest works of this material are the *kapkap* of Melanesia and the headbands of the Marquesas Islands;

FIG. 8

those parts consisting of turtle-shell are frequently cut out in a delicate manner, almost like lace. Cylinder-shaped arm rings, abundantly decorated with engraved and notched ornamentation, are particularly highly esteemed in the Sepik district and on the northern coast of New Guinea. Only in the islands in the Torres Straits, however, is turtle-shell used for figures, masks and head-dress.

Teeth of the most varied provenance are used everywhere for decorative purposes. The tusks of the boar are particularly popular in Melanesia, and those of the sperm-whale in Polynesia. They frequently serve as an emblem of dignity and rank. In the western parts of Polynesia especially, the ivory from whale-tusks is fashioned into small human figures.

Animal and human bone, too, is often worked. Small bone figures and richly decorated ornaments of the same material are, for example, characteristic of the Marquesas, and engraved or carved daggers of cassowary or human bone are found in many parts of New Guinea. Even human skulls are often artistically modelled for purposes connected with head-hunting and ancestor worship. Magnificent skull masks are to be found in the Sepik district (in northern New Guinea) and in New Britain, and heads modelled

FIG. 9

over skulls in the Sepik valley, central New Ireland, Choiseul (Solomon Is.), and the New Hebrides.

Feathers, birds' beaks, animal and human hair, and pieces of hide and skin are used everywhere as ornaments and for decorative purposes, and — last but not least — also to give the final decorative touch to carvings and masks. In addition to the feather head-dresses of fantastic size made in the eastern part of central New Guinea and in the Maprik territory (Sepik district) mention must be made of the wonderful feather mosaic work, such as is found in the southern Sepik area (Keram) in the form of shields, and in central New Ireland, where it is used for headbands, and finally in Hawaii, where we find particularly fine capes and helmets, as well as idols.

PLATE P. 161

The use of spider-webbing in the New Hebrides in the fashioning of certain types of mask is presumably unique.

Raw materials: vegetable

Wood plays much the most predominant part in the production of implements and works of art of every kind. The bark-like outer surface of the stems of palm-trees and buttress roots are used to make two-dimensional figures and architectural elements. Sculptures of tree-fern pith are found in the New Hebrides and the north-western part of New Guinea. In the Sepik district and the Maprik territory (northern New Guinea) small decorative masks and heads used in harvest ceremonies are produced from balsa wood, which is light in weight and easily worked. Very heavy ebony is popular on St. Matthias I. for dancing staffs, clubs and spears.
The *malanggan* carvings from northern New Ireland are made of very soft wood, while in northern New Guinea preference is given to hardwoods for making carved figures. Engravings, notched decorations and poker-work are frequently to be found on bamboo canes and gourds. In the Maprik territory and on the upper Sepik figures in the shape of birds are made from bamboo canes, and in the same areas, as well as on the coast of the Gulf of Papua, suitably shaped roots and branches are fashioned into snakes and other figures.
In Melanesia rattan, withes and stems of all kinds are used in different ways to produce masks and figures. We have space to note only the *malanggan* doll-like figures in New Ireland and, of special merit, the basketry masks of the Sepik district. In various places in New Guinea, New Britain and Hawaii even masks, parts of masks and figures are made of string.

FIG. 32 — *Wooden lime spatulae with depressions filled in with lime. Curvilinear style of Massim province.* Right: *eastern tip of New Guinea. Length 14½ in.* Left: *Kiriwina, Trobriand Is. Length 10½ in. Cf. p. 120.*

Painting from a cult-house at Ulupu, northern Maprik district. Sheaths of palm-leaves are sewn together and painted with earth pigments and soot. They served as interior decoration of cult-houses during

In Melanesia painting is applied to the spathes of the areca palm and to the leaf-sheaths of the sago-palm, which are beaten out flat and scraped thin, and more rarely to bark and boards. Leaves and bark fibres are used both to bedeck mask-bearers and to make the masks themselves. The same is true of bark-cloth, which when painted is frequently used as decoration, as well as for clothing and ornaments.

There are countless different kinds of seeds and fruit which are worked to serve decorative purposes or to make implements, and which often bear decoration as well. In the western parts of Oceania silvery-grey Job's tears and the red seeds of one kind of shrub are special favourites. Coconut-shells and other hard fruit, and especially gourds, are frequently engraved and decorated with poker-work.

FIG. 12

Colouring

Vegetable dyes are mainly used for the decoration of bark-cloth or to dye corded or bark fibre material, in reddish-brown and yellow — but also in shades of greyish-blue and blue. The only organic substances used for painting on wood, bark or spathes and leaf-sheaths are rhizomes of curcuma, and less frequently greenish seaweed, and the red pulp of the fruit of the annatto tree, which has recently been introduced from America and is now wide-spread. But otherwise the main materials used in painting are coloured earth (white, yellow, red and brown), ores (black), fired limestone (white), charcoal and soot. The pulverized material is as a rule ground and prepared with water and saliva, less frequently with the sap of plants or oil. Fixatives are almost entirely lacking. For applying the colour chewed or frayed stalks, pieces of wood, or feathers are used; but often the artists are obliged to rely on their own fingers.

Tools

The tools employed by Oceanic artists are extremely primitive. In former times carvers had at their disposal only implements of stone, or of vegetable or animal material. By far the most important tool is the adze with a polished blade. In some parts of Micronesia and Melanesia where suitable stone is lacking or rare, blades are also made of pieces of shell from large clams or sea-shells. There are variations not only in the shape of the blade but also in the method of hafting and in the angle of the blade to the shaft. Very frequent use is made of the adze (an axe with the blade set at right angles to the handle), which resembles a small hoe. It is employed in Melanesia for all purposes, for rough as well as for delicate work. Even today it is still much used, with an imported 'plane-iron' taking the place of the primitive stone blade. In Melanesia the adzes employed for various purposes tend to differ from one another only in their size, but in Micronesia and Polynesia a

FIG. 13

initiation ceremonies. Similar faces, arranged in rows and combined with other motifs, also embellish the gables on the front of the cult-houses. Like the large sculptured figures, they represent clan spirits. Typical northern Maprik style. *Museum für Völkerkunde, Basle. Height 51⅛ in., width 31½ in. Cf. p. 114.*

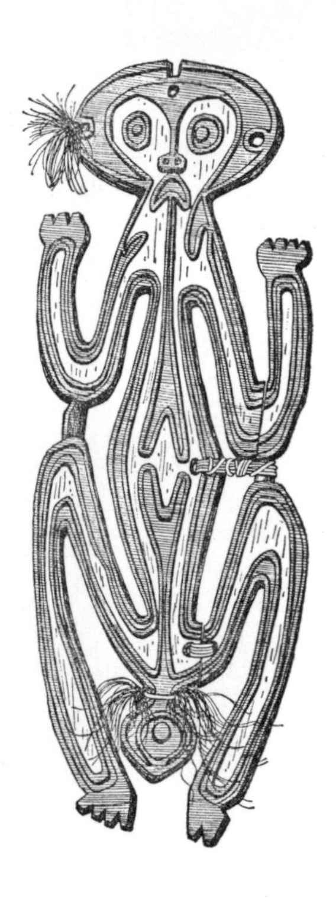

Fig. 33 — Skull idol. Male figure, carved from a single board in shallow relief, painted in parts with lime and with rattan tied on. To carvings of this kind, kept in the cult-house, were affixed the skulls of men killed in head-hunting. Style typical of the eastern coastlands of the Gulf of Papua. Wapo-Gope area, to the west of Purari, Gulf of Papua. Height 24¾ in. Cf. p. 132.

large number of special types are known. Since the main tool in use is the adze, the wood is not so much carved as hewn. Proper wood-carving knives were not known —not, at least, in former times. Tools in two pieces, stone implements like chisels, bivalve shells and bones or teeth, used together with mallets, are only found in a few places in Melanesia (for example, in the Sepik district), but are more frequent in Polynesia and Micronesia. They are signs of notable technical progress, of a level of development generally not attained by primitive peoples. Only for the most elaborately executed work are cutting tools used, such as splinters of stone and obsidian, shells with sharp edges, boars' tusks, and the teeth of mammals and fish. The same devices are used for engraving, and sometimes also for polishing, but in such cases they are frequently supplemented by rasps and files made from branches of coral and the skin of the ray and shark. Not only wood, but also turtle-shell, bone, ivory and even stone are treated in this way. Objects of stone and shell are polished as well as sawn and drilled. For this purpose arenaceous quartz and rattan fibres, or hollow bamboo drills, are utilized. For more delicate work drills with quartz points are used. The polished finish of many wooden objects is brought about by abrasion with plants containing silicic acid or by rubbing with oil.

Fig. 14

It has already been pointed out above that the shortage or absence of certain raw materials can also have an effect upon art. The art of pottery, and thus also of pottery decoration and clay sculpture, is out of the question where no clay is available. Stone figures cannot be fashioned in areas that are lacking in stone, or at best can only be made from imported materials; but on the other hand they are common in areas where wood is in short supply. This has been pointed out with particular reference to Easter Island; and it is also held that as a consequence of the shortage of wood here all available material was fully utilized, down to the last inch, which led to the figures acquiring a distorted shape such as is found nowhere else in

Basketry mask, made of rattan with withes tied on, from Numbungai, southern Maprik district. Traces of painting with earth pigments. These basketry masks are, apart from imitations of them in wood, the only type of mask found in the Maprik district. They are regarded as female representations of mythological figures and play a part (often of a somewhat grotesque character) in initiation ceremonies. *Museum für Völkerkunde, Basle. Height 21½ in.* *Cf. p. 114.*

Oceania. Of greater significance than the natural conditions in determining the development of Oceanic art forms is the fact that, because of the primitive nature of the tools employed, the mode of workmanship has to be adapted to the material. In any case the peoples of Oceania have not the means of changing their raw materials to such an extent that they become unrecognizable, or of simulating something that does not exist in nature. They are obliged to be true to their materials; and this constitutes one of the claims to greatness of Oceanic art. It will also readily be appreciated that the raw materials and tools available may exert a certain influence upon the style adopted, i.e., that stylistic characteristics may be determined by technological factors, and need not always be the result of past contact between different cultures or of independent cultural development.

Art forms

As is also the case with us, in Oceania a distinction has to made between three-dimensional, or plastic, art and two-dimensional surface delineation. Within the former group a further distinction can be made between sculpture, i.e., hewn or carved objects, and plastic art, where objects are modelled out of the raw material (e.g., clay). The second group is divided into painting and surface decoration. In the former case we are dealing with objects that are of importance in their own right, whereas in the latter case it is a matter of supplementary decoration, surface alterations and particularly ornamentation. It is not always possible to draw a sharp dividing-line between these two groups. The term surface decoration sometimes includes sculptures in high or low relief, while two-dimensional surface delineation often forms an integral part of three-dimensional art and can hardly be considered independently. But in spite of this it is necessary to divide art forms into two main groups, each with its special styles. For technical and formal reasons each group is subject to laws of its own – a point which must not be overlooked when making comparative studies.

A distinction is also often made on the basis of the use to which works of art are put, between art in its own right on one hand and architectural and applied art on the other. But here, too, a clear-cut distinction is often scarcely possible.

Art in the broader sense of the word also includes architecture proper, and not only the decoration of houses. This will only be treated incidentally in this study, but it may be pointed out here that there is fine architecture in many parts of Oceania. The enormous men's houses and cult-houses in the Sepik district or in the area of the Gulf of Papua in New Guinea are as worthy of admiration as are certain other wooden structures in Micronesia and New Zealand, or stone constructions (platforms, terraces and pyramids) in eastern Polynesia – to name only a few examples.

THE ARTIST'S SOCIAL STATUS

In the discussion of the fundamentals of Oceanic art it has already been pointed out that an interrelationship exists between the society, the culture, the artist and his work. It has also been noted that in most parts of the area there are no artists who can live exclusively from the proceeds of their work. Professional specialization is a sign of an advanced stage of development where conditions approximate to those in high cultures. Interestingly enough, it is only found in Polynesia. Carvers and stonemasons here belong to the nobility and in general occupy a privileged position. On the other hand, in Micronesia, and especially in Melanesia, knowledge of certain techniques is usually handed down from generation to generation within individual families. A certain degree of specialization can just as frequently result simply from individual predilection on the part of the artist or a particular talent for artistic expression. Such artists, like other craftsmen, produce a surplus above their own requirements and in certain circumstances even to some extent manage to live from the proceeds of their work, but are not obliged to do so. Like the other members of the tribe, they could if necessary support themselves by agriculture, fishing, etc., and in most instances this is indeed the normal practice.

Social status

Unfortunately very little is known about the social status of the artist, except in Polynesia. But it may be assumed that in Melanesia as well he enjoys considerable esteem, and that the fashioning of religious works in particular gives sculptors and painters a high position in society. This is not solely due to their special accomplishments as artists and craftsmen, although these abilities, it is true, are often related to supernatural forces by virtue of their uniqueness. The artist's prestige is enhanced still further by his knowledge of religious and magical practices and formulas, which are often thought to be as essential as skilled craftsmanship or artistic talent in the proper manufacture of implements and works of art and in ensuring that they are correctly adapted and applied. This is why the artist often enjoys not only particular esteem within his community but may also perform the functions of a priest or magician. Also worthy of note in this connection is the fact that painting and carving are entirely in the hands of the menfolk, just as ritual, in the broadest sense of the word, is also primarily a male responsibility.

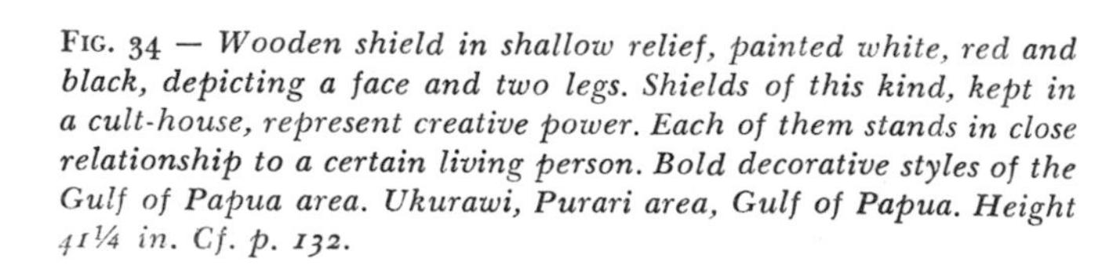

FIG. 34 — *Wooden shield in shallow relief, painted white, red and black, depicting a face and two legs. Shields of this kind, kept in a cult-house, represent creative power. Each of them stands in close relationship to a certain living person. Bold decorative styles of the Gulf of Papua area. Ukurawi, Purari area, Gulf of Papua. Height 41¼ in.* *Cf. p. 132.*

This rule is carried to such an extent that, for example, in the Sepik district basketry masks and corded objects (figures and parts of masks) may only be fashioned by men, although elsewhere weaving techniques of this kind are the province of women alone. Even certain decorations on jars (carving and notching) are here applied by men, whereas the jars themselves are made by women.

Artistic sense

We have already touched briefly upon the question whether Oceanic art may be considered as genuine art, or whether it should not rather be treated as a craft; this point must now be broached again in connection with the question of the degree of individual judgement exercised by the artist. Oceanic art is no doubt utilitarian art in that it primarily serves ritual purposes. It is also definitely collective in character, for its motifs and styles are very deeply rooted in tradition. This is shown most convincingly, perhaps, in the fact that in some areas there are privileges governing the production of certain art forms, which can be bought and sold: for example, the large paintings on spirit houses by the river Keram (Sepik district) or the *malanggan* ritual carvings in northern New Ireland. In spite of all these restrictions works may be created which are imbued with profound content. For this reason we may undoubtedly assume that such works were made by men possessed of artistic sense. During my own journeyings in the Bismarck Archipelago and the Sepik district of New Guinea I have been convinced time and again of the existence of sculptors and painters who in evaluating their own works and those by other artists take into account, not only the perfection of craftsmanship displayed or simply the function served, but also artistic content, and who are very frequently prepared to discuss this very point. In the evaluation of an artist and his work by the public the situation in Oceania does not seem to differ very much from that in the Western world. There, too, craftsmen who are excellent copyists but have no real inner feeling may receive the plaudits of the crowd, whereas eminent artists may be insufficiently appreciated.

The art of the South Seas is folk art. Even in cases where its significance from the standpoint of content and function is not commonly understood, it can exist within the framework of the community as a whole and the culture to which it belongs. But it would be erroneous for this reason to call it anonymous. This term has been applied to it in our collections because too much attention has been paid to the work and not enough to the artist. But in Oceania, on the other hand, the names of great artists are often still familiar after several generations have come and gone. Frequently such artists and their works acquire a supernatural character and are brought within the scope of mythological tradition. Even in such cases very ancient works of art are exceptional, as is evident from the fact that wood and other vegetable material is rapidly destroyed by weathering and pests of various kinds.

IV. STYLE PROVINCES AND STYLES

We shall now proceed to consider Oceanic art in greater detail, dealing in succession with the three major style regions: Melanesia, Polynesia and Micronesia. By 'style region' or 'style province' is meant an area clearly delimited in the geographical sense that has its own typical artistic style. Clearly we are here concerned in the first instance with the purely formal qualities of a work, for its style is in fact the product of a certain unique and immutable selection and combination by the artist of elements which can also occur, in a different composition, in other styles. For reasons of technique alone the styles adopted in various forms of artistic expression, such as sculpture, painting and decoration, are governed by different laws. They are therefore not strictly comparable with one another and have to be considered independently within each of the various style regions. Obviously it is also important, when describing the stylistic characteristics of a certain region, to note whether all art forms (e.g., carving, painting, etc.) are present or only some; which are predominant; and whether decoration is lacking or overshadows all others. The motifs employed are also of importance. One ought really to compare the styles of each motif independently, but this is unfortunately not possible here – mainly because only very few studies of style according to purely formal principles have as yet been undertaken in Oceania. However, by and large it may be said that throughout the South Seas the principal motifs are human, as a result of the preponderantly religious character of Oceanic art and the general tendency to represent supernatural forces in personified form. In view of this fact the following survey can be confined largely to the stylistic characteristics of human figures.
Considered geographically, the various style provinces do not constitute historical entities. Nor are they co-extensive with cultural regions. They serve merely as an aid to the description of the various artistic styles.

MELANESIA

In Melanesia the history of population movements is complex. Some districts remained isolated for a long period of time. Owing to these factors one finds a greater number and variety of style provinces than in other areas of Oceania. These provinces do not always comprise whole islands or archipelagoes. Often they only embrace parts of an island, or even small stretches of territory; this is particularly the case in New Guinea and the Bismarck Archipelago. In a concluding chapter an attempt will be made to tabulate the typical features of Melanesian art and to compare them with the specific features of Polynesian and Micronesian art.

NEW GUINEA

The island of New Guinea has not yet been fully explored or investigated. From the upper reaches of the Mamberamo and the Sepik in the north

Wooden male and female cult figures, bearing traces of painting, from a men's house at Jerik on Umboi Island. Typical forms of the Tami style, except for the position of the arms: with the male figure *(left)*

across the central mountain ranges and plateaus to the valley of the Digul there stretches a vast area that is still almost entirely virgin territory. The same holds good of the inland areas of the Vogelkop peninsula, the coastal ranges east of the Ramu and the plateau country south-west of the Huon peninsula. Any attempt to distinguish between styles must therefore necessarily remain incomplete. A reasonably adequate amount of information is available only for the coastal districts and some of the larger river basins. But in the present state of our knowledge it is permissible to assume that on the whole the inhabitants of the mountainous central districts have nothing of particular merit to offer in the way of art. This has been established with regard to the eastern highlands, which by and large are very poor both in sculptural works and two-dimensional surface delineations, whereas this district is almost unimaginably rich as regards ornaments, particularly the use of feathers.
In the northern parts of the island, which are mainly inhabited by peoples of Austromelanid culture, six style provinces are generally distinguished.

North-western New Guinea

This province embraces the islands off the coast of western New Guinea, some places on the Vogelkop peninsula, the coast of Geelvink Bay and the Schouten Islands, and extends as far eastwards as the estuary of the Mamberamo. Although there are several local styles, this district is in general very uniform, with one single style of sculpture and equally characteristic styles of decoration. The only paintings known are reproductions made by priests of mythological creatures (men, snakes and dragons); masks are wholly lacking.
Although there are some sculptures of animals (fish, snakes and crocodiles), the principal motifs here are human. Human figures were featured on the ends of the supporting posts of the great men's houses, which have now disappeared, and were also carved in relief on the longitudinal beams and crossbeams of these houses, where they were sometimes found in association with crocodiles and snakes. There are also some large cult figures. But the typical style is seen to best advantage in the smaller human figures termed *korwar*, some of which were used as skull-containers. These standing or squatting figures occasionally have tendril-like forms or smaller figures on the front. The head, which rests upon a short neck, is invariably larger in proportion to the rest of the body, and is carved with straight lines at right angles to one another. The face is often almost rectangular, and is cut off horizontally at the base, with the very broad mouth, open and often showing the teeth, placed close to this edge. In many instances the whole jaw protrudes like a snout.

PLATE P. 36

these are folded behind the back; with the female figure they rest upon the abdomen. *Museum für Völkerkunde, Basle. Height of male figure 57½ in., of female figure 58¼ in. Cf. p. 119.*

Fig. 35 — Detail of a bark belt worn by men, with engraved anthropomorphic ornaments. The depressions are filled in with lime. Kerewa area, Gulf of Papua. Width 5½ in. Cf. p. 134.

The nose consists of a narrow vertical ridge and clearly-marked flaring nostrils (anchor form); the eyes are inset beneath a very angular bulge on the forehead, usually horizontal, and are suggested by slight elevations or perforations; the top of the head is slightly domed. The shape of these figures, which are of dark and menacing appearance, is so typical that the style of the whole district has been termed the *korwar* style after them.

Fig. 16

The style of decoration is equally characteristic: it consists of tendril-like ornaments with sharply curving hooks. The best examples are to be seen on canoe ornaments and head-rests in open-work, where they are featured together with human heads, and in the decoration engraved on bamboo quivers.

The rigid rendering of the human figures, and especially the squatting posture, as well as the use of the tendril ornament and the style of painting, to some extent resemble Indonesian styles; they are found nowhere else in New Guinea.

Humboldt Bay and Lake Sentani

This style province extends from the mouth of the Mamberamo approximately as far as the frontier between Dutch and Australian New Guinea. It embraces a narrow belt of coastland, together with the islands lying off-shore, and stretches into the interior some distance beyond Lake Sentani. Local centres are to be found both in the latter region and also in the area around Humboldt Bay. Here again artistic sculptures and decoration prevail at the expense of painting. Most motifs are human, but there are also some animal figures (fish, crocodiles, lizards, snakes and birds). There are no masks in this province either.

Plate p. 40

The sculptures are to be found on the men's houses, which are built on poles and have pyramid-shaped roofs. These human figures are generally rounded and full-bodied. In the western coastlands they are somewhat reminiscent of the *korwar* style (anchor-shaped noses), whereas in the eastern parts the noses are broader and curved, as in the Sepik district. Most of the figures are shown erect, though some are squatting or seated; they are strikingly rigid, with the arms hanging down or close to the body (holding the abdomen). The face is oval-shaped, usually with a pointed chin. The eyes, ears and mouth (which is turned up at the corners), and sometimes the nose as well, are as a rule only suggested. There are also some animal figures in

Painted wooden dance shield from the Trobriand Islands. The surface is decorated with serpent motifs and elegant designs typical of the Massim style province. *British Museum. Height approx. 22½ in.* *Cf. p. 120.*

Wooden ancestor figure from the Lorentz river, Asmat, painted with earth pigments; the head and ear ornaments are made of cord, bast, cassowary feathers and grass seeds. Figures of this kind are found up to the present day only in the environs of the Lorentz river. Typical Asmat style. *Museum für Völkerkunde, Basle. Height 35½ in. Cf. p. 127.*

Fig. 36 – *Decorative combs used by men. The little wooden sticks are tied together with rattan and cord, which is then coated with resin-like fruit pulp. The figurative representations are of the same material. Manus I., Admiralty Is.* Left: *face and crocodile head. 10¾ in.* Right: *male head with ancient hairdress. 9⅝ in. Rounded type of figure. Cf. p. 139.*

wood (emblems of individual clans), and human guardian figures which served as roof decorations. In the Lake Sentani area we also find very fine roof-posts on the houses of chiefs, which are decorated with reliefs or almost fully three-dimensional figures of human beings and animals (lizards). They terminate in wing-like projections carved in open-work and decorated with curvilinear ornaments and animal motifs. The prows of canoes also bear lavish decoration featuring human, birds'head and fish motifs; as well as these spirited compositions there are some very life-like bird figures. Carvings of this kind seem to have more vigour than the ritual figures, and in their treatment are partly very reminiscent of the styles found in the Sepik district.

The predilection for rounded and curved forms, which has been noted already in connection with sculptured figures, is particularly evident in all decoration. Designs in the shape of arcs and circles are found on wooden bowls, bamboo containers, gourds, suspension hooks in the shape of boards, daggers made of cassowary bone, hour-glass drums, and much else besides. The most popular design, especially in the Lake Sentani area, is a regular arrangement of double spirals. This type of surface decoration has with justice been termed the 'curvilinear style'.

Fig. 17

The exceptionally fine paintings on bark-cloth are very rare nowadays. They used to be the property of particular clans and were suspended in the men's houses. The fabrics of this type found in the Lake Sentani area generally only bear designs of curvilinear ornaments, while those from the area around Humboldt Bay have fish, snakes and birds – in a traditional style, but arranged freely. Food-jars also used to be painted with such motifs for clan festivals.

Plate p. 44

Sepik district

The Sepik district, which extends from the frontier between

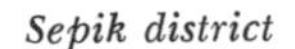

Fig. 37 – *Figures on handles of wooden lime spatulae. They are of the more rounded type, with ancient hairdress and incised ornaments.* Left: *overall length 13⅜ in., of figure 3¼ in.* Right: *overall length 15 in., of figure 4 in. Bipi I., Admiralty Is. Cf. p. 139.*

Detailed map of lower and middle Sepik district on p. 189

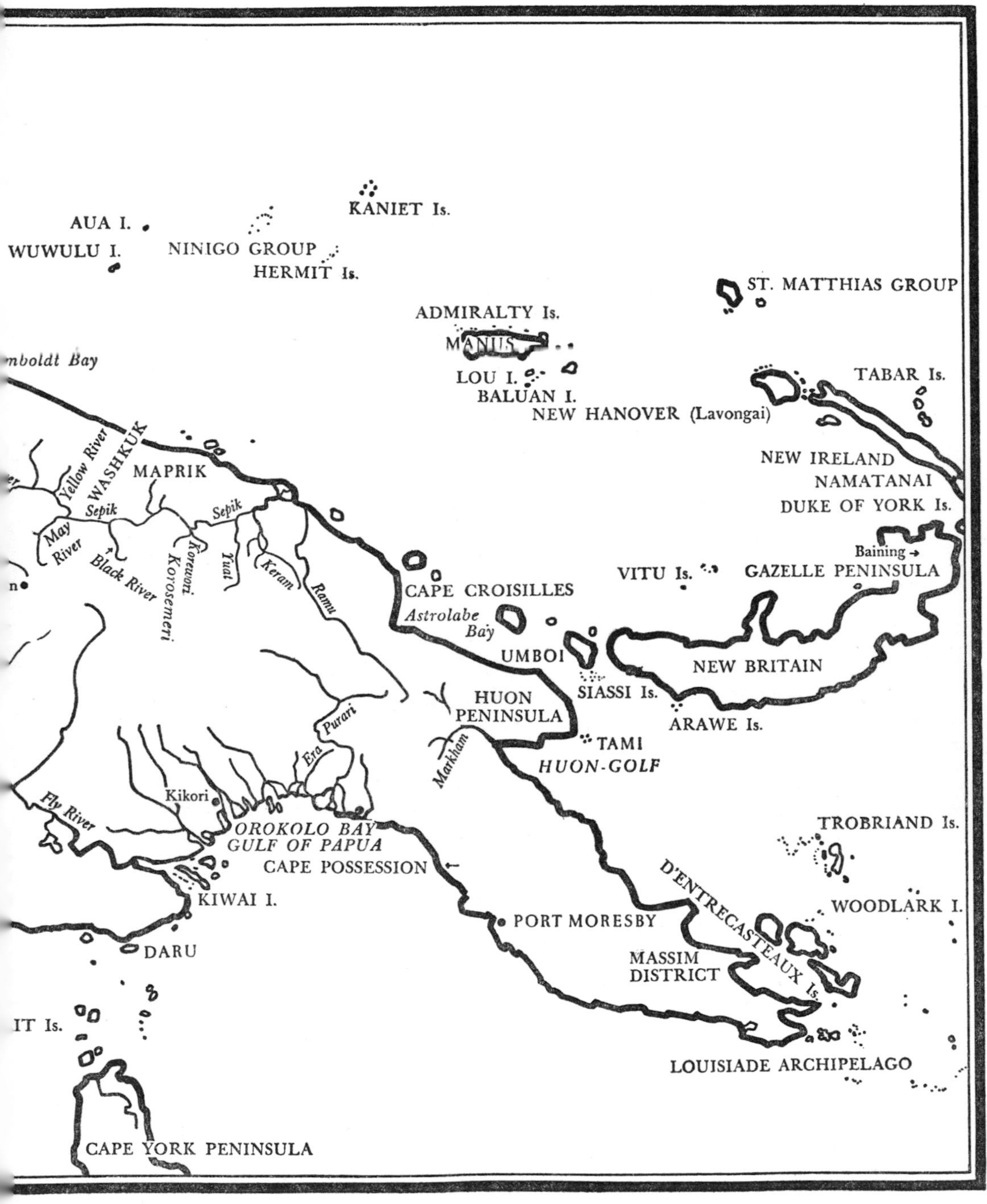

KANIET Is.
AUA I.
WUWULU I.
NINIGO GROUP
HERMIT Is.
ST. MATTHIAS GROUP
ADMIRALTY Is.
MANUS
mboldt Bay
LOU I.
BALUAN I.
TABAR Is.
NEW HANOVER (Lavongai)
Yellow River
WASHKUK
MAPRIK
Sepik
Sepik
May River
Black River
Korewori
Korosemeri
Yuat
Keram
Ramu
NEW IRELAND
NAMATANAI
DUKE OF YORK Is.
Baining
VITU Is.
GAZELLE PENINSULA
CAPE CROISILLES
Astrolabe Bay
UMBOI
NEW BRITAIN
SIASSI Is.
HUON PENINSULA
ARAWE Is.
Purari
Era
Markham
TAMI
HUON-GOLF
Kikori
Fly River
OROKOLO BAY
GULF OF PAPUA
CAPE POSSESSION
TROBRIAND Is.
D'ENTRECASTEAUX Is.
KIWAI I.
PORT MORESBY
WOODLARK I.
MASSIM DISTRICT
DARU
IT Is.
LOUISIADE ARCHIPELAGO
CAPE YORK PENINSULA

Dutch and Australian New Guinea roughly as far as Cape Croisilles and reaches far inland in the area of the rivers Sepik and Ramu, is acknowledged to be the most important cultural centre in New Guinea, and even in the whole of Oceania. It is frequently referred to as a province with a uniform style, but this is not correct. There are actually at least six groups of styles here, and each of them has distinct local varieties, many of which could also be considered independent style provinces.
Within the Sepik district the inhabitants of the coastal region, the Maprik mountains, and in particular the lowlands along the lower and middle Sepik, have an incredible wealth of works of art, related through clans and kinship groups to ancestors and mythological figures. This artistic wealth is connected with the very impressive dramatic ceremonies which they hold. These centre on their spirit houses – buildings that are unique both from the architectural and artistic point of view, which often also serve as men's houses. A major role is played in ritual not only by sculptures, masks, paintings and implements but also by musical and sound-making instruments: wooden slit-drums, hour-glass drums, wooden trumpets, transverse flutes (which sometimes attain a considerable size) and bull-roarers. The latter are lancet-shaped little boards which emit a humming note when swung on the end of a cord. Many cult objects are kept secret, but some, especially certain masks, play a part in public festivals. The motifs employed in rituals are repeated in architecture, as well as on weapons, boats and implements of all kinds.
The profusion of works is not the only striking point: also noteworthy is the great wealth of styles. This does not result from a variety of motifs, as one might think – for here, too, human figures predominate, and there are few animals other than birds, crocodiles, lizards and snakes. Much more important are the numerous variations in style and in the bold manner of combining different elements, and the surprisingly wide latitude of freedom employed in design, so that the works often seem to have departed a long way from tradition. However, the confusing picture thus presented becomes clearer when one takes into account the strong emotional quality with which these works of art are imbued and the uniform character of the basic decorative styles. Throughout the area curves of one kind or another predominate; and in addition much use is made of colour.
In other parts of this district the level of artistic achievement is generally speaking poorer and has not the same wealth of variety. This is true already

Ceremonial poles (*bis*poles) from the coastal area of the Asmat district, south-western New Guinea. Each represents a canoe standing upright, and is topped by an exaggeratedly large ornament. The human figures depict men killed by the enemy. These poles are erected during great fertility ceremonies. *Koninklijk Instituut voor de Tropen, Amsterdam. Overall length 19 ft. 2 in.; of details shown 17 ft. and 17 ft. 4 in.* *Cf. p. 127.*

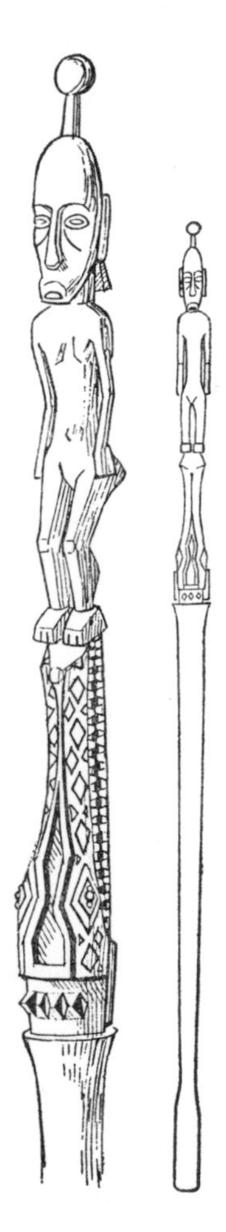

FIG. 38 — Left: *wooden lime spatula. Crocodile head and male figure with ancient hairdress. Elongated type of figure, but of a more rounded form. South coast of Manus I., Admiralty Is. Overall length 19¾ in., of carving 7½ in.* Right: *wooden spearhead, with a spine of a sting-ray inserted, tied on with cord and decorated with glass beads. The hat-like projection of the figure is inserted into the spear-shaft. Angular elongated type of figure. South coast of Manus, Admiralty Is. Length 16 in. Cf. p. 139.*

of the southern border of the Sepik lowlands and of the whole mountainous area along the coast except the Maprik territory. There is also a gradual decline in artistic standards as one follows the Sepik upstream; and the inhabitants of the mountainous areas near the uppermost reaches of the river must be ranged with those other peoples of central New Guinea who have little to boast of in the way of art.

The profusion of styles in some parts of the Sepik river area is closely connected with the fact that there is extensive contact between the various groups of peoples. Already in early times, in spite of traditional hostilities, feuds and head-hunting, commodities, ritual figures, masks, and even ceremonies and songs were interchanged over a wide area. This often led to modifications in their significance, but the external forms remained the same, and were emulated or fused. This is why some styles are disseminated over such a wide area, and especially why it is often hardly possible to distinguish between different style provinces and local variants. Quite often there are to be found in the same settlement masks and sculptured figures that differ completely from one another. The following classification into style provinces can therefore be regarded only as approximate.

Coastal area

PLATE P. 49

The coastal area presents a relatively simple and clear picture. Already in the western part the human figures and facial masks bear features that occur in more pronounced form in the immediate vicinity of the Sepik and Ramu estuaries. The bodies are usually thick-set, with legs and arms bent and a short neck. The oblong heads have large tufts of hair. The face, too, is long and tapers to a point at the chin. The nose, which is always very convex, is broad at the top and is often extended downwards over the whole body. Characteristic, too,

FIGS. 18, 19

are the slanting eyes pointing towards the medial line and the sharp ridge between the forehead and the nose. Often a bird-like impression is conveyed, with the nose representing the beak: hence the term 'beak style'. It is disseminated over an area that comprises the lower reaches of the Sepik and Ramu rivers as well as the tributaries that flow into them here.

In the lower Sepik area we find magnificent canoe prows, among other things, bearing heads of crocodiles and human beings, carved in open-work, as well as complete bird and human figures, some of which are prolonged, with fully plasticity, into the hollowed-out part of the log. Distinct local styles are to be found here, particularly along the right-hand tributaries, the Keram and Yuat, as well as in the transitional zone leading to the central Sepik area. On the Yuat the Mundugumor are distinguished as artists and merchants who, for example, knew how to utilize for their own purposes the famous spirit figures of the neighbouring bushmen. Their sculptures are among the finest works in New Guinea. Most of them are lavishly decorated with clam-shells, hair and feathers. This is also true of their masks, from which two types are derived: one with a typical hooked nose, and possibly also a second type with a bulbous nose, found throughout the entire central Sepik area. The masks that are flatter in form, made from wood or the front parts of human skulls, over which faces were modelled in resin or clay, presumably originate from the villages on the river Sepik in the area of its junction with the Yuat. Throughout the whole district one finds, as well as figures, poly-chrome paintings on palm leaf-sheaths. These were used especially for the decoration of cult buildings.

Lower Sepik

Yuat

PLATE P. 52

FIG. 20

FIG. 19

PLATE P. 56

Influences from the lower reaches of the river Sepik make themselves felt far upstream. In any case, elements of the beak style are to be found in the next style province, the middle Sepik. This begins in the broad trans-itional zone above the Yuat and extends along the river as far as Ambunti and beyond. It too, has several typical less refined local forms which can hardly be distinguished from one another any longer. Furthermore, it is in this area that the influence of all adjacent territories has been felt most strongly. Finally, in many places this style has come to overshadow older forms, traces of which can still be made out in some works.

Middle Sepik

PLATES PP. 58, 64, 68

All the areas skirting the central Sepik area have their own very distinct local styles. In the mountainous country on either bank of the river above Ambunti (Washkuk and Yeshan) the art styles of the central Sepik area

Washkuk, Yeshan

FIG. 39 — *Wooden food-bowl with handles added. Incised ornamentation. Typical spiral handles topped by lizards or croc-odiles. Geometric designs. Iru, Manus I., Admiralty Is. Diameter 15¾ in., height 7 in. Cf. p. 139.*

Canoe ornament in wood, painted with earth pigments, from the Eilanden river, Asmat district. The human figures are more lavishly decorated than are the cult figures from the same district. Typical is the pronounced curvilinear tendril-like ornamentation. *Museum für Völkerkunde, Basle. Length 32½ in. Cf. p. 128.*

have fused with styles reminiscent of Maprik, particularly in their colourfulness. Cruder Sepik styles are to be found – also in this case together with transitional styles leading to Maprik ones – throughout the savannah country north of the river. In the south the art and culture which today is confined to the upper reaches of the tributaries seems to have been superseded by other styles only at a relatively recent date.

Korewori

A particularly well-developed local style exists on the Korewori, best illustrated by the gigantic ritual crocodile figures from this area. Among the ritual objects of the middle Sepik area a leading place is taken by mythological figures, ancestor statues and masks of all shapes and sizes. It

PLATE P. 75
FIG. 21

FIG. 40 — Top of a woman's ebony dance staff. Incised ornamentation filled in with lime. Typical St. Matthias style of sculpture and ornamentation. Mussau I., St. Matthias Group. Overall length 46½ in., of male figure 10¼ in. Cf. p. 140.

would take far too long to list even the most important of them. Here, too, faces are modelled over the skulls of persons who have died or been killed in head-hunting. The ritual houses are incredibly lavishly decorated with carvings and paintings featuring human faces or figures and curvilinear ornamentation. Among the best-known implements, which are likewise almost invariably decorated in an artistic manner, are ceremonial stools, footstools, head-rests, and also hooks (from which bags, etc., are suspended) which are lavishly decorated with figures; these are almost entirely confined to the middle Sepik area.

PLATE P. 78

FIGS. 22, 23

FIGS. 4, 10, 15

Upper Sepik

The third style province comprises the low-lying areas by the Sepik upstream from Ambunti, apparently as far as the May river area. As one proceeds up the river one at first notes a gradual decline in artistic quality. In the same way the stylistic influence from the middle Sepik and the highlands of Washkuk and Yeshan makes itself felt to an ever-diminishing extent, although in the beginning it is still apparent. Except in the transitional zones in the lowest reaches of the river three-dimensional works and particularly masks seem to be largely missing. Sculpture comprises only the heads on so-called canoe shields, which, however, are used here for house decoration and as dance emblems, and to ornament canoe prows and paddle-shafts (cf. Fig. 24). It is the usual practice to depict heads of crocodiles and birds, but they are reduced to essentials and carved so freely in open-work that it is often hardly possible to recognize the motifs any longer. In the lower area the decoration of the large shields consists mainly of curvilinear ornaments, but faces are depicted as well; this points to influences from the middle Sepik. As we move further upstream, particularly following the May river, the decoration becomes more abstract; although an-

FIG. 41 — Striking part of ebony club used for killing pigs. Fish and snake carved in relief, depressions filled in with lime. Typical St. Matthias ornamentation. Mussau I., St. Matthias Group. Overall length 22¾ in. Cf. p. 140.

thropomorphic features are frequently still recognizable, the typically curvilinear designs tend to disappear, indicating affinities with the mountainous areas of the Sepik district. This is also true of the paintings on palm-leaf sheaths, used as decoration on houses and doors (cf. Plate p. 81).

The Yellow river forms the starting-point of a style province which apparently also stretches northwards a long way into the mountains of the northern coastal range and even as far as the central range. There seems to be very little in the way of art here that is worthy of note. On the Yellow river itself it is mainly restricted to decoration on shields, bamboo containers and pipes for smoking; this is also true of the Green river and Telefolmin, the last two Australian administrative posts, situated in territory that is otherwise completely unexplored. Of great interest is the decoration on the shields found everywhere in these areas. Certain technical features (designs of raised portions on a hollowed-out ground), already known in the low-lying areas on the upper Sepik, bear a great resemblance to those found at Asmat in south-western New Guinea; so too do some of the styles of decoration, though these are much cruder. Possibly cultural links may exist between this area and the basins of the rivers between the Digul and the Lorentz. If so, this would constitute a parallel to the many cultural and artistic links that connect the peoples settled on the Gulf of Papua in the south and those in the Sepik district in the north.

The style province of the border areas to the south of the Sepik lowlands comprises the upper reaches of the rivers Korewori, Korosemeri and Blackwater, and from there stretches in a great arc southwards as far as the Black river above Ambunti. Its exact extent is not known. But formerly it no doubt included areas situated further to the north, and there is even some evidence that it is closely related to the ancient art forms to be found in the mountain ranges on the northern border (Maprik); these areas may once actually have been connected. Today it seems to be very strongly influenced by the art of the middle Sepik area, which in some places has superimposed itself upon and ousted the older styles. Only the flat spirit figures, with their characteristic abundance of hooks, can be ascribed to it with certainty. Smaller figures of this kind are used as amulets and

PLATE P. 84

Wooden shields used in battle, painted with earth pigments, from the Asmat district, south-western New Guinea. The shield on the left is from the Lorentz river area, that on the right from the Eilanden river area. The decoration on both shields is apparently derived in the main from anthropomorphic motifs, but only on the shield on the right is a human figure still identifiable. On the left-hand shield the ornamentation is completely asymmetrical, while that on the right-hand one is built up around a medial line. *Museum für Völkerkunde, Basle. Maximum width of shield on left 19¼ in., of that on right 16½ in. Cf. p. 128.*

dance emblems, whereas the larger ones stand in men's houses, where they serve primarily as oracles, which are consulted before campaigns and hunting expeditions, and personify a mythical figure. This may also be the cradle of the basketry masks which are known throughout the middle Sepik area, since particularly large and fine specimens are to be found in the southern border region.

Maprik

Maprik, a style province situated on the southern slopes of the Prince Alexander range, extends over a very small area with uncertain boundaries, but after the much larger middle Sepik area it is the most important art centre in the Sepik region. From a stylistic point of view, especially in so far as religious art is concerned, it is also characterized by astonishing variety. Preference is given to such motifs as human beings, birds and snakes and in isolated instances other animals as well. Especially in carvings in relief they are often found combined in astonishing ways. Here, too, as in the middle Sepik area, sculptures are carved in open-work. Though there are several local variations the character of this singular style is basically uniform. A common feature are, in the human motifs and often in the paintings as well, T-shaped faces, formed by the bulging forehead and straight narrow nose; also common are the combination of the face with various kinds of birds and large decorative motifs, and especially the glaring colours. In general it is thought essential that sculptures should be painted, and the colours are frequently considered more important than the figures themselves as transmitters of supernatural power. Works of art which are intimately related to the clans play a special part in initiation ceremonies and harvest festivals. Also religious in character are the gigantic paintings on the triangular facades of the gables on cult houses, as well as the sculptures that are affixed to them. They are also connected with clans and yam cultivation. As in the southern border areas, so also in the Maprik territory the only masks known are of the basketry type, or in any case wooden imitations of them. They are found in many different variants. Linguistic and cultural idiosyncrasies indicate that the inhabitants of Maprik made their way here from the middle Sepik. Certain artistic affinities also suggest this conclusion. For this reason it is all the more surprising to find that Maprik art

PLATES PP. 87, 90

PLATE P. 93

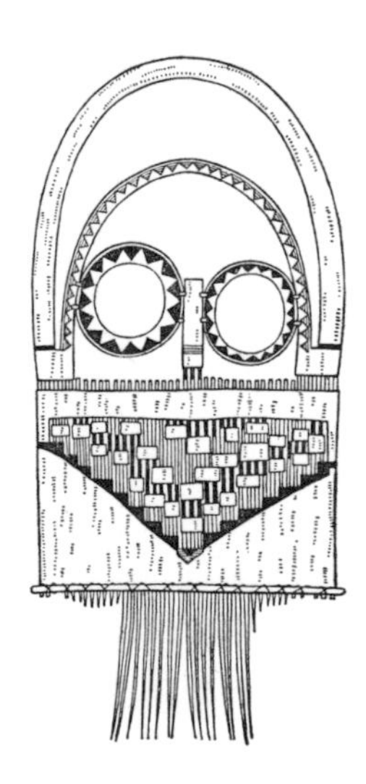

FIG. 42 — *Decorative comb used by men, made of small sticks; the plate and decorations are of cordage and withes, coated with lime and painted white, red and black. Mussau I., St. Matthias Group. Length 22¾ in., width 10 in. Cf. p. 140.*

FIG. 43 — *Middle piece of a hood worn by women when dancing, made of bark-cloth and painted red, blue and black. Lelet plateau, central New Ireland. Length 11¾ in., width 8 in. Cf. p. 142.*

developed along lines of its own and evolved a completely independent style. The next style province in northern New Guinea, which is very uniform in character, comprises a narrow coastal strip extending from Cape Croisilles approximately as far as the base of the Huon peninsula, together with the adjacent islands. Although surface decoration is by no means lacking, the whole area is dominated by sculptures and wooden masks which are treated in a fully three-dimensional manner; these are regarded as embodiments of spirits. Besides small male and female figures, usually plain, there are some that are for the most part painted, which measure some three to six feet in height; the same styles are also to be found on the posts of the men's houses. In the case of the standing figures the shoulder-belt and the hips are block-shaped. Frequently the feet rest upon another block, or else the legs terminate in one. The arms hang down loosely, with the hands resting on, or close to, the hips. The head projects directly out of the shoulders; the face, which is frequently fashioned like a board, is set so low down that the shoulders seem to be on a level with the ears. The bulges on the forehead form a straight horizontal line, from which the narrow nose leads downwards vertically; it is often anchor-shaped. The parts beneath the forehead are inset. In the triangular or pentagonal face the eyes protrude in the form of cones; instead of eye-brows, and often below the eyes as well, there are semi-circles or triangles. The mouth is at the bottom of the chinless face, and frequently features decorative ornaments used in battle or dances. The head is often topped by a hemispherical cap; ears and head-dress are often combined with motifs of hooks and spirals to form a decorative board-like structure carved in open-work. Sometimes several figures or heads are

Astrolabe Bay

FIG. 25

FIG. 44 — *Wooden face mask carved in open-work, painted white, yellow, red and black. Snail-shells for eyes. Face reduced to rectangular form, with mouth, two teeth and eyes. Large wing-shaped ears. Omo, north-western New Ireland. Width 25¼ in. Cf. p. 145.*

Shield mask from the Wapo district, west of Purari, Gulf of Papua. Bamboo and rattan frame, covered with bark-cloth and painted with earth pigments; the painted panels are divided by tied-on withes. At

FIG. 45 — *Wooden head mask. Rattan frame; hair crest of yellow and light brown fibres; prickly fruit over the forehead; cords on either side of the hair crest. Opercula of snails for eyes, painted white, yellow, red and black. Personification of a deceased person. One of the most common types of mask in the area where* malanggans *are found. Typical bent nose, snout-like straight mouth with teeth showing, distended ear-lobes. Nemassalang, north-western New Ireland. Height 19¾ in. Cf. p. 146.*

placed one on top of another. From a stylistic point of view these sculptures bear a great resemblance to the religious figures from Yuat in the Sepik district. These, too, are combined with animal motifs and are devoid of any decoration, or have only few ornaments. Small human figures executed in the same style are frequently to be found on the handles of dance rattles made of fruit-rind. But just as often birds are represented on these as well. Sculptures in the round also occur in the shape of birds and fish.

All decorative art is emphatically geometrical and there is a complete absence of human and animal motifs. Preference is given to straight lines and combinations of lines: chevrons, toothed designs, triangles and squares. Spirals and curves occur very rarely. The same designs are to be found time and again on bamboo combs, large cylindrical turtle-shell clasps with incised decorations filled in with lime, bamboo quivers, hour-glass drums, mostly with arched handles, flat wooden bowls, clubs, bull-roarers and circular shields which very often bear a sort of Maltese cross.

Paintings in a reddish, and in rare instances a black, colour occur on blankets and loin-cloths made of bark-cloth. Here, too, geometric designs are employed, most of them linear and angular.

Huon Gulf, Tami

This style province comprises the coastal area of the Huon Gulf and the off-shore islands, particularly Tami, after which this style is often called. Off-shoots are to be found to the north on Umboi and Siassi and as far afield as New Britain.

the bottom a part projects forth like a snout. The decorative motifs serve as clan emblems. Characteristic of the Gulf of Papua. Bold ornamentation, probably derived from a facial motif. *Museum für Völkerkunde, Basle. Height 5 ft. 5 in., max. width 2 ft. 6¼ in. Cf. p. 132.*

Head mask from the Purari district, on the Gulf of Papua. Rattan frame, covered with bark-cloth and painted. It has sewn-on withes, decoration of cassowary feathers, and huge ears affixed to it. Masks of this kind represent bush spirits, the appearance of which serves to protect the crops. In material and form they are typical of the eastern parts of the Gulf of Papua style province. *Museum für Völkerkunde, Basle. Height 3 ft. 11 in.* *Cf. p. 132.*

This area is noted for a characteristic style of sculpture and special types of masks, paintings and decorative designs. The sculptures, most of which are cult objects, bear strong resemblance to the style found in Astrolabe Bay. But here the face is basically square in outline, although narrower at the bottom than at the top; the cheeks and forehead are usually on the same plane; the eyes do not protrude but are incised in outline and are slightly inset. The nose forms a straight or slightly bulging line; nostrils are either missing or are turned downwards, and are often actually seperate from the nose. The mouth, at the bottom of the face, is not particularly wide; the teeth are shown, and often the tongue as well. Here, too, the shoulders and hips project considerably, and the head appears to be set very low down. As with the Astrolabe Bay figures there is a strongly-marked tendency towards treatment in breadth, thus making the style heavy and very static. All the figures are as a rule painted, with preference being given to red and black ornaments on a white ground. Frequently — in renderings of faces, for example — painting takes the place of modelling.

Figs. 26, 27

Plate p. 98

Two types of mask in particular are known from Tami: firstly, those with pointed frames covered with bark-cloth and painted, which resemble wooden sculptures; and secondly, wooden masks executed in the same style. Animal motifs (e.g., pig, opossum, lizard, crocodile, snake, bird, fish, turtle) occur frequently, but are not rendered in association with human figures — at least, not in the case of cult objects. The crocodile appears as a complete figure on canoe prows and paddle-handles, in this case very often in combination with a human being, bird and fish. The crocodile is to be found depicted in carvings in relief on planks of canoes, posts of houses, and ornaments affixed to dwellings.

In the decoration of wooden bowls, suspension hooks, head-rests, lime spatulae and other implements predominance is given to highly stylized and extremely conventionalized animal motifs (snake, fish, bird). Representations of human beings also occur. The designs are almost invariably incised and filled in with lime. On the Huon Gulf two types of shield were formerly

Fig. 46 — *Wooden cult figure* (uli). *Face in parts modelled in resin; eyes of mother-of-pearl with opercula of snails; fringed beard of fibres of roots. Lime coating, painted in white, yellow, red and black. Konos, central New Ireland. Height 49 in. Cf. p. 146.*

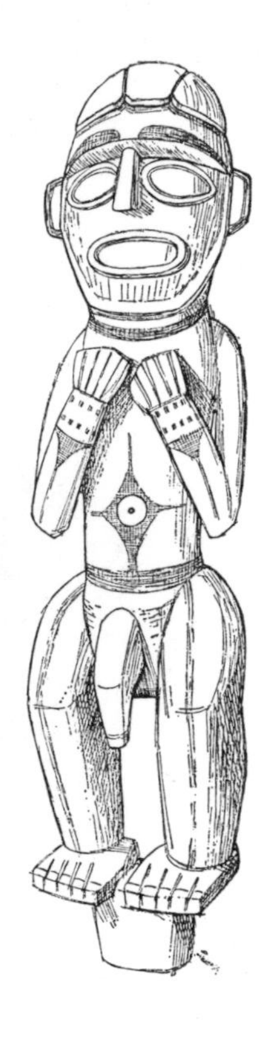

Fig. 47 – Limestone ancestor figure, parts of which are painted red. Central New Ireland. Height 21⅝ in. Cf. p. 146.

in use: one was wooden, oval and slightly curved, and the other consisted of several layers of bark-cloth. Both types were painted (reddish-brown and black) with simple circular ornaments, faces and complete human figures wearing head-dress (cf. Figs. 12, 28, 29, 30). Already before the arrival of the white man the Tami Islands were an important trading centre for the exchange of implements of all kinds, and particularly of wooden bowls, which found their way even as far as the Admiralty Islands.

In the extreme eastern part of New Guinea is the so-called Massim style province. It comprises the eastern tip of the island, and especially also the D'Entrecasteaux, Trobriand and Woodlark Islands, as well as the Louisiade Archipelago. As in the Tami area this region is very homogeneous from the artistic point of view. Massim art consists mainly of two-dimensional surface delineation, with very delicate refined styles of decoration. By comparison carved figures in the round are rarely met with; painting, too, plays only a very minor part. The art of this district seems in general to be based far less on religious ideas than in other parts of New Guinea. This may be the reason why more emphasis is laid on technique of rendering than on emotional content.

On the Trobriand Islands are sculptured human figures, usually represented in a squatting posture, seldom standing, which bear some resemblance to the *korwar* style of north-western New Guinea in the rendering of the head and face. The decorative character of these figures in very striking owing to the richness of ornamentation; the designs are incised and often filled in with lime. Lavish decoration is, however, a particularly typical feature on many implements. It is unique in its wealth of variations and fondness for delicate small designs. The ornamentation mainly consists of curvilinear elements such as spirals, S-shaped lines, meanders, circles and arcs, but there are also chevron and toothed designs, often occurring in combination with human and animal figures (snake, fish, bird). Besides large garland-like ornaments on canoe prows (particularly well-known in the Louisiade Archipelago), mention must be made of such typical objects as dance shields, ceremonial weapons (staffs, clubs, spears), net sinkers and lime spatulae, as well as the painted facades of gables and carved beams on small yam storehouses.

Figs. 31, 32

Plate p. 101

As has already been pointed out, all the style provinces of New Guinea so far mentioned come within the sphere of Austromelanid hybrid cultures. Although Papuan elements are unmistakably present – they are particularly

Wooden door-jambs, painted with earth pigments, from the entrance to a dwelling-house, found on Pitiliu I., Admiralty Is. These ancestor figures stood on either side of the entrance. Both of them show Christian missionary influences: the male figure is depicted in a praying attitude; the female one wears a cross as a breast ornament. *Museum für Völkerkunde, Basle. Height 6 ft. 8¾ in., 5 ft. 9¼ in.* *Cf. p. 137.*

Cult-house with *malanggans* from Medina, north-western New Ireland. The house is made of wood, bamboo, small palm-leaves and croton-leaves; the figures are carved in soft wood, painted with earth pigments and yellow oil-colour. The house was erected to commemorate 14 deceased persons from the village. The sculptures represent mythological scenes, ancestors, totem birds and fish. On the block of wood, decorated with leaves, was placed the shell money for payment of the carvers. Typical *malanggan* style. *Museum für Völkerkunde, Basle. Height approx. 8 ft., length approx. 16 ft. 4 in., depth approx. 10 ft.* *Cf. p. 142.*

pronounced in the middle Sepik area — Austronesian influence makes itself felt as the connecting link between different artistic styles. This results in the existence of certain common features and explains why in most cases it is impossible to draw sharp dividing-lines between the various style provinces.

Southern parts of New Guinea

We shall now examine the slopes of the mountain ranges in the south of the island, where conditions are different. Apart from areas to the east of the Gulf of Papua which can boast of very little in the way of artistic achievements, we are dealing here with Papuan cultures proper, in which Austronesian influences are minimal or even altogether absent. As a consequence we find distinctive local artistic forms that are particularly archaic. Thus, for example, throughout the southern region masks are predominantly pointed or cone-shaped, and (in contrast to the Sepik district, which is also largely Papuan in character) are not even provided with wooden heads or faces. The plaited masks of the Gulf of Papua, and the string ones produced further to the west (Asmat and Mimika), correspond to the basketry masks of the north. But in contrast to the Sepik district all the art forms to be found on the Gulf of Papua are predominantly two-dimensional in character. Only in the south-west do we find sculpture of any quality. But here too (and this incidentally also applies to the Sepik district) the artists are not content with three-dimensional rendering alone, but attach very great value to decoration as well.

The southern style provinces are as a rule divided into four: the south-west, the Marind-anim, the Gulf of Papua, and the islands in the Torres Straits. The area in the extreme west, including some regions on the McCluer Gulf where there is much evidence of recent Indonesian (and partly even Islamic) influences, seems to have very little to offer in the way of art; this is also true of the so-called central district along the south coast of the eastern part of the island, in the vicinity of Port Moresby.

The south-western area extends from Etna Bay in the west to the basins of the rivers Mapi and Digul. In some parts we find works that can vie with those of the Sepik district (not to mention other areas of New Guinea) in their design and dramatic emotional treatment, although there is not the

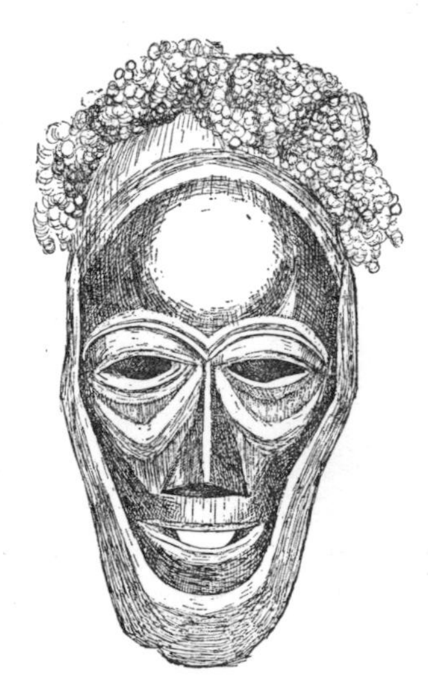

FIG. 48 — *Skull mask. Front part of a human skull, modelled over with resin and clay and painted in white, red and black. Bleached human hair is stuck on. Gazelle peninsula, New Britain. Height 11 in.* *Cf. p. 150.*

FIG. 49 — *Dance mask. Frame of bamboo covered with bark-cloth, painted red and black. Baining, Gazelle peninsula, New Britain. Max. width 18¾ in. Cf. p. 149.*

same wealth or variety of styles. Although a distinction is often made between various groups of styles, and even between different style provinces, it is the characteristics common to them all that are really striking.

In two-dimensional representation the predominant technique is one already mentioned in connection with the upper Sepik area, in which the most prominent features project in the form of narrow ridges. In the west the ornaments are mainly angular, but as we proceed further eastwards curvilinear forms become more and more evident. Most of the designs are anthropomorphic in character, but one can perhaps note the influence of Indonesian tendril-like ornamentation, as is also the case in the area of the *korwar* style in the north. One gains the impression that there are affinities in two-dimensional surface delineation with Australia, particularly Queensland. This is of significance in that this area of New Guinea is more likely than any other to yield cultural remnants of the Australian settlers. As we move further eastwards, the ornamentation generally becomes more refined and a more important part is played by colour (mainly red and white, less frequently black).

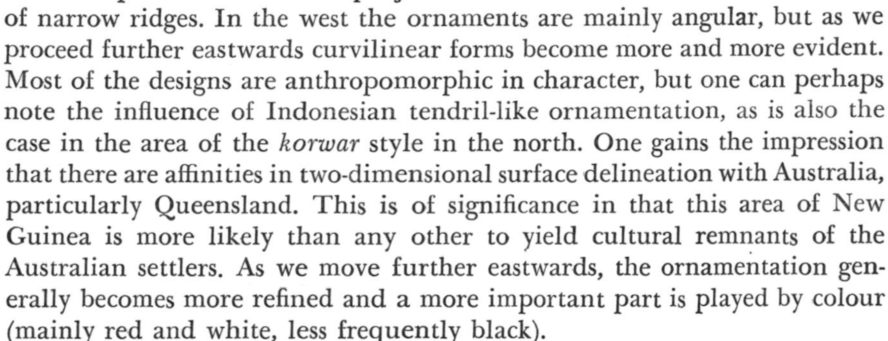

Three-dimensional art, which in this area chiefly treats human subjects, is rarer in the east and finally disappears altogether. In the western part, the district of Mimika, human figures are rendered with long narrow heads, the nose straight and perforated, the chin prominent, the small mouth half-open, and the eyes oval-shaped. One stylistic group comprises female figures with elongated torso, legs short and slightly bent, protruding abdomen, and arms bent or raised up to the head. They are decorated with a sort of network of triangles. Another group is formed by large ancestor poles, used mainly in initiation ceremonies; these frequently consist of two figures of deceased persons placed one upon another and topped by a projecting wing carved in open-work. The post and the base of the figures are often hollowed out. Human figures, and often human heads as well, are also featured on board-like canoe ornaments, which in their angularity, like the other Mimika figures, are somewhat reminiscent of the *korwar* styles of north-western New Guinea. Particularly characteristic of these boards is the tendril-like ornamentation, carved in open-work, the design of which chiefly consists of straight angular

Mimika

Head of a *malanggan* doll-like figure from Burra, north-western New Ireland. Wood, painted with earth pigments and soot, and trimmed with cord on either side of the head. This head belonged to a huge seated figure made of rattan and cord, with raised arms and hands of wood, which personified a mythological

FIG. 50 — *Wooden paddle. The figure stands out in very low relief and is painted white, red and black. Buka I., Solomons. Height of figure 18 in. Cf. p. 153.*

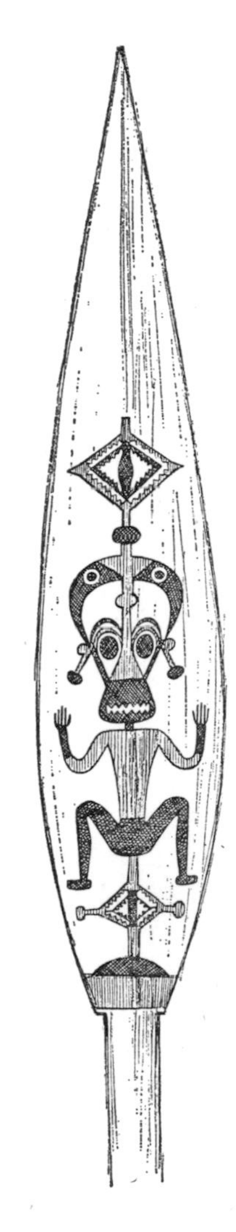

elements. Some of these can be made out as arms, legs and torso, which in combination with the top of the board form a human figure. In addition to representations in relief on the sides of canoes, paddle-blades, wooden stools and sago-pounders, mention may be made of the light oval or rectangular ceremonial shields, shaped like boards, with a handle and a piece at the top carved in open-work. They, too, often have a net-like asymmetrical decoration identical with that found on canoe tops.

Masks consist of a frame of wickerwork and rattan, over which is stretched a cover of cordage in interlocking technique. They are either pointed or helmet-shaped and cover head and shoulders. They are used in ceremonies to commemorate the dead, where they personify those who have died since the last such festival.

The art centres of the Asmat area are situated between the rivers Kampong and Eilanden and the Digul. Here, too, human beings are by far the most prominent subjects. Individual figures with a marked three-dimensional quality have so far only been discovered in areas on the river Lorentz. They are personifications of ancestors known as 'skeleton figures': slender female figures, shown squatting, with the elbows supported on the knees and the chin resting in the hands. The thin cylindrically-shaped torso is overshadowed by the highly accentuated limbs. The head is pointed and egg-shaped; the ears are barely indicated; the face is very narrow; the nose is shown with nostrils; the eyes are oval-shaped; and the mouth is slightly turned up at the corners, with the tongue showing. The hair is rendered in the form of a cap. The whole figure is very symmetrical. On the limbs are long grooves filled in with paint, which follow the natural curves and are interrupted by diagonal ridges. Standing figures are also produced in the same style. Frequently the arms, and especially the legs, are accentuated to such an extent that the impression of the human form is largely lost. From the coastal area between the rivers Lorentz and Eilanden come enormous ceremonial posts, the lower parts of which are frequently hollowed out as with a canoe, presumably to suggest a boat; over them are two or more human figures placed upon one another in

PLATE P. 107

character. On the head, rendered in an austere simple manner, emphasis is given to the hairdress (crest) formerly worn by men, and to the double nose ornament, which consists of small pieces of shell. In essence this is a typical *malanggan* style. *Museum für Völkerkunde, Basle. Height 33¾ in. Cf. p. 145.*

the style already mentioned. In front of the uppermost figure there rises a triangular wing-like projection, carved in open-work and often decorated with curvilinear ornaments in combination with figures (birds' heads and human beings). Also in this case the human figures are representations of deceased members of the village community.

Sculptured figures taken from mythology are commonly found as canoe ornaments; and there are also flat oblong wooden bowls in human shape. These are stylistically akin to the forms already mentioned, having raised arms and bent legs, with the feet turned inwards. The hollowed-out part is in the torso. Human beings, often in association with birds' heads and apparently non-representational ornaments, occur in relief on paddle-blades measuring several feet in length and above all on heavy shields used in battle. As is suggested by the head- or stick-shaped projections with faces on the top, the whole figure seems to resemble a human being. Also the tendril-like ornaments on the surface, which are usually symmetrical and consist of raised patterns, are no doubt in most cases derived from human motifs. Likewise raised and worked in the same style are the decorations to be found on trumpets and bamboo megaphones used in head-hunting, on leaf-shaped projections on spear-shafts, and on boats.

PLATES PP. 110, 113

Here, too, masks made from cordage occur, some of them supplemented by wooden parts; they cover the head, shoulders and the upper part of the body. They resemble those noted in the Mimika district but are much finer in shape.

The entire ornamentation of the Asmat region, particularly the decorations on shields and the stylized renderings of the human body on fretted board ornaments, recall, as has been mentioned above, the styles of the upper Sepik area (shields) and the southern border areas of the Sepik lowlands (hook figures). A common basis may exist here, and indeed even relatively recent historical connections.

The next style region to the east comprises the Marind-anim tribes. They live in the coastal area and parts of the interior east of Frederik Hendrik Island. These tribes, whose knowledge of technol-

FIG. 51 — *Idol from a war canoe. Blackened wood, inlaid with mother-of pearl. Human figure with dove. Maravo Lagoon, New Georgia, Solomons. Height 7 in. Cf. p. 153.*

Malanggan frieze from Fessoa, north-western New Ireland. Wood, painted with earth pigments and sap of curcuma. Snail opercula are used for the eyes of the birds and snake. All the animals represent mythological figures and events, details of which are, however, not known. Typical *malanggan* style, partly executed in open-work with figurative designs and gaily painted in a manner largely independent of the plastic forms. *Museum für Völkerkunde, Basle. Length 4 ft. 3 in., height 1 ft. 9 in.* *Cf. p. 145.*

ogy is still on a very primitive level, are known for their complex and highly dramatic ritual ceremonies, which in some ways recall Australian totemistic cults and are exceptionally interesting for the light they shed on myths. The deities from whose bodies, according to tradition, food-plants, animals and cultural products sprang, mainly appear during great initiation ceremonies in the guise of masked figures; they personify at the same time the founders of the various clans and an animal, plant or cultural product. These masks are characterized not so much by plastic rendering as by a fantastic wealth of ornaments and attributes of all kinds, which completely conceal the body. A painted leaf or leaf-sheath devoid of any human features

Mask from the Gazelle peninsula, New Britain, belonging to a secret society. The head, which is of sacking, is painted and decorated with a cluster of feathers, leaves then being added as well. The mask represents a *tumbuan* of the Dukduk secret society, which in contrast to the male *dukduk* is thought to be female. Primitive form (conical or pointed mask), no wood being used. *Museum für Völkerkunde, Basle. Height 4 ft. 11 in.* *Cf. p. 150.*

FIG. 52 — *Wooden gable figure. Tern, represented in a lifelike manner, with wings tied on. The head is painted white, the other parts black. Guadalcanal, Solomons. Length 14⅜ in. Cf. p. 155.*

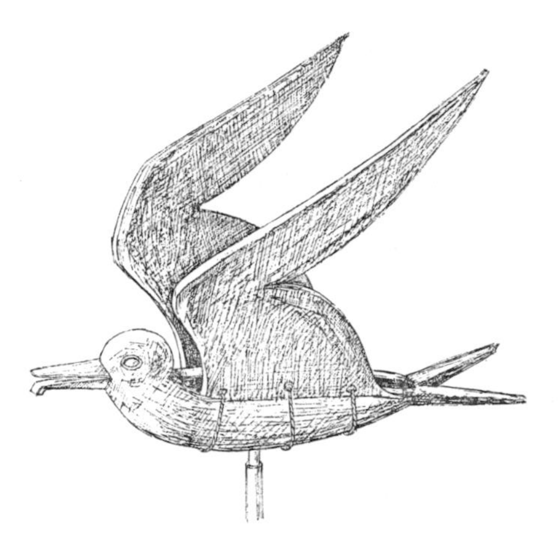

is fastened over the face; among the attributes there are some rather crudely worked animal or plant figures. By comparison sculpture and two-dimensional surface delineations take a very secondary place. Stylistically the few roughly worked figures recall those from the middle reaches of the Fly river and the Sepik.

The Marind-anim were the only inhabitants of New Guinea who knew how to cover the skulls of the enemies they had killed, after cleaning, with the skin from their heads, and to preserve them in this form.

Gulf of Papua

The style province comprising the vast alluvial plains between the Fly river and Cape Possession has very marked features so far as its art is concerned. In the cultural sphere there is a highly developed dramatic ceremonial life, with festivals at which ample use is made of masks. These festivals often last for a number of years. Everywhere in the area sculptured figures play only a very minor part. The artist concentrates his creative urge entirely upon two-dimensional surface delineation. In this ornamentation and colour are the most important factors; the main subject is almost always a human figure or face, but even these are subject to conventions as regards decoration. As a rule — particularly in the ritual sphere — large objects are used as well as bold renderings with distinct contour lines. Cult objects and secular implements are largely identical in style, whether they are bas-reliefs, incised or engraved motifs, appliqué (sewing on withes, or sticking on seeds and fruit) or painting. The colours preferred are white (grey), red (brown), black and yellow. The entire decoration is dominated by curvilinear designs, concentric circles, arcs of circles, S-shaped designs, spirals and meanders.

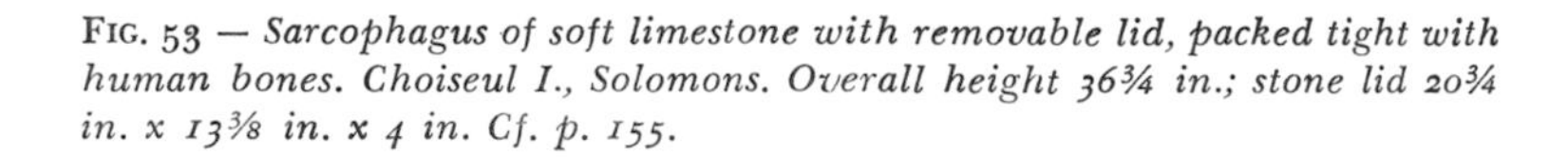

FIG. 53 — *Sarcophagus of soft limestone with removable lid, packed tight with human bones. Choiseul I., Solomons. Overall height 36¾ in.; stone lid 20¾ in. x 13⅜ in. x 4 in. Cf. p. 155.*

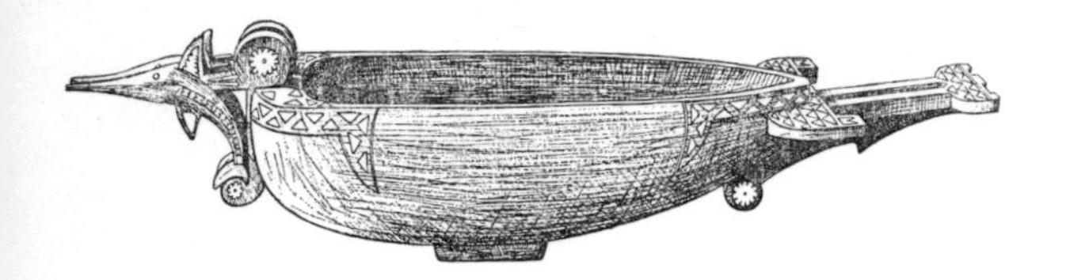

FIG. 54 — *Food-bowl of blackened wood, inlaid with mother-of-pearl. The bowl is in the shape of a bird with twin heads and tail. In front of each beak is a dolphin. San Cristoval, Solomons. Length 34¼ in. Cf. p. 155.*

In the west the most important cult objects are flat figures carved in the shape of boards, in which often the head alone can be identified, while in place of the body we find a shield-like fretted structure with 'stopped out' hooks. But this part can also be carved in the outline of the body, in which case the surface is covered with raised patterns running parallel to the contours of the body. In the east, especially in the Orokolo Bay area, we find, instead of these, tapering oval-shaped ceremonial shields, frequently measuring more than three feet in length. Fitted at the bottom with a handle, they generally have highly stylized faces, and less frequently full-size figures of which, however, the face is also emphasized. Both types are of sacral significance as abodes or personifications of bush or sea spirits. The same is true of very long bull-roarers, the incised decoration on which is again mainly anthropomorphic in character. Lastly, human figures are also depicted in ornaments on hour-glass drums, one end of which often takes the form of wide-open jaws.

FIG. 33

FIG. 34

Even more striking than the wooden cult objects are the masks, most of which also serve ceremonial purposes. From the east we know of various types of mask, but all of them consist of a wooden frame, rattan and bark-cloth. In this area there occur monstrous constructions, one part of which projects vertically and another horizontally, the latter part being provided at the end with jaws; we also come across oval-shaped shield-like objects, often measuring more than 19 feet in height, which are painted and have a face projecting outwards like a snout. In addition to these there are small cone-shaped masks and helmet-masks featuring snout-like faces or topped by crests in animal shape. These mainly personify mythological figures, but the last-mentioned type of mask seems to be much more of a grotesque than a sacred nature. In the western part of the Papuan Gulf area there predominates a type of mask consisting of wickerwork covered with clay, with faces bearing animal features.

PLATE P. 116

PLATE P. 118

Among the large number of decorated objects, most of which are secular, shields are particularly characteristic. Almost rectangular or oval in shape, they are provided with a broad indentation on the upper end. During battle

Wooden battle and dance shields from New Britain (*left:* from Nakanei, Gazelle peninsula; *right:* from Beechey Cape, south coast (Sulka tribe)). Shallow carving, painted. The shield on the right has a plaited rattan border, affixed by means of perforations, and also bands of rattan, dyed red, tied around it.

Museum für Völkerkunde, Basle. Shield on the left: height 4 ft. 5 in., width 7¾ in.; shield on the right: height 4 ft. 5½ in., width 12½ in. Cf. p. 152.

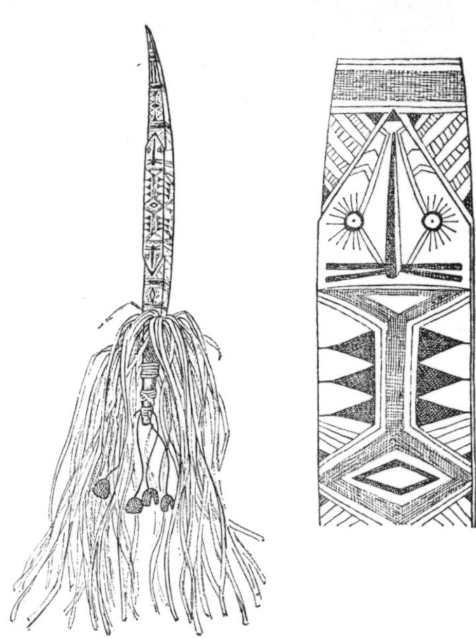

FIG. 55 — *Dance club* (left). *Wood, bast and nut-shells. Detail* (right) *painted white, red and black. Nitendi, Santa Cruz Is. Length of club 34½ in., of detail 7 in. Cf. p. 157.*

they are slung in front of the left-hand side of the body, and the left arm, in which the bow is held, is placed in this indentation. Here, too, as in the case of ceremonial shields and cult figures, ornamentation is carved in relief, the motifs again being predominantly anthropomorphic. But there are also some ornaments consisting of spirals and circles. Particularly fine examples of decorative art are the bark belts worn by men coiled around the waist several times. The ornaments, which are arranged symmetrically, painted and carved in relief on a hollowed-out ground, either derive from human faces or are curvilinear.

FIG. 35

The striking affinities between the art of the Gulf and the Sepik districts have long been known. Even if the preference for two-dimensional treatment is lacking in the north, colour and decoration play the same prominent part in both areas. In ornamentation pride of place is taken by the curvilinear style, in which anthropomorphic motifs and an over-accentuation of the head are characteristic features. Also common to both areas are board-like sculptures, carved in open-work, head trophies, and masks that are cone-shaped in plan but are mostly not made of wood.

Torres Straits Islands

The style province of the islands situated in the Torres Straits, between Australia and New Guinea, also includes the lower reaches of the Fly river and the islands that lie off the coast at this point. The art in this area is predominantly two-dimensional, with rectilinear design elements often arranged in bands; curvilinear motifs occur less often. The islands situated in the Torres Straits and Daudai (Fly) river are characterized particularly by chevron designs, herring-bone patterns and toothed designs. Wooden combs with huge decorated grips, engraved stems of tobacco-pipes, and hour-glass drums are all decorated in this way. Very fine human heads and motifs of crocodiles or snakes are to be found on arrows. Canoes feature

Female funerary figure from Bougainville, western Solomons. Painted wood, with loin-cloth made of fringes of leaves. Statues of this kind, and sometimes just heads, are produced when a death occurs, and erected in front of the house of the deceased; after the ceremony they are normally burnt. The form of the figure and the style of painting are typical of the western Solomons. *Museum für Völkerkunde, Basle. Height approx. 5 ft. 8 in. Cf. p. 153.*

Fish figure from Wango, San Cristoval I., eastern Solomons. Blackened wood with inlaid decoration of mother-of-pearl discs with jagged edges; the base and fins are inserted. Significance not known. The perfect naturalistic form is typical. *Museum für Völkerkunde, Basle. Length 22¾ in.* *Cf. p. 155.*

very distorted human faces, and in isolated instances anthropomorphic motifs also occur on hour-glass drums. Small magic figures and decorations in the form of animals (fish, sea-cow, turtle) on dance staffs are all distinguished by great realism and fine workmanship. Animal motifs (crocodile and pig's head) also appear on magic objects made of small coconuts which are decorated to excess.

The best known of all objects from this style province are the face masks used in burial rites and the fish figures worn on the head. They apparently represent actual and mythological tribal ancestors. They are composed of turtle-shells that have been affixed together (sometimes in a heated state), with pieces of mollusc-shell melted on. These are veritable masterpieces, judged from the standpoint of technique. The eyes of the masks are of mother-of-pearl, black paste being used to suggest the pupils. The mouth is open, with the teeth showing. Ornaments in bands are usually engraved on the forehead, round the eyes, on the nostrils and round the border of the face. Sometimes a beard is affixed as well. Often the face is framed by a border in which triangular designs are carved in open-work, real human hair or bark fibres being inserted in the perforations to suggest head and hair. The treatment of the fish figures in particular is remarkably realistic. From the islands situated in the west of the Torres Straits wooden masks, which were used in fertility rites, are also known. Oblong and angular in shape, they bear a distinct resemblance to the standing figures from the Fly delta, which have arms hanging down loosely. Masks personifying the deceased, in which human and animal motifs are combined, are mainly limited to the Fly delta. Those that occur in very large sizes are very often made entirely of turtle-shell, while others are of wood.

This archipelago is inhabited by four groups of peoples: (i) the Ussiai in the interior of the main island of Manus; (ii) the Matankol along the shores of this island and on a number of coral atolls in the north; (iii) the Baluan on the island of that name and also on Lou and Manus; (iv) the Manus, who live on the south coast of Manus and also on a number of small islands, in houses supported by piles. Within these groups there are cultural variations and some very marked linguistic differences. On the other hand, they form a cultural unit with a very characteristic style of art, originating mainly with the Matankol. Throughout the area sculpture prevails, and two-dimensional surface delineation plays a subordinate role. Masks are absent, and painting is rare — although it occurs, for example, as decoration on houses on Baluan.
In the religious sphere there are striking ancestor statues of various sizes, which are placed in club-houses or dwellings. Figures identical with these are found on the door-posts of men's houses and on the well-known bedsteads, which have four legs, a frame consisting of four parts, and a board to lie on; but in this case, more frequently than on the door-jambs, only the heads are shown, and often they appear in association with crocodile heads or sculptures bearing geometric designs. The same styles, and also fish motifs, are to be found on the handles of scoops, on lime spatulae used for betel-chewing — some of which are particularly delicately worked — and also on an ornament made with frigate-bird feathers worn by men on the neck when dancing or in war. They also appear on canoe prows and on the ends of logs more than 30 feet long placed on forked poles and

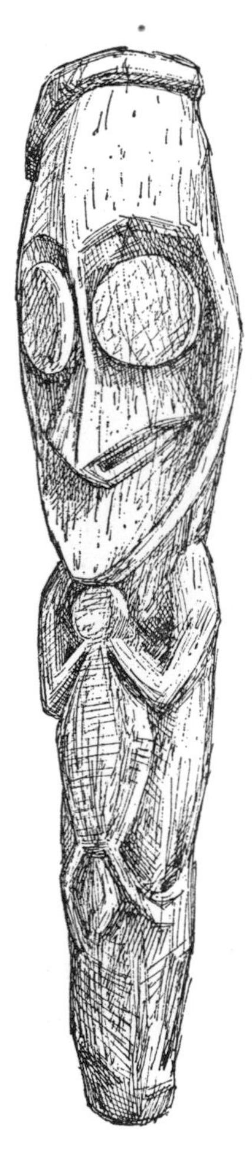

FIG. 56 — *Ancestor statue of tree-fern wood, not painted. Human figure with lizard (tutelary spirit). Ambrym, New Hebrides. Height 6 ft. 2¾ in.* *Cf. p. 159.*

Mask from southern Malekula, New Hebrides, belonging to a secret society. Tube made of tree-fern wood open at the bottom of the back, coated with clay and modelled; the trimming consists of staffs with tassels and boars' tusks; it is painted with earth pigments. These masks, placed over the head so that they representing canoes, on which men perform dances on ceremonial occasions. Finally, there are also spears with wooden, sting-ray spine and obsidian points, and obsidian daggers frequently decorated with complete figures, heads, faces and crocodile motifs; in most cases, however, these are not wooden carvings but are modelled plastically from the pulp of the Guinea plum (*parinarium excelsum*). The fine wooden bowls of this archipelago often take the shape of crocodiles and birds; some especially large ones measuring more than seven feet in diameter have spiral-shaped handles carved in open-work.

FIG. 36

FIG. 39

There are two types of three-dimensional human figures: one, which is rare, is characterized by cylindrical and rounded forms, while the other appears to be more angular and rectilinear; in both cases these are standing figures. Well-proportioned and somewhat simplified, with the arms hanging down and the legs slightly bent, these styles give the impression of being static, yet not at all rigid. The face sometimes wears an agressive expression, is either oval-shaped or angular, and oblong; the nose is straight and narrow, often without nostrils, the mouth, set very low down, is also narrow and straight, and usually protrudes markedly; the eyes are small and oval-shaped; the ears are almost invariably clearly indicated and are rendered with distended lobes. Another characteristic feature is a hat, or a tuft of hair which stands up and is held in position by a cylindrical tube. All these elements of the second type of figure somewhat resemble the *korwar* style, but are most reminiscent of that of Tami. In this connection it is of interest to note that the Manus had trading links with Tami, and that the well-known wooden bowls from Tami found on the Admiralty Islands were already no rarity even in early times. The bowls in the shape of birds also call to mind the Tami style, especially in their ornamentation. In both cases it is organically combined with the object itself; it is either in delicate bas-relief or incised, most of the designs being rectilinear; anthropomorphic and animal motifs are much less important. An especial favourite are bands of chevron lines and lozenges formed from combinations of such chevrons with almost rectangular crosses. Crosses also occur very frequently on their own, whereas spiral-shaped and curvilinear forms appear rarely, except on the handles of bowls and ornaments on canoe prows. The painting is generally applied in a restrained manner, red and white being the chief colours, whereas black is used only to accentuate certain parts of the decoration.

FIG. 37

FIG. 38

FIG. 39

Poker-work is usually only employed to decorate dumb-bell-shaped gourds in which pulverized lime is kept for betel-chewing. These containers feature ornaments which are very different from the decorative style common

FIG. 11

hang down in front of the body, are used by the secret societies to terrorize the population. This type, distinguished above all by the tubular form and long nose, is limited to southern Malekula. *Museum für Völkerkunde, Basle. Height 45¼ in. Cf. p. 160.*

FIG. 57 — *Stone amulet. Twin figure carved in soft stone. It is held in the hand when trading pigs. Ambrym, New Hebrides. Height 3½ in.* *Cf. p. 160.*

elsewhere. The same is true of the widely disseminated *kapkap* ornaments, consisting of turtle-shell carved in open-work, which are mounted on discs of clam-shell.

The culture of these islands is closely connected with that of New Hanover (Lavongai) and New Ireland, but is also linked to the Admiralty Islands and manifests strong Micronesian influences. All this finds expression in art, in which decoration plays the most prominent part. Well-known, however, are the carved ancestor figures; so, too, are representations of human beings on posts of houses and dance staffs, fish and bird sculptures on decorative boards on houses, as well as canoes; identical motifs are also found painted on houses and on women's kilts made from areca-palm spathes. The treatment of the figures appears clumsy; this is especially true of the human ones, which are made of wood. The subject is shown standing, with the arms hanging down or bent in front of the abdomen, in a style somewhat resembling those of New Ireland. But there are also some affinities, especially in animal motifs, with the Admiralty Islands (Fig. 40).

More characteristic are the ornaments on cult objects and utensils, some of which are painted, but which are generally incised and filled in with white lime, and have two-dimensional surface delineations featuring animal figures. Examples of these are to be found on spear-shafts, lime spatulae and clubs (Fig. 41), as well as on sculptured figures. Ornaments are almost always arranged in the form of bands or rectangular panels; the design elements are small and with a few exceptions entirely geometric.

In addition to leaf-shaped motifs we frequently find lozenges, toothed designs, crosses, circles, star-shaped and horseshoe-shaped forms, and combinations of all these. Their delicate design and the way in which they are arranged bear a strong resemblance to Micronesian decorative styles from the Carolines. The poker-work decorations on lime containers made of gourds are of curvilinear character, in the form of circles and arcs. Small ear-pendants of turtle-shell, large decorative combs for men, and univalve shells used as penis ornaments are decorated with purely geometric designs.

FIGS. 11, 42

New Ireland

This style province comprises, in addition to the main island, New Hanover and the Tabar island group. The very low level of technological development in this whole area stands in contrast to the high standard of artistic achievement, which in some areas is astonishingly advanced and is unique throughout Oceania as regards its fantastic forms and the virtuosity of the

Paintings from a cult-house at Gaua, Banks Is. Wooden boards, painted with earth pigments. They were formerly suspended on the facade of a small cult-house. The human figures and faces, and the birds as well, are representations of ancestor spirits. Remarkable are the extremely simple treatment of the faces and the rectilinear geometric ornamentation. *Museum für Völkerkunde, Basle. Height 2 ft. 11½ in. and 5 ft. 3 in.* *Cf. p. 160.*

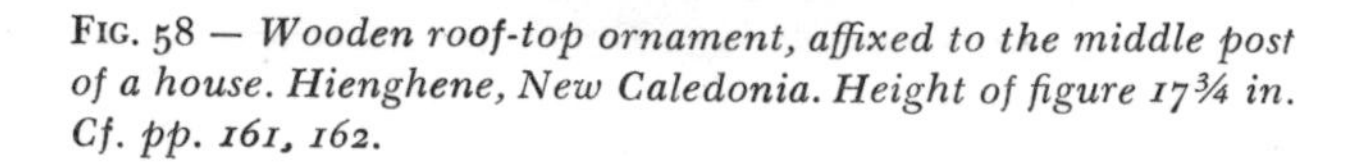

Fig. 58 — *Wooden roof-top ornament, affixed to the middle post of a house. Hienghene, New Caledonia. Height of figure 17¾ in. Cf. pp. 161, 162.*

carving. Sculptures, decoration in relief and masks are by far the most predominant objects. Paintings on wooden boards or bark are used to decorate houses, for instance, and in central New Ireland painted bark-cloth caps are worn by women when dancing. But far greater importance attaches to the painting and decoration of plastic objects. Apart from Maprik in northern New Guinea and the New Hebrides there is no other area in Oceania where colour is used in quite such profusion as here. The most important colours are red, white, yellow and black; sometimes also a greenish hue is obtained from seaweed, and recently laundry blue has come to play a part as well. In the ornamentation of figures and masks it is characteristic that often the colour seems to be unrelated to the plastic form; in any case it is never quite as organically adapted to it as is the case in the Admiralty Islands.

Within this style region four local areas can be distinguished: (i) the New Hanover Islands, known only for their masks; (ii) north-western New Ireland and the Tabar Islands, which possess the greatest number of carvings and a variety of masks; (iii) central New Ireland, the home of the *uli* figures and rayed discs (*kapkap* ornaments), where there may originally have been no masks; (iv) the south-eastern parts of central New Ireland, where there are chalk figures and in some districts masks as well. The south has probably little to offer in the way of art, but so far little is known about this area.

North-western New Ireland Tabar Is.

Plate p. 122

The art of the north-western area and the Tabar Islands is by far the most impressive. Carvings and masks predominate. The masks are called *malanggans* and form the focal-point of the religious ceremonies known by this name. These ceremonies are primarily festivals in memory of the departed, but at the same time they are also concerned with the initiation of young men, and last but not least are regarded as an important means of enhancing the prestige of the organizers. The preparations alone for these occasions often take as much as several years, and the festivities themselves last for months. The carvings used for this purpose stand or hang in special houses in courts secluded by a high stockade of bamboo or wickerwork. All in all they constitute a magnificent gallery of mythological figures and acts, personifications of the departed, ancestors, totem animals and a unique rendering of all historical and mythical events in sculptured form. Most of the *malanggan* carvings are owned by individual families, who are entitled to sell the right to produce them. The sculptor, however, is granted

Wooden door-jamb from Ouebia, New Caledonia. The front is flat and convex, the back concave; in cross-section it is crescent-shaped. Traces of painting. Representation of a female figure (recognizable by the characteristic lozenge-shaped ornament close to the ears). Also typical are the broad face and rectilinear ornaments. *Museum für Völkerkunde, Basle. Height 5 ft. 5 in., width 3 ft. 2 in.* *Cf. p. 161.*

Dance mask from Bopope, New Caledonia. Cylindrical basket-work, of thin withes, with inset face of blackened wood, trimmed with human hair. The body is enveloped in a mesh net, into which feathers are knotted. Such masks, which represent water demons, occurred singly. *Museum für Völkerkunde, Basle. Length of face 9 in.* *Cf. p. 162.*

a good deal of personal freedom in the manner of execution, and this fact, together with the large choice of motifs, makes for wide variations. Most of the *malanggans* – whether they are fully three-dimensional or *malanggan* frieze-like reliefs – consist of one piece, which is carved in open-work. Very frequently, however, figures occur which are combined from several parts. Besides ordinary single sculptures there are figures placed one upon another, and often whole rows of figures, not infrequently hewn from a single tree-trunk. The *malanggan* doll-like figures constitute a special type. These are small statues, entirely carved from wood, seated upon a cross-beam with raised hands, or figures larger than life-size, the body of which consists of leaves, grass and cords, while the head and hands are made of wood. The most interesting pieces are truly dramatic in their wealth and variety of motifs. These include human beings in association with birds, fish, snakes, crabs, pigs, and marsupials, or mythological symbols (moon, sun), dance emblems, implements and weapons, often featuring animals or men fighting or even devouring one another. Animals, and especially fish, are also represented on their own. Furthermore, in the case of board-shaped forms entire parts are ornamented all over; often the animal motifs occurring on them are hardly recognizable any longer (cf. Plate p. 129).

PLATE P. 126

The *malanggans* are characterized by the fact that they are mostly carved in open-work with a fantasy that knows no bounds. Only in the Maprik territory and on the Sepik do there occur sculptures which can to some extent match them in this respect – although they are not comparable in style, since the open-work is limited to two-dimensional surface delineations and is not three-dimensional.

The masks of north-western New Ireland are not worn in the way usual in New Guinea, where the whole body is enclosed in bark-cloth and leaves, but with kilts made of these materials, and sometimes with a covering of bark-cloth worn on the upper part of the body like a shirt. From a stylistic point of view the most important and largest forms are entirely *malanggan* in character, and they are no doubt likewise personifications of mythological figures. With regard to motifs and forms we find the same magnificent wealth as in the case of cult figures. Especially characteristic are the large inserted ears, and in many cases also board-shaped noses, which again may comprise combinations of all sorts of motifs. The use of additional paraphernalia may be even more popular here than is the case with sculptures. Hair is often suggested by bark fibres, fruit-rind, roots, shells of marine animals rather like worms, etc., and sometimes also by the insertion of small sticks of wood; bark-cloth is also used. In a more simplified form which occurs frequently the facial part consists of wood but the other parts of the head are made of rattan and bark-cloth, the area round the temples being coated with lime; in the centre is a hair-crest of dyed bark fibres, which corresponds to the traditional hairdress worn by men. Masks of this kind are seen in public, frequently performing grotesque acts despite the fact that they

FIG. 44

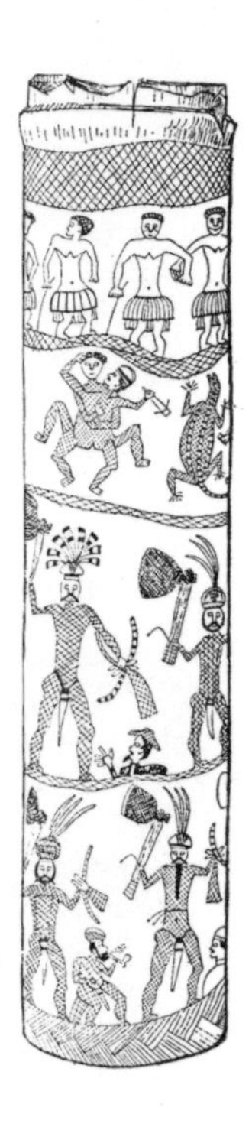

FIG. 59 — *Engraved bamboo with scenic compositions. Oubatche, New Caledonia. Length 15 in. Cf. p. 162.*

personify departed souls. Some typical forms have prominent rectilinear snout-like jaws with a straight mouth displaying the teeth. This form (but only this one) is also known in New Hanover. Another type, a helmet-like mask, is made entirely of bark-cloth, rattan, withes and small pieces of wood. On Tabar it is referred to as man's mysterious double who lives in the bush.

From a cultural and artistic point of view the central area of New Ireland and particularly the plateau (Lelet) is known for its *uli* rites and figures. Here, too, we are concerned with festivals in memory of the departed (in which an important part is played by carefully prepared skulls of deceased persons); here, too, as in the north, they serve as re-enactments of mythological events. This cult, which is secret, centres upon the impressive great *uli* figures, which are often truly monumental in their effect. These are heavy sculptures having a high degree of plasticity, with voluminous breasts and accentuated male genitals, entwined with tendril-like forms detached from the body; they often have little subsidiary figures on the forepart of the shoulder, in front of the abdomen or on the base. The head usually has a central comb-shaped crest, such as we have already noted in connection with the *malanggans* and masks of the north-west. The forehead is set fairly high, the nose is large and curved, and often provided with flaring nostrils. The eyes, shaped in various forms, are always represented by the opercula of a certain kind of sea-snail, giving them a steady stare and so enhancing still further the threatening and irate impression created by the very large head. The ears are clearly shaped; the lower part of the face projects outwards in triangular form, often tapering to a kind of beard which may be connected with the tendrils. The mouth is straight and broad, with the teeth visible. Characteristic, too, are the cylinder-shaped torso, the arms hanging down or held before the abdomen, and the short slightly-bent legs. Also related to the *uli* ceremonies are the so-called 'suns': disc- or wheel-shaped and brightly painted objects measuring some nine feet in diameter, made from withes, sticks and bark fibres tied together. These may be symbols of the sun, in which case they would be related to the mythological celestial deity.

Namatanai

In the south-eastern part of central New Ireland (Namatanai district), and only in this area, we find chalk figures, which in most cases are only lightly painted; they were used in a secret death cult. They may have been

FIG. 47

Striking part of a wooden club from the Tonga Is. The characteristic ornamentation, which is predominantly geometric and rectilinear, consists of small design elements, but human figures and birds can also be identified. *Institut für Völkerkunde, Göttingen. Length of detail approx. 12 in.* *Cf. p. 167.*

Handle of fly-whisk, made of wood and cord, from Tahiti. It was used in ceremonies and may even have been regarded as the manifestation of a deity. The top of the handle consists of two interconnected squatting figures, which taken as a whole have an ornamental rather than representational character. *Museum of Primitive Art, New York. Length of entire fly-whisk approx. 23 in.* *Cf. p. 169.*

personifications of the departed. A similar form is also known in the eastern parts of New Britain. From a stylistic point of view they are much simpler than all the other New Ireland sculptures. In spite of this it is possible to establish formal affinities between the *uli* figures and the *malanggans,* which may indicate that they had a common source. Masks from the Namatanai district, on the other hand, bear a great resemblance to those found in the Duke of York Islands.
By comparison with religious works of art secular forms play a minor part throughout New Ireland. Canoe ornaments from the north-west, usually with a head as the main motif, show a very marked *malanggan* style. From north-west and central New Ireland come the finest styles of *kapkaps* in Melanesia.

New Britain

Of this island, the largest in the Bismarck Archipelago, only the coastal areas and the Gazelle peninsula are fairly well-known, whereas the mountainous interior by and large still awaits exploration. This area, which in itself shows little homogeneity from the cultural point of view, also includes the Vitu Islands situated off the north coast, the Duke of York Islands to the east of the Gazelle peninsula, and the Arawe Islands off the south coast. In the east there are particularly close links with New Ireland, while in the west strong influences from New Guinea make themselves felt; in the interior especially, ancient Papuan cultures have been authenticated. In the parts of New Britain that have been explored sculptures and painted objects play a minor part by comparison with decorative work, and in particular with masks, the styles of which are among the most impressive and interesting in Oceania. These masks are mainly connected with male secret societies, except in the case of the semi-nomadic Baining in the interior of the Gazelle peninsula, where they appear publicly on occasions such as harvest festivals and other socially significant events. Here the wearers of the masks represent the departed, ancestors and mythological figures; in former times, when they were worn by those in charge of the societies, they probably were used for police functions and to punish those who infringed laws and customs. But later these societies became terroristic organizations which exploited the population unscrupulously.
The New Britain masks are so diverse that they cannot really be held to constitute a local style; one ought rather to distinguish between several style provinces, the number of which has yet to be established. The Baining masks,

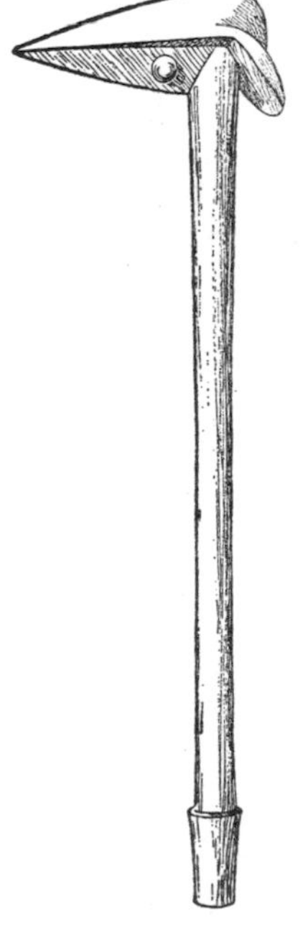

FIG. 60 — *Wooden war club, so called bird's-head club. New Caledonia. Overall length 31½ in., of head 11½ in. Cf. p. 163.*

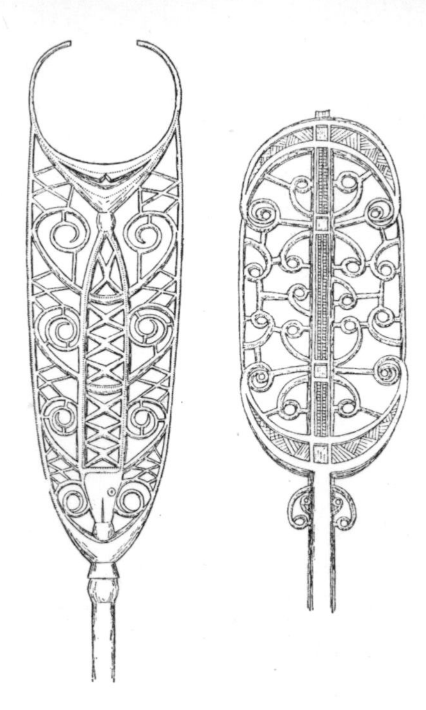

FIG. 61 — *Handles of lime spatulae. Wood carved in open-work. Curvilinear tendril-like ornamentation. Kaniet, Para-Micronesia.* Left: *overall length 20 in., length of handle (with fish motif) 11 in.* Right: *overall length 24 in., length of handle 8¼ in. Cf. p. 164.*

however, constitute a distinct group. The frames, frequently of gigantic size, are covered with bark-cloth, bark or leaves. Some of them measure over 130 ft. in height and could naturally only be worn with the assistance of other people. They are distinguished by their fantastic shapes and relatively moderate use of colour. Particularly impressive are the figures in the shape of animal heads with enormous eyes and snouts.

South coast; Gazelle peninsula

In the southern coastal area we find masks which consist simply of cord meshes covering the entire head, to which cloaks made of leaves are affixed. These are the prototypes of the pointed masks in which the head has the shape of a cone, which are used by the Dukduk secret society on the Gazelle peninsula, and by some other peoples as well. Grotesquely shaped, they also appear on the Vitu Islands and with the Sulka on the main island. They are made of wood, bark, leaf-sheaths, bark-cloth and cane frames, and are trimmed with lengths of pith that are sewn together. A particularly characteristic feature among the Sulka are the enormous umbrellas or hats with which they crown the actual masks.

PLATE P. 130

Wooden masks are rare throughout this area. Helmet-like masks are known in the Vitu Islands, masks like boards worn over the head among the Menge, and masks fastened over the face from the Duke of York Islands. In the coastal areas of the Gazelle peninsula skull masks have also been found. They are made of the front part of skulls, over which a resinous material is modelled and painted; frequently human hair is then stuck on. They are held between the teeth by a cross-bar inserted at the back of the mask (Fig. 48).

In spite of the distinct local styles of the masks, affinities may be noted (except in the case of the unique Baining specimens) with adjacent areas.

Hollow wooden image of a deity from Rurutu, Austral Is., with a removable lid on the back. This figure, unique in its genre, represents the sea god in the act of creating other gods and men. It bears a stylistic resemblance to other sculptures, different in form, from the Cook and Austral Is. *British Museum. Height 44 in. Cf. p. 172.*

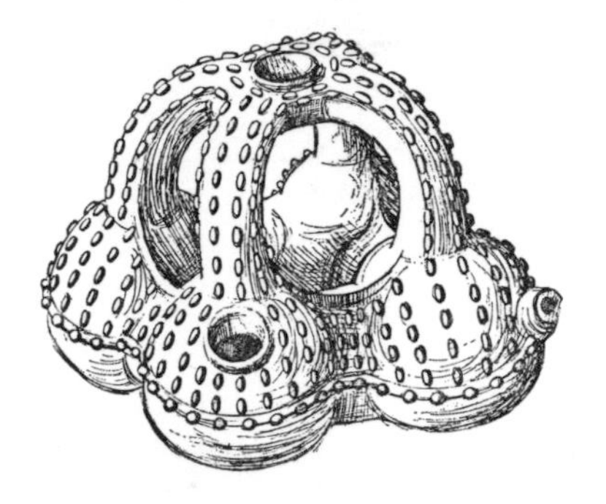

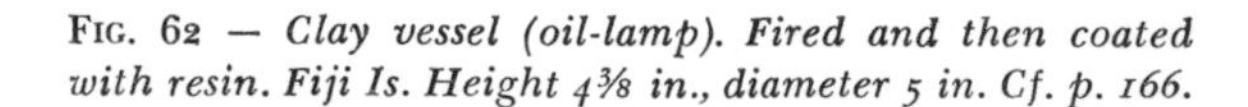

FIG. 62 — *Clay vessel (oil-lamp). Fired and then coated with resin. Fiji Is. Height 4⅜ in., diameter 5 in. Cf. p. 166.*

Where faces are represented, they bear a great resemblance to those from Tami, from where, incidentally, they have been adopted directly in the western parts of the island. On the other hand, the wooden masks in the Duke of York Islands correspond by and large to the central New Ireland type. Such connections are also evident in the human and animal figures of the Ingiet magic society on the Gazelle peninsula. They are produced from tufa and bear a great resemblance to the New Ireland chalk figures. So far as decorative representation is concerned, mention may be made of the linear and mouth-shaped canoe ornaments, featuring elegant spirals, from the Gazelle peninsula; ornaments on canoes in the shape of figures (recalling the Tami style); the shields carried in battle by the Sulka, on which anthropomorphic figures are painted; and finally, the lavishly painted dance shields from the Vitu Islands and the south coast. Here curvilinear ornaments are widespread.

PLATE P. 133

Solomon Islands

In spite of great cultural diversity the artistic styles of this archipelago may be grouped together and treated as a single style region. Making allowances for the distinct local styles, three-dimensional representations appear everywhere as frequently as two-dimensional surface delineations and decorations, although large-size figures are rare, and frequently decorative art plays a preponderant part. An unusually highly developed sense of form makes itself felt in all three groups, but so also does a restraint that prevents sculptural forms from being heavy and exaggerated — without, however, depriving them of their vitality. Often we are reminded of principles that are also of importance in the art of the Admiralty Islands. A common feature in both areas is the sparse use of colour and the organically adapted decorations, mostly arranged in the form of bands. In two-dimensional surface delineation preference is given to black, while in decorative designs white and red are used; very often we also find mother-of-pearl inlays. In most of the three-dimensional representations or two-dimensional surface delineations the head dominates the work either owing to its size or by reason of its style. The figures are more frequently posed sitting or squatting than standing.

FIG. 63 — *Wooden war club. Fiji Is. Length 3 ft. 4¼ in. Cf. p. 166.*

In the western Solomons human subjects are especially predominant; of other living things only birds are depicted, and then but seldom. On Bougainville deceased persons are represented by life-size figures and heads. From this island we also have male sculptures measuring some three feet in height, which are fitted with handles and are carried about by initiates as emblems; they probably personify spirits. The shape of the head is characteristic in both cases: with the male figures the hair tuft is spherical, while the female ones have a truncated cone, a very bulging forehead, and a prominent chin with a broad and deep-set mouth. The same characteristics are repeated in some of the seated figures used in the western Solomons to decorate canoes. In the west there are also to be found figures measuring between 9 and 12 ft. in height, consisting of a torso and head; these personify spirits and are worn in the form of helmet-like masks at initiation festivals; elsewhere in the Solomons masks are lacking. On the paddles from Buka (Fig. 50) and Bougainville there occur very fine painted human figures, carved in bas-relief, depicted in a seated posture with hands raised or with facial ornaments which can hardly be identified any longer. In addition there are round wooden dance shields, dance boards and paddle-shaped clubs in bas-relief, frequently decorated with designs filled in with lime. This form of ornamentation is in most cases of a markedly geometrical and rectilinear character.

In the central Solomons large carved figures are lacking, whereas smaller ones representing either human beings or animals are among the finest sculptures found in this archipelago. Squatting figures with heads larger in proportion to the rest of the body serve both as ornamentation and as 'guardians' of plank-built canoes, which measure up to about 120 ft. in length (Fig. 51). These are presumably representations of spirits. Special characteristic features are the projecting jaws and concave noses — styles found again in decorative

Image of a deity (Tiki) from the Marquesas Is. It is carved from volcanic rock and may have been used for magical purposes. *Musée de l'Homme, Paris. Height approx. 6 in.* *Cf. p. 172.*

FIG. 64 – *Wooden throwing-club. Fiji Is. Length 16½ in. Cf. p. 166.*

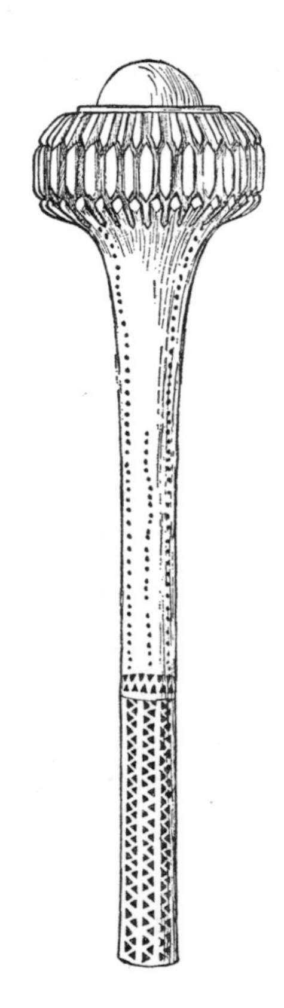

figures on bowls and other utensils. The same is true of most of the figures of volcanic rock or coral-rag, which are apparently confined to the central Solomons, and the stone net sinkers with figured designs. Quite unique is a stone sarcophagus from the interior of Choiseul; in its basic form, but not in its ornamentation, it bears a resemblance to the pieces found on the Minahassa peninsula in northern Celebes. More rounded in form than most sculptures are the re-modelled human skulls, which are decorated – like many other wooden objects – with an inlay of mother-of-pearl discs in various shapes. In the decoration of bowls, implements and weapons one frequently finds, in addition to human subjects, birds, fish or dolphins: these also occur in painting, in the form of open-work designs (wooden combs, paddles) or in inlays with mother-of-pearl – the latter especially in the New Georgia group. Choiseul is known for its thick *tridacna-shell* discs in open-work, bearing human figures or motifs derived from them. They serve as grilles to secure the small houses in which the skulls of chiefs are kept.

FIG. 14

Eastern Solomons

In the eastern Solomons there are human figures that occur in burial places and on the posts of boat- and cult-houses. They have rectangular or round faces and short bent legs. Very similar styles are also featured on the very finely worked spears to be found in this area. Highly characteristic of secular art is the profuse use of animal motifs (frigate-bird, snake, fish and dolphins, pig) as well as human figures. They are to be found on cut-out clam-shell ornaments and on disc-shaped breast ornaments similar to the *kapkaps,* and also on the handles of wooden bowls and on dishes. Seen as a whole they often have the shape of birds or pigs. Bird figures are also found on canoe prows.

PLATE P. 136
FIG. 52
FIG. 54

From a stylistic point of view the Solomons constitute a hybrid zone. In their rigidity the figures often recall the *korwar* or Tami style, but in

Wooden temple figure from Kailua, Hawaiian Is. Poles topped by sculptures were erected as guardians in the fences enclosing temple complexes. The figure portrayed presumably represents the god of war.

FIG. 65 — *Wooden war club. Tonga. Length 3 ft. 9½ in. Cf. p. 167.*

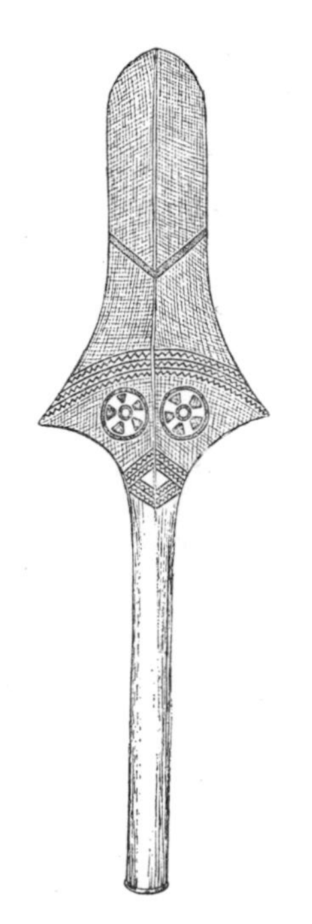

addition to them there also appear forms that are very definitely rounded. The ornamentation includes both consistently curvilinear designs and those of the rectilinear type. The general preference given to rectilinear forms in sculpture and ornamentation is reminiscent of the Admiralty Islands. Objects inlaid with bivalve shells, on the other hand, are found elsewhere only in Micronesia, and stone figures of hard volcanic rock only in Polynesia.

In the small Santa Cruz group a unique form of art has developed. Here figures play a very minor role; the only known examples are human statuettes of wood and figures in relief on cuttle-bone. These mainly serve magical purposes, as do the small carved figures of birds and fish. The huge funerary posts, which are nowadays simply ornamented, were in former times apparently carved in human form, while dance staffs were given the shape of bird figures. But now this motif is scarcely recognizable any longer. The staffs are painted with extremely fine rectilinear designs which without exception derive from fish and bird motifs. Identical design elements occur on gourds, on the superb *kapkap* breast ornaments, and in plaiting and weaving. In detail they bear a resemblance to the designs in the Admiralty Islands and on St. Matthias Island — where, incidentally, weaving is likewise known, as it is in Santa Cruz.

FIG. 55

FIG. 8

Banks Islands, New Hebrides

Although the culture of this whole area is fairly homogeneous in character, from the point of view of art only Ambrym, Malekula and the Banks Islands are of interest. The eastern and especially the southern New Hebrides have very little to offer.

In the central areas and the Banks Islands plastic art plays the preponderant part, although painting is by no means absent and there is also a good deal of ornamentation. The carved figures and masks are closely related

Characteristic features are the hairdress, shape of the mouth, squat body and pendant arms. *British Museum. Height of figure 30¼ in. Cf. p. 175.*

Head of the Hawaiian god of war. Plaited work, covered with a fine-mesh net into which feathers are knotted. Mother-of-pearl and wooden buttons serve as eyes; in the mouth are fitted polished dog's teeth;

FIG. 66 — *Wooden war club. Samoa. The striking part has angular teeth, giving the impression of a rectilinear geometric ornamentation. Length 37¾ in. Cf. p. 167.*

to deceased persons, secret societies and the Suque. This is an organization of a socio-religious character, open to membership by men who can afford to buy their way into it. It is constructed on a hierarchical pattern, each rank having its appropriate price. The prestige of the individual and his status after death depend upon the rank he holds or held. Among the emblems associated with the Suque are the famous figures made of tree-fern trunks. On Ambrym and the Banks Islands they are erected near the men's houses or ancestor houses, and are considered to be the abodes of spirits. Other figures that fulfil the same function are made of wood or are modelled in clay over a frame of palm-leaf fibres. There are also tree-fern statues, which may depict one or more full-size figures, or half a figure, or alternatively just heads and faces; only rarely do we find animals (birds) represented. In most cases the heads are excessively large in comparison with the body. The posts frequently differ from one another in style, although in general the faces are pointed and oval-shaped, with discs suggesting slightly slanting eyes; the noses are large, with flaring nostrils; the mouth is turned up at the corners; the limbs are bent.

FIG. 56

In Malekula we find ancestor figures made of bamboo, barkcloth and other materials. Deceased persons of distinction are also personified in cult figures; often the main feature of these is a skull, over which a face is modelled in clay; it is then painted and bedecked with hair. It may simply be impaled on a decorated post, but frequently it tops a complete sculptured figure. In rare instances the modelled head is preserved on its own.

and on the head there is human hair. Typical plastic feather-work, with stylistic features that also occur in wooden sculptures. *Institut für Völkerkunde, Göttingen. Height 18½ in. Cf. p. 175.*

The large slit-drums featuring one or more carved faces are likewise connected with the grades of the Suque society. In style they bear a resemblance to the chief forms of the tree-fern statues; they are set upright and frequently measure several feet in height. It may be added that the very widespread magic amulets made of soft stone often take the shape of figures.

FIG. 57

Masks mainly personify ancestors and mythological figures. They, too, are often connected with such hierarchical societies, but in some areas also belong to secret societies. Some types are made of wood, others of tree-fern tubes over which figures are modelled in clay, and others again consist of a frame covered with bark-cloth and spider-webbing. Adornment with bark fibres feathers, hair etc., is invariably a major feature. A particularly favourite decoration on funerary figures are boars' tusks; these also serve as ornaments. The masks are often conical, in which case the top of the cone forms the face and the legs and arms are attached lower down; alternatively, the face by itself may take up the whole space on top of the cone. The lozenge-shaped face is generally composed of two segments joined together at the centre. Helmet-like masks or face masks may have this angular shape, but they are also found in an oval shape.

PLATE P. 138

In the north painted wooden boards serve to adorn the gable ends of cult-houses. They feature greatly simplified human figures with arms raised and legs bent, as well as faces and birds.

PLATE P. 141

On secular implements human figures frequently occur, the heads of which are highly stylized, being divided into sharply angular segments by deep indentations. These figures generally appear holding the abdomen.

The stylistic features of the carved figures bear most resemblance to the beak style and other formal idiosyncrasies of the Sepik district. This is also borne out by the great importance attached to colouring. Even the tree-fern figures are painted, after having first been coated with clay.

Animals are represented relatively rarely. On the Banks Islands birds and snakes are to be found in sculpture and painting. Elsewhere animal motifs are featured only in the northern areas of the central New Hebrides; fish on dance emblems; and birds on masks, canoe prows and magic posts in the fields, as well as on the ends of the gable-beams on men's houses and the small ancestor houses erected for the preservation of skulls. A bowl from Aoba (Omba), now in Basle, has the shape of a boar and is made of soft sandstone . Its significance is not known; it may have served sacrificial purposes or been used for making *kava*. More frequent are flat decorated wooden bowls with fretted handles. The ornamentation on cult or secular implements is simple, and consists in many cases of bands, lines of triangles or chevrons, lozenges, and more rarely circles or rings.

New Caledonia, Loyalty Islands

In the art of these islands pride of place is taken by three-dimensional human figures, which occur both as single statues and architectural parts. Animal figures are a great rarity and paintings seem to be absent; masks, on the other hand, are in evidence. Colours (red and black) and incised designs

Feather cape from the Hawaiian Is. Network with feathers knotted into the mesh. *British Museum. Height 4 ft. 1 in., max. diameter 9 ft. 6 in. Cf. pp. 89, 175.*

are employed sparsely as decoration. The ornaments are very frequently composed of parallel lines, bands of lozenges and herring-bone patterns. The cult figures, most of which are whole but measure less than three feet in height, are apparently personifications of ancestors and spirits; they are regarded as guardian or magic figures. They are often of clumsy workmanship. The bodies and faces are rounded; the arms are bent and held in front of the abdomen. Of better quality are the faces of the so-called heads of money, which are suspended from strings of sea-shells, which serve as currency. The largest and most striking figures are the architectural parts and the decorations on large houses, which are circular in plan. In the interior of these houses they are to be found on side-posts and roof-beams, and outside on door-jambs and on the sill. Faces are throughout the principal

Fig. 58

Plate p. 143

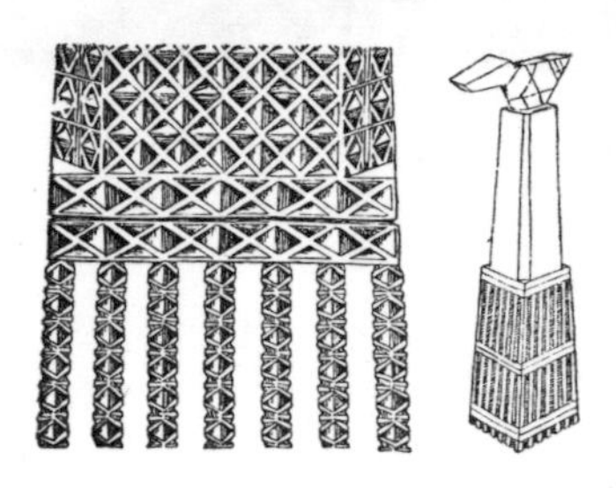

FIG. 67 — *Ornamentation on a ceremonial adze. Wood carved in open-work, stone blade. The delicate simple ornamentation is characteristic. Hervey I., Cook Is. Overall length 17¾ in. Cf. p. 170.*

motif. In the oblong structural part geometric ornaments take the place of the body — a design which recurs in the faces.

Where these ornaments occur on door-jambs, they are usually rectangular, the breadth being greater than the height. Typical features are: pointed and oval- or lozenge-shaped eyes below pronounced bulging foreheads; pointed beak-like noses with flaring nostrils; and a small mouth, often with the tongue hanging out. In other architectural features of this kind, particularly in the interior of the huts, the face is oblong, often terminating at the bottom in an arc; the eyes project like buttons; the nose is straight and frequently rather narrow, without nostrils; the mouth is open fairly wide, showing the teeth and a protruding tongue. A beard is sometimes suggested by vertical incisions in the chin. All these figures are thought to represent ancestor spirits whose function it is to protect the house. They are also to be found as representations in relief on coffins.

FIG. 58
The central post of the conical roofs of club-houses and the houses of chiefs are surmounted by spire-like carvings, often in the shape of a figure. But just as frequently they are abstract in form, often carved in open-work, and at best one can make out a human face. These roof spires are regarded as insignia of the family or symbols of ancestors.

These two styles of architectural figures recur in masks. Those that are smaller are long and narrow, and are mainly rectilinear. The larger type of mask, PLATE P. 144 personifying a water demon, on the other hand, corresponds more to the hook-nosed faces, such as are found chiefly on door-frames; but in the case of masks they are often more rounded, and the nose especially is differently shaped — often almost semi-circular, turned downwards as well as inwards, and furnished with nostrils in the shape of cups. Those parts of the masks that make up the face are made of heavy wood. Attached to them is a cylinder-shaped piece of plaiting or cordage, extended at the back in the form of flaps, and in part bedecked with human hair. At the bottom of the face there is a beard of the same material, and a feather costume is likewise attached to the mask, which covers the body of the wearer down to his knees.

FIG. 59
Particularly well known among New Caledonian decorated objects are the bamboo canes with incised or burnt-in geometrical designs, featuring figures of all kinds as well as whole scenic compositions. Some of these at least are

presumably insignia of rank and office. So, too, are the staffs and ceremonial adzes of the chiefs, which are fitted with disc-like blades; some of them, however, are just individual works devoid of any ceremonial or social significance.

Among purely utilitarian objects there is space to mention only the clubs. With regard to their workmanship and form, they show the same consummate skill in technique as the masks and figures. The New Caledonians had a highly developed sense of form.

FIG. 60

Para-Micronesia (outlying islands of north-western Polynesia)

In that part of Melanesia that is nearest to Micronesia and Polynesia there are a number of small islands which from a cultural point of view belong rather to these two regions than to Melanesia. This whole area is called Para-Micronesia, but sometimes it is referred to as the outlying islands of north-western Polynesia, in which case the western islands in the Bismarck Archipelago are not included. It is necessary to mention these islands since it is here that we find wooden figures that are very important for the history of Oceanic art and culture. Although they all personify ancestors or mythological figures, they differ from one another in style. One type, represented by a group from Nukumanu, comprises large figures of which some measure as much as 16 ft. in height. Their bodies are flat, almost board-like and rectilinear. The head, set low down, seems to be placed between the shoulders when viewed from the front. The face is triangular, with the hint of a beard at the bottom. Also characteristic are the sharply delineated horizontal lines above the eyes and the straight narrow nose. The arms hang down and are rather elongated. Except for a cockscomb-like structure on the head, all these features bear a great resemblance to the styles that occur by the Huon Gulf and on Tami. The same is true of the smaller wooden figures that are found on Tauu in particular. Although in this case the body is more voluminous, it is still typically angular. As with the figures from the Huon Gulf, the hips are sharply gradated and the feet terminate in a block. A third group, also known to exist on Tauu, comprises small very rounded figures measuring little more than 18 in. in height. The head projects above the shoulders; the face is oval-

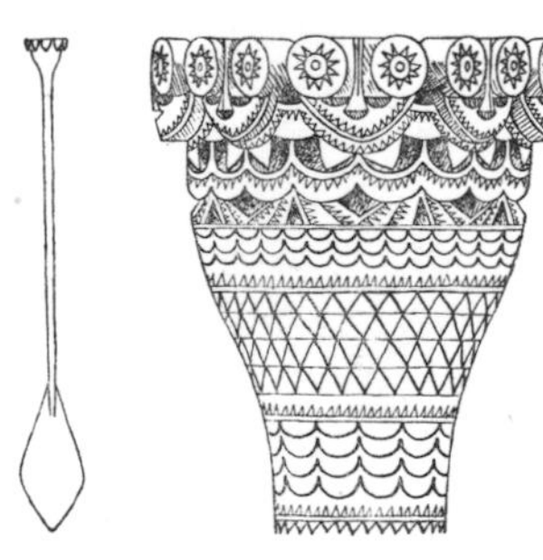

FIG. 68 — *Wooden ceremonial paddle* (left). *The top of the shaft* (right) *is ornamented all over with carving, including highly stylized human faces. Mangaia or Hervey I., Cook Is. Overall length 38¼ in. Cf. p. 170.*

Detail of a *tapa* cloth from the Hawaiian Is. Beaten bark-cloth, printed with stamps and painted. *Institut für Völkerkunde, Göttingen. Width of detail 25¼ in., height 18½ in.* *Cf. p. 176.*

shaped or tapering; and the ears, in contrast to the other styles, are depicted in detail. But here, too, the arms are shown hanging down and the legs again have a block for feet. Thus in their most important characteristics these small figures tally with the large ones, and belong to the same style category. Even if affinities with other styles make themselves felt here, these figures have one typical feature: none of them have arms close to the body or raised.

FIG. 61

So far as ornamentation is concerned, the north seems to have been strongly influenced by northern and western New Guinea.

POLYNESIA

It has already been pointed out that, in contrast to Melanesia, the culture of Polynesia is much more homogeneous. But from this we should not draw the conclusion that there are no local cultures or style provinces. Although the mode of economic life as well as the socio-religious pattern

FIG. 69 — *Bottom of a wooden food-bowl with designs carved in relief. Ornamentation typical of the Marquesas Is. Nuku Hiva, Marquesas Is. Height 5 in., diameter 12 in. Cf. p. 173.*

do give the impression of being more uniform, there are great differences in points of detail. The same is true of art forms and styles. In some areas there are no figures, but elsewhere they are all the more important. Although decorative designs are as a rule characterized by sparse use of colour and small surface ornaments, and in many areas these constitute the only form of art, they are not of the same importance in all areas, and often have typical local variations. Painting occurs seldom, apart from the ornamentation of *tapa,* but is not totally absent. Finally, the shortage of certain raw materials has led to local specialization.

This survey is limited to the most important style provinces. A number of island groups that are not important from an artistic point of view will have to be left out of account.

Fiji Islands

The Fiji or Viti group forms a transitional zone between Melanesia and Polynesia. From a physical anthropological point of view the inhabitants belong to Melanesia; but their culture is hybrid, and their art is preponderantly Polynesian in spite of all its individual traits. Neither plastic art nor painting play an important part here. Of much greater significance is the ornamentation of implements.

Among full-length sculptures there are figures of wood and ivory (from the tusks of the sperm-whale or from imported walrus-tusks). These are mainly regarded as representations of deified human beings, which are venerated as tribal gods. They are large wooden figures with a long torso; the head is low-set between highly accentuated shoulders; the face is oval-shaped and tapering; the nose is relatively straight; the eyes are narrow and horizontal; and the mouth is a horizontal slit. Figures in high relief, too, which presumably served as door-posts, possess the same stylistic features. As in the outlying islands of north-western Polynesia, the small figures have rounded heads and bodies, some with arms hanging down but others with them held before the abdomen; the legs are slightly bent. Both types give the impression of being very impersonal and lifeless.

Among secular works of art much the most important are wooden bowls, clubs and ornamented bark-cloth (*tapa*). Bowls frequently used for ceremonial purposes, e.g., for *kava*-drinking and anointing priests and chiefs, boast an exquisitely fine form, but they are usually not decorated. Occasionally they take the shape of an animal (turtle). Also well known are the clay

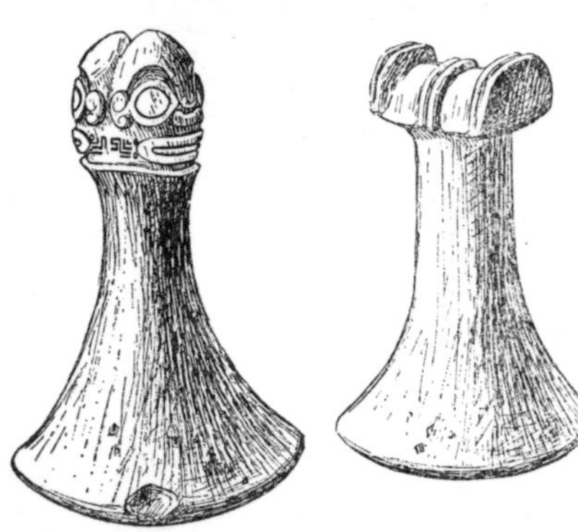

FIG. 70 — *Bread-fruit pounder of volcanic rock.* Left: *Marquesas Is.; the two heads are a typical Marquesas style. Height 7¾ in.* Right: *Tahiti. Height 7¼ in. Cf. pp. 169, 173.*

FIG. 62

vessels, often made up of several different containers, which again reveal a perfect sense of form.

FIGS. 63, 64

Ornamentation of the most delicate kind is to be found on various clubs used in fighting. A few exceptions apart, such decorations are completely geometrical and rectilinear. Only seldom are motifs of faces recognizable in them. The designs, most of which are arranged in panels, are incised.

Bark-cloth (*tapa*), which is worked by the womenfolk, is nearly always ornamented in black. The designs are usually rubbed in with the aid of matrices. Also in this case, except for one plant motif and small animal figures, the ornamentation is rectilinear and geometrical throughout. Some fabrics bear an astonishing resemblance to those from Indonesia, with their bold designs placed lengthwise in the centre and at either end fine motifs arranged in transverse bands.

Tonga, Samoa

The peoples of these two groups are closely akin, despite important social and political differences. Differences also occur as regards technology and especially the form of their implements, weapons, etc., and in their art as well. Carved figures occur extremely seldom: in Samoa no finds at all are known, and in the Tonga group they are known to be produced only on one island. But apparently in former times they were made more generally in both areas.

Tonga figures are representations of deities, who are thought to take up residence in them for part of the time or to furnish them with some of their power. Those that are fairly large in size, measuring up to 18 inches in height, are made of wood, and smaller ones of ivory. Usually they are female, with bodies rounded and the shoulders and hips accentuated; other characteristic features are the sharply pointed breasts and particularly the arms, which hang down loosely.

A fine sense of form and skill in the arts of working wood are even more highly developed in Samoa and Tonga than in Fiji. This is shown by the incomparable beauty of the bowls, head-rests, weapons and other implements; by comparison decoration plays a minor part. Samoa is, moreover, known for its bowls in the shape of turtles. There is a complete absence of painted decoration, and incised ornament is likewise extremely rare. Only clubs,

Wooden ancestor figure from Easter I. Male figure, represented mainly in skeleton form. *British Museum. Height 18¾ in.* *Cf. p. 178.*

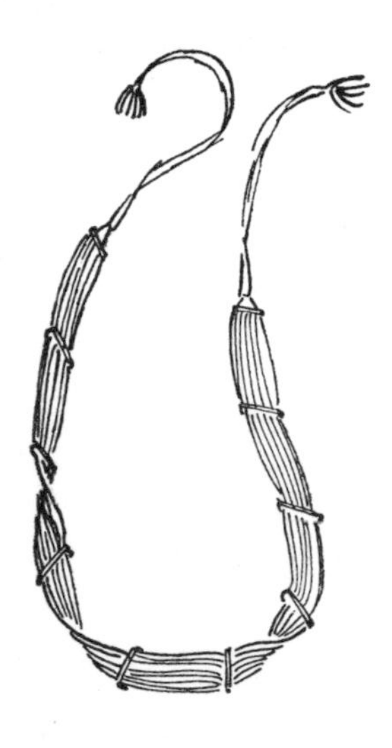

as a rule, have delicate incised ornament of rectilinear design; in Tonga they are often provided with a broad striking end which in cross-section is flat and lozenge-shaped; in Samoa, on the other hand, they taper to a short hook and are furnished on the outside with long teeth. In both areas decoration is applied not at once, but gradually in the course of time, after victorious battles, as commemorative emblems; it is thought to have a magic connotation.

Samoa and Tonga are both centres where ornamented *tapa* is produced. Here, too, the designs are rubbed in by means of matrices and geometrical forms are by far the most prominent. Animal motifs arranged in long bands, with stylized heads, several pairs of legs, and a fan-like tail are to be found only in Samoa.

In this ancient centre of Polynesian culture, too, figures are rare. As in Samoa and Tonga most of the deities, and particularly those that are supreme, are not represented as figures but in the form of symbols of various kinds. For this purpose frequent use is for example, made, of cordage bedecked with red feathers. But in former times representations in human guise seem to have played a greater part than they do nowadays. This is suggested by the existence of isolated ancient stone figures, and the few wooden sculptures that have survived may perhaps also represent deities. As a rule, it is true, they are termed spirit figures, and are used by magicians. They seldom measure more than 18 inches in height, may be either male or female, and (apart from a few very realistic specimens) are always fashioned in the same style. Rounded forms are typical: the abdomen is prominent and protrudes from the torso; the head is pointed and egg-shaped; the nose is straight and distinctly formed; and the eyes are narrow and usually suggested by two curved bulges. The horizontal mouth, too, is narrow, like a tiny slit. The ears are clearly recognizable. The legs are always bent, as are the arms, which are shown resting on the abdomen.

Figures are also to be found on implements, but in this case

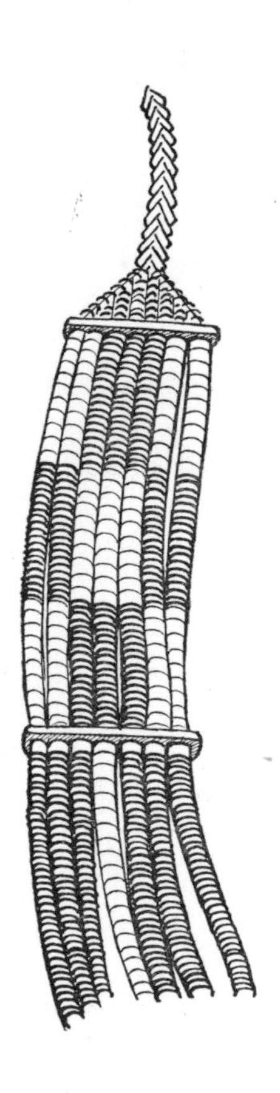

FIG 71 — *Belt. Discs of white mussel- and black coconut-shell threaded on a cord, with small wooden transverse slats. Oleai, Caroline Is. Overall length 37½ in. Cf. p. 179.*

Plank of a gable on a men's house from the Palau Is. Wood, with traces of painting. It is all carved in one piece except for the head of the female figure, which is affixed. On the plank itself is an incised scenic composition. *Hamburgisches Museum für Völkerkunde und Vorgeschichte. Length 12 ft. 1 in., height of figure 2 ft. 9½ in. Cf. p. 179.*

they are even more stylized in form. On the handles of fly-whisks for ceremonial use we find extremely impressive squatting figures with heads almost resembling enormous beaks, and with pointed projections on the forehead. Again the arms are bent, crossed on the chest or abdomen. Other pieces that are often highly stylized include magic objects of wood or stone, in which animal subjects can occasionally be identified.

PLATE P. 148

Cult objects and utensils are decorated with simple incised designs, but are as a rule polished smooth. They are very rarely painted. Ornaments are purely geometrical and bear some resemblance to those from the Cook Islands. The designs on *tapa* are also chiefly geometrical. The use of matrices is not known in this area, and its place is taken by painting.

FIG. 70

Cook and Austral Islands

From a cultural point of view these archipelagoes are closely related to the Society Islands; from an artistic point of view they constitute one of the most interesting regions of Oceania. They show affinities with the Tahiti group in the style of human figures, whereas their ornamentation, typified by small motifs and design elements that are in the main geometrical, calls to mind Samoa and Tonga. Both in plastic art and ornamentation we are dealing here entirely with indigenous forms – renderings which differ very much even from one locality to another. Also in this area lavish carved ornamentation is mainly restricted to cult objects or objects used for ceremonial purposes of some kind. Secular implements are in most cases left plain.

In the ritual sphere ornaments have come to play such a predominant part that they must be considered the most characteristic feature of the area. Often they cover not only the entire surface of an object but are so deeply incised as to produce open-work designs; indeed, the object may be reduced to a state in which the original form is no longer recognizable. Most of these pieces are representations of deities which, as one would expect from the predominance of design elements, are present in the ornaments rather than in the object itself. In Samoa and Tonga we came across the practice of decorating clubs after victory in battle. This idea is developed further here in a consistent fashion: ornaments represent the force obtained either from enemies that have been killed or from deities. The exaggerated value attached to them may perhaps derive from the fact that the arrangement of the ornament is interpreted as symbolic of the equally rigidly organized socio-religious structure.

FIG. 67

The ornamentation is in the main extremely geometrical. Fine examples are to be found on all ritual objects, ceremonial adzes, ladles for libations, bowls, paddles, etc. Only in isolated instances do human subjects occur, and bird figures are very seldom met with. The human motifs are limited to bands of small figures connected to one another, portrayed with arms raised and legs bent, and to the rendering of triangular heads and faces, with discs for eyes, which are likewise arranged in bands.

FIG. 68

On the basis of the anthropomorphic motifs featured in decorative art, and for other reasons as well, it may be assumed that the divine powers may also have been represented in the form of figures, and that they may indeed have been of greater importance in former times, before they were ousted, than they are nowadays. This assumption is substantiated by the fact that in both island groups sculptures of deities occur which range from those of a typically figurative character through various transitional forms to abstract and ornamental renderings, as well as to representations of divine force in the form of various objects made of cord, feathers, *tapa,* etc. The sculptures of a purely figurative character are mainly made of wood. Stone figures, some of which are of monumental size, are also found. They were erected on stone platforms – the latter are absent in western Polynesia – or preserved in cult-houses and only exhibited during festivals. They are mostly represented in a squatting posture, or at least with the knees bent, whereas the arms are shown almost without exception resting on the chest or the protruding abdomen. All the limbs are short. The top of the head is relatively flat, and the two halves of the face meet at the centre in a line, which may or may not be clearly indicated; this leads from the forehead to the chin and suggests the nose. The oval-shaped pointed eyes, extending from the nose to the region of the ears, project and are framed by two curved bulges. Other bulges are to be found close to the eyebrows. The ears have the shape of bowls and are circular. They very large mouth is lozenge-shaped, showing well-developed lips and the suggestion of a protruding tongue.

Detail of a painted beam from a men's house at Yap. On the left, two dugongs. *Hamburgisches Museum für Völkerkunde und Vorgeschichte. Height 4 ft 11 in., width 1 ft. 4¾ in.* *Cf. p. 180.*

In the Cook Islands the slant of the two halves of the face is often so greatly accentuated that in cross-section the head has a cuneiform shape. This form is also characteristic of the deities represented on staffs from the same area. Such sculptures generally feature at one end a head, or one or two figures placed lengthwise, followed by small human figures crosswise, often hardly identifiable as such. These may perhaps be genealogical representations, possibly of deities and their descendants. This motif is expressed in a more effective fashion in the wooden sculptures from Rarotonga (Cook Islands) and Rurutu (Austral Islands): in the first case small figures are affixed to the chest and arms of a large male figure; in the second case these figures are depicted crawling about, as it were, on the torso and limbs; they are also used to suggest eyes, nose, mouth and ears and are even to be found inside the hollow torso, which has a lid at the back.

PLATE P. 151

Deities represented on staffs, too, may be furnished with heads or figures at one end, but usually bear ornamentation, either overall or with this forming the principal decoration. Finally, overall decoration is to be found on the ceremonial adzes from Mangaia (Cook Islands), which may also represent deities and apparently were mainly used for ritual purposes in peace negotiations.

Marquesas Islands

Although likewise typically Polynesian, the culture of this group differs distinctly from that of central and western Polynesia. The population is divided into numerous small tribes which formerly used to be in a permanent state of hostility with one another. The social structure and the rites were based on these units; and in addition to this there was a very well-established cult of the dead. Deceased persons were mummified and at a later stage (where those who had died were men of distinction), after the death rites were completed, the skulls were preserved. Sculpture and decoration are of equal value: both forms are highly developed as regards craftsmanship as well as level of artistic achievement.

In plastic art wood, stone, bone and ivory, and in ornamentation mollusc- and turtle-shell, were treated with the same consummate skill. Idols made of wood and stone, frequently measuring more than 9 ft. in height, served to adorn splendid terraces and other stone monuments. They were similar to those employed elsewhere in eastern and central Polynesia as places of worship, but here they were in most cases much simpler in form. Such figures were also erected in dwelling-houses, where they often served as architectural parts. Smaller figures, mostly of stone, were used as magic objects.

PLATE P. 154

All the anthropomorphic representations display the same stylistic features. As is the case in central Polynesia, the squat figures are depicted in a crouching posture, or at least with short stout legs; the arms are bent and always rest on the abdomen. The excessively large head has facial features that are only slightly raised. The eyes are as a rule rounded and encircled by rings – especially on stone figures, whereas wooden sculptures generally have curved bulges instead. The short nose, closely linked to the eyes and often to the ears as well, possesses two distinctly modelled nostrils. In the very wide horizontal mouth the lips are clearly shown and the teeth and tongue are often visible as well. Frequently the wooden figures are covered all over with incised designs in flat relief; in their patterns they resemble the tattoo-marks in the Marquesas, which have attained a particularly high level of development. In contrast to the central and western parts of Polynesia, secular implements, tools and weapons are also often decorated with figures, and even on personal ornaments human figures play a much greater part. The style is uniform and has distinctive features.

Individual variations are more evident in purely ornamental forms of decoration than in figures. As a rule they are bolder and less monotonous here than in the western parts of Polynesia, and above all are found here in much greater profusion. Basically the designs are curvilinear, but there is a definite tendency for circles, spirals, meanders, pointed oval-shaped and horseshoe-shaped elements to give way to rectilinear motifs; thus rectilinear designs (lines in series, herring-bone patterns, etc.) also occur frequently. Magnificent examples of figured and ornamental decorative art are to be found, for instance, on stone pestles used for crushing bread-fruit, on war clubs which widen out at one end and have a face on either side, on the foot-supports of stilts, which are modelled in the form of figures, and on wooden bowls and trumpets. In the sphere of ornaments especially worthy of note are the headbands made of square-shaped pieces of turtle- and bivalve shell, some of which are carved in open-work, as well as discs like *kapkaps,* bone ear-plugs, which are frequently modelled in the shape of figures, handles of fans, and decorative necklaces of cylinder-shaped beads. *Tapa* is known but is not ornamented.

FIG. 69

FIG. 70

FIG. 72

One of the distinguishing features of Hawaiian culture is the well-defined feudal social structure and the autocratic system of government. The nobility, and the ruling families in particular, were accorded divine adulation. For this reason a great part was played in ritual, not only by individual, family and craft deities, but also by representatives of the state religion, with the god of war at their head. The walls of places of worship were adorned with posts crowned with carved heads, and before the place of worship itself were numerous standing wooden figures, which served decorative purposes or as guardians. But the most important cult objects, the actual manifesta-tions of deities, frequently consisted of small unpretentious objects such as, for instance, a *tapa* scroll decorated with feathers. Besides these there were heads and figures, frequently measuring more than six feet in height, which were also regarded as representatives of gods. These were seldom made of

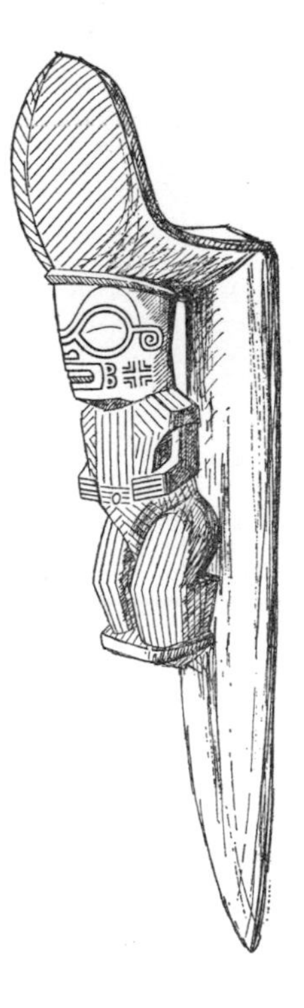

FIG. 72 – *Wooden foot-support on stilt. Marquesas Is. Height 11¾ in. Cf. p. 173.*

Wooden image of a deity. Nukuoro, central Carolines. *Hamburgisches Museum für Völkerkunde und Vorgeschichte. Height 5 ft. 3¾ in., width 1 ft. 4¾ in.* *Cf. p. 180.*

wood, but usually of cord or wickerwork, and could be carried about. Smaller stone or wooden figures, on the other hand, were identified as representatives of family or craft deities. All these cult figures were once to be found in abundance, but in 1819, still before the white man influenced Hawaiian culture, they fell victim to a religious and social upheaval. Later such figures only remained popular as ornamentation on implements of all kinds.

In three-dimensional art two main styles can be clearly distinguished. In both cases the body is squat, and the legs are stout and bent. The arms, too, are bent, and in this case we cannot speak of them as holding the abdomen. The head is in one instance excessively large; the hair is often parted and modelled in the shape of a cap, and hangs far down the nape of the neck, calling to mind the styles in New Guinea and the Admiralty Islands. Such figures convey an impression of extreme vitality. The facial expression is particularly ferocious. This is brought about to a large extent by the form of the mouth, which is very large, often in the shape of a figure 8 lying horizontally, with gnashing teeth and the tongue visible. The nose is short but is furnished with large curved nostrils. The great pointed oval-shaped eyes are frequently turned downwards and outwards, and are enclosed within curved segments.

Plate p. 156

This same type also includes figures bedecked with feathers and heads made of bundles of withes. Here the threatening expression is intensified still further by the insertion of teeth, mother-of-pearl eyes with wooden pupils, and human hair.

Plate p. 158

In the second style, represented mainly by smaller figures, the heads most resemble those from central Polynesia. Hairdress is lacking; the mouth is smaller and straighter; the nose has no nostrils. Sculptures of this kind were also made of stone; they are to be found above all on wooden bowls, drums and gaming-boards, often in incredible contortions and carved with much imagination. In former times there seems to have existed a third style, characterized by long low-set heads and faces, long narrow noses, very prominent chins, thinner bodies and relatively long legs. The more ancient of these figures bear a striking resemblance to those from northern New Guinea (Huon Gulf, Astrolabe Bay).

Apart from incised lines, usually following the contours of the mouth, there is no ornamentation at all on the surface of the figures. Such forms of decoration are also almost invariably lacking on utensils, except for gourds. Even in the ornamentation of jewellery and clothing preference was given to bold motifs, as may be seen distinctly from the superb cloaks worn by nobles on state occasions and in battle. These consisted of cord meshes with feathers knotted into them, mostly red and yellow in colour, forming shield-shaped panels, often also with black borders and contours. The same technique is also employed in making the crested helmets which are worn with these cloaks.

Plate p. 161

PLATE P. 164 The Hawaiian *tapa* is considered to be the finest bark-cloth in Oceania. It is painted or printed with the aid of wooden stamps. Leaf motifs occur relatively frequently, as do geometrical ornaments as well.

Easter Island The culture of this Polynesian island, the remotest in Oceania, has distinctive features, owing to external economic and technological factors: for example, the absence of the coconut-palm and some tuberous plants, and the very great shortage of wood. Here, too, the social organization was based on class stratification; at its head was a king who may have exercised purely religious functions. Deities seem by and large to have played a minor role, apart from one mythological being with a bird's head in human guise, such as is found elsewhere in Polynesia as well. The well-known gigantic stone figures may also be idols, but they are more likely to be ancestor figures or monuments erected in their honour and for their protection. They are mainly sited close to the shore, on platforms which serve as places of worship and burial-grounds. All the wooden sculptures undoubtedly represent ancestors. The way in which they are fashioned in itself points to the fact that the dead were thought to live on in the form of skeletons. They were used mainly in fertility and harvest rites. The small stone sculptures discovered recently, too, though possibly modern products, may be connected with such rites. Small wooden figures of different kinds may likewise have had a ritual significance, but no doubt also partly served as ornaments, since wood was such a rare and costly material. Apart from drift-wood, which is occasionally available, the only material for wood carvings comes from the gnarled branches of a certain kind of bush. It was natural that such material should be utilized so far as possible in its natural form; and this is the only reasonable explanation why the small figures are often most grotesquely contorted. The shortage of wood may also have resulted in the fact that figures were carved in stone much more frequently on Easter Island than elsewhere in Oceania; the painted figures consisting of a frame covered with *tapa* are suggestive rather of the feather figures in Hawaii.

So far as motifs are concerned, human beings are by far the most prominent. Birds, lizards, fish, whales, animals with human heads and boats are frequently depicted. Great differences of style are apparent between stone and wooden figures, as well as within the two groups. The monumental works of volcanic tufa as a rule depict at the most the upper part of the body, the head and arms. Often the outstretched arms are placed close to the sides of the cylindrically-shaped torso, but they may just as often be held over the abdomen. The most frequent means of rendering heads is one in which, when viewed from the front, they resemble elongated rectangles, and when viewed from the side, seem pointed and trapezoidal; they have a flat crown, formerly topped by a wig of red stone. The face has a protruding forehead and deep-set eye-sockets; the nose curves slightly inwards and has clearly shaped nostrils; the mouth is small and horizontal, with prominent lips and small ears with very distended lobes.

Wooden face mask from Mortlock, central Carolines, painted with lime and soot and bearing incised geometric ornamentation. *Hamburgisches Museum für Völkerkunde und Vorgeschichte. Height 17¾ in., width 19¾ in.* *Cf. p. 180.*

Only in isolated instances do large squatting stone figures occur. Fragments of smaller stone sculptures resembling them in style have also been found. The entire body, but above all the head, is fashioned in a more rounded form; details of all these forms bear great resemblance to those from central Polynesia.

PLATE P. 167

The male wooden ancestor figures are as a rule very uniform in style. The slender body is often portrayed leaning slightly forward, and is rendered in the form of a skeleton, with the chest and spine standing out particularly clearly. Although the slightly bent legs are relatively short, the vertical line is accentuated. This is chiefly due to the long arms, which are likewise slightly bent, but hang down and are placed close to the hips. The accentuated treatment of shoulders and hips that is an invariable feature seems to be deliberate. Below the almost spherical upper part of the head is a very oblong face with a small beard. The nose is narrow and very curved; the protruding eyes are often inlaid with discs of shell, set with deep curved bags below them and bulging eyebrows, also curved, above them. The protruding mouth with gnashing teeth resembles the horizontal figure 8 in Hawaiian sculptures. The ear is frequently spiral-shaped, with distended lobes. The cranium is often ornamented with animal and human motifs carved in flat relief.

In sharp contrast to these sculptures are the female figures, which are fashioned throughout in rounded forms, give the effect of being broader, and are represented holding the abdomen.

Figurative representations are also to be found on ceremonial staffs and ornamental plates, wooden paddles and clubs, either in the form of whole figures or heads. Sometimes they are simplified to such an extent that the motifs can hardly be made out any longer. There are also some isolated bird figures and combinations of birds and human beings (a man with a bird's head), as well as other animal figures; these are met with as decorative motifs as well.

Tapa is known, but is dyed in no other colour than yellow, and painted only when it is used as a cover for head-dress and for roughly worked figures.

FIG. 73 — *Wooden architectural part from a men's house. Palau Is. Height 18 in. Cf. p. 179.*

MICRONESIA

The view frequently held that the culture of Micronesia, like that of Polynesia, is very homogeneous is due to an excessive emphasis on the material aspects of culture. In the sphere of social organization and religious beliefs there are very marked differences, and the same holds good for the forms of art related to them. By and large these are no doubt less striking than in Polynesia, let alone Melanesia, and in many areas of Micronesia, it is true, one can look in vain for figures or paintings of any kind. Instead there occur magnificently decorated mats and fabrics, as well as ornaments and implements of perfect workmanship. These may justly be considered the expression of creative artistic volition, even though the results may often appear prosaic and sober. But in Micronesia in particular, there are also areas where, within the sphere of plastic art, painting and decoration, works have been created which can vie with those from Polynesia and Melanesia, and indeed even surpass them. They are, however, confined to the Palau island group and the Carolines, whereas the Marianas, Marshall and Gilbert Islands cannot boast of anything of the kind. Only as a consequence of contact with our civilization have stone and wooden figures been produced here, as they have in other parts of Micronesia as well. From an artistic point of view, however, these are in most cases of very little value. In Micronesia as well as in Polynesia mythological figures of deities are represented mainly on objects that apparently serve a secular purpose (staffs, shell-trumpets, etc.). Apart from Nukuoro in the Carolines, figures of wood and stone are only known in the Palau Islands.

Fig. 71

Palau Islands

Here carvings are also to be found on the handles of spoons, and on clay lamps, in the form of small figures placed upon the rim of the vessel. By far the most significant, however, are the carved figures in high and flat relief, and paintings and decorations found on various buildings: men's houses, boat-houses, and small cult-houses. The houses of young men in particular can vie in every respect with the ceremonial buildings of Melanesia in regard to artistic workmanship. Their gable side is decorated with a fully carved female figure and planks bearing incised and scenic compositions of mythological and historical events. The posts and beams on such houses are likewise carved and painted. The posture of the figures, seated with legs astraddle, bears great resemblance to that of the female figures from the middle Sepik which support the ridge beams of the spirit houses, and other forms found on the Huon Gulf, whereas scenic compositions of this kind are not known elsewhere in Oceania.

Fig. 73

Plate p. 169

In the sphere of decorative art Palau has become well known for its lidded bowls of wood inlaid with mother-of-pearl, which are often modelled in the shape of a bird. They bear in the main purely geometrical designs, but in some cases the pieces of mother-of-pearl are combined to form human and animal figures as well.

Yap

Yap is less important from an artistic point of view. The posts of club-houses – and also, for example, some of the boards in their walls – are adorned with carvings or are painted in white and black. Human figures carved in high relief have stylistic affinities with the elongated figures found in northern New Guinea and other parts of Melanesia, the hanging arms being of particular significance in this respect. Incised decoration, as well as notched and burnt-in designs and others executed in poker-work, consist predominantly of rectilinear geometrical ornaments. These also occur frequently in painting, but fish, sea-cows, turtles and human beings are PLATE P. 171 among the motifs depicted here. Roughly worked bird and fish figures may be suspended on the gable ends of men's houses.

Carolines

Sculpture and painting are rarer here than in the west, but there are nevertheless some outstanding works of art. This is particularly true of the PLATE P. 174 Polynesian enclave of Nukuoro. From the standpoint of technique alone the wooden figures are of the highest quality; but especially striking is the extreme limitation of the formal elements, which are reduced to essentials. The pointed egg-shaped head is very often represented without any detail. From very broad shoulders the arms hang down freely; if hands are indicated, they rest on the hips. The slightly bent legs terminate in a base, or else the feet may be reduced to a sort of block. The maximum of expression is here achieved with a minimum of resources, in a way unknown anywhere else PLATE P. 177 in Oceania.

The second exception are the wooden masks from Mortlock. They represent a benevolent spirit and are used to ward off dangerous typhoons. In their dignified restraint and simple style of painting they differ radically from other South Sea masks. They are incidentally the only types of mask known in Micronesia.

Figurative decoration on architectural parts is likewise rarely met with in the Carolines. In isolated instances we find house posts bearing human figures with raised arms, or painted human figures and animals, in which case black and white are invariably the main colours used. The spirit boats PLATE P. 182 from Truk used in ritual may be decorated with carved bird figures; here, too, we find splendid canoe ornaments in the form of two very simplified bird figures. On the same island purely geometrical ornamentation, with small incised rectilinear designs, has also attained a very high level of development. The decoration on parts of boats and dance staffs, in which the indentations are filled in with lime, bear striking resemblance to the forms of decoration on St. Matthias Island. Similar ornaments are to be found on Ponape (on dance paddles) and Kusaie (on the trestles used in weaving) as well as on basket-work objects and fabrics of many kinds.

V. THE ART STYLES OF OCEANIA AND THEIR HISTORICAL SIGNIFICANCE

In this necessarily brief survey of the individual style provinces of Oceania, in which only the most important points could be touched upon, reference has occasionally been made to the affinities and relationships existing between the various art centres. An attempt will now be made to give a general picture. At first we shall deal with the three major regions of Melanesia, Micronesia and Polynesia, and then Oceania as a whole. Finally, we shall consider the question what light, if any, the study of art styles can throw upon the history of culture and settlement in Oceania.

It should be clear from the foregoing that there are few stylistic features common to all three main areas. Not even Micronesia and Polynesia, let alone Melanesia, can be regarded as homogeneous regions in this respect. But we cannot help but be struck by several important phenomena which, though not universally met with in these regions, are nevertheless prevalent there.

Melanesia

Melanesia is much the richest and most varied art region of Oceania. Generally speaking, all three forms of art are represented here: three-dimensional art as well as two-dimensional surface delineation, and within the latter group both painting and ornamentation. So far as technique is concerned, however, the main emphasis lies upon sculpture, and as regards motifs upon figurative representations; (the latter holds good for all three art forms). Just as impressive as the unbelievable wealth of artistic products is the emotional quality of these works – which achieve an intensity of expression attained elsewhere only in Hawaii. This is closely related to the spectacular cults that exist in Melanesia. These cults are also related to masks, which are more or less limited to Melanesia. Lavish ornamentation, exaggerated forms, and profuse use of colour all help to enhance the power of expression in each of these art forms. Another striking feature is the predilection for the use for secular purposes of what were originally cult motifs, as in the decoration on all manner of implements, which again is less common in Polynesia and Micronesia. Art which is basically religious in character overshadows all other types and illustrates in a superb manner how greatly, and in what a direct way, the modes of thought and life of people in this area are influenced by their religious beliefs.

But just as we do not find these characteristics in such pronounced form everywhere, so we cannot expect to find that certain styles are general throughout Melanesia. Our survey has shown clearly enough how diverse the styles are within the various provinces. But despite all these local differences it is still possible to determine certain facts on the basis of

Wooden canoe ornament, carved in one piece, from Truk, central Carolines. *Hamburgisches Museum für Völkerkunde und Vorgeschichte. Height 17¾ in., width 19¾ in.* *Cf. p. 180.*

which we can establish the relationship between these provinces, and draw certain conclusions. Unfortunately only few comparative studies are so far available. But it is already clear from those that have been made that the dissemination of certain basic styles corresponds largely to the process of settlement in Melanesia.

As is only to be expected, no distinct art forms or styles can be ascribed to the earliest immigrants. The Tasmanians and Australians left no traces of their presence in New Guinea that can be identified with certainty. In any case, as typical nomadic hunters and food-gatherers they probably had very little to boast of in the way of art. It is only with the Papuan immigrants that we can reckon with important artistic products. All the Papuan cultures still extant are distinguished by their spectacular cult objects, especially masks made of withes, rattan, bark-cloth, string, leaves, etc. (but not — or only to a small extent — of wood), and by the fact that two-dimensional surface delineation plays the preponderant part; it is not here that the carving of figures developed. These features are typical of the art of all Papuan peoples or of areas that have been under considerable Papuan influence, such as the southern areas of New Guinea (the Gulf of Papua in particular), the Sepik district, and with the Baining and Sulka in New Britain.

Papuans

Everywhere in Papuan areas curvilinear ornamentation is to be found to a greater or lesser extent. This may therefore be ascribed to the Papuans; but it could possibly also have been characteristic of the round adze culture, the next culture to reach Melanesia, which is also typified by a profuse use of colour and the frequent occurrence of masks. But these masks, or at least parts of their faces, are largely of wood, which indicates that carving flourished greatly in the round adze culture. Melanesian sculpture is mainly rooted in this culture so far as style is concerned: preference is apparently given to rounded forms for the head and torso, and especially for the arms, which are either bent (holding the abdomen) or raised (in a posture of adoration).

Round adze culture

Wood-carving is of course also one of the principal characteristic attributes of the southern Austronesian immigrants. But from the standpoint of style their carving has different features: accentuation of straight lines on the torso, head and limbs, great emphasis on the shoulder- and hip-line, and fusion of the part around the feet to form a block. In two-dimensional surface delineation the chief ornamentation is geometrical and rectilinear. As a rule Austronesian art has less vitality and imagination than that of the round adze or Papuan cultures. All these peculiar features are clearly shown in the art of those areas of northern New Guinea that are predominantly Austronesian (Astrolabe Bay, Huon Gulf, Tami).

Southern Austronesians

The fusion of the basic types of style of the round adze people and the southern Austronesians, which can be seen over large areas of New Guinea and in other Melanesian islands, indicates very clearly the Austromelanid hybrid character of the cultures of this area. The very fact that one type or

Austromelanids

the other can occur, or predominate, in the present-day local cultures may yield welcome evidence as to the respective roles played in their development by either of these two basic types. Thus the styles in the areas situated on Lake Sentani and Humboldt Bay, as well as the whole Sepik district, have clearly been very strongly influenced by the round adze culture; the same is true to a lesser degree of New Ireland and the New Hebrides. On the other hand, as has already been mentioned, the art of areas on the Huon Gulf and Astrolabe Bay, and also possibly the Admiralty Islands and some of the Solomons, was much more exposed to powerful southern Austronesian influences. In western New Guinea it is more difficult to assign spheres of influence to these two groups, since in addition to the two ancient cultures a stimulus has been received here in more recent times from Indonesia, which finds expression above all in striking forms of ornamentation carved in openwork, and in the case of sculpture possibly also in the *korwar* style.

Indonesians

Polynesia

Ornamentation plays a preponderant part in Polynesian art, expressed in its most characteristic form in the island groups of Tonga and Samoa, as well as the Cook and Austral Islands (at least with regard to ornamentation). It is distinctly rectilinear and geometrical, with a predilection for small and even minute motifs, and with a tendency towards endless repetition. Plastic and particularly figurative representations are rare, at least in the west, and are often limited to small forms. Masks are completely absent, and colours are hardly used at all. To a large extent artists concentrate on creating sober and distinct forms, which seem to reveal a strong inclination towards order and regularity. There are no traces here of the impulsiveness we find in Melanesian art. These styles lack an emotional quality; the sense of form has stifled the religious feeling that is expressed so distinctly in Melanesia. In other areas of Polynesia these main characteristic features are to be found only to a limited extent or not at all. In the Society Islands, Hawaii and Easter Island ornamentation plays a very minor part. In the Marquesas it is based upon other motifs, derived from curvilinear elements, and in addition is executed much more boldly. Curvilinear designs are also predominant in New Zealand art. Of greater importance, however, is the fact that in all these marginal areas we have three-dimensional sculptured figures, which most probably played a much greater part in former times than they do today. They occur very frequently in New Zealand, but they are also no rarity on Fiji, and in the outlying islands of north-western Polynesia, and especially on the Society Islands, Cook and Austral Islands, Marquesas, Hawaii and Easter Island. Here, too, these statements corroborate the findings made in studies of the history of settlement; and investigations into artistic styles can in turn provide fresh clues as to the process of settlement. The northern Austronesian immigrants, who introduced the central Polynesian cultures, must have had little to boast of in the way of figurative art, but they apparently possessed a highly developed form of decorative art, with motifs that were decidedly geometrical. It was only on the islands mentioned above, particularly on

Northern Austronesians

Tonga and Samoa, that they were able to come into their own fully both in their culture and their art. In those areas of Polynesia where there is sculpture or curvilinear ornamentation, art forms and styles were retained which derive from earlier settlers, in part perhaps from the round adze people, but certainly from Austromelanid elements. This is why one finds reproduced in Polynesian sculpture the two basic types already mentioned: figures holding the abdomen and figures with arms outstretched or hanging down. The latter preponderate in the west; thus here evidently the southern Austronesian elements are especially pronounced. In the east, on the other hand, we in part find the very reverse: the Cook and Austral island group, the Society and Marquesas Islands have figures holding the abdomen. But in Hawaii again we find figures with arms hanging down, and on Easter Island both types occur, with those holding the abdomen prevailing.

Southern Austronesians

Micronesia

Seen as a whole, Micronesia is the area of Oceania that has least to offer in the way of art. It is almost entirely restricted to rectilinear geometrical ornamentation, distinguished by very sparing use of materials, simplicity and a prosaic approach, but also by a very great elegance in the treatment of form. Three-dimensional figures, figurative painting and ornamentation are just as rare as masks; they derive no doubt from Melanesian or late Indonesian influences, or are connected with cultural phenomena related to western Polynesia. From an artistic point of view, the greater part of Micronesia is thus closely connected with the heart of Polynesia.

General characteristics of Oceanic art

It is even more difficult than it is in the case of the three main regions to establish the characteristic features of Oceanic art as a whole. But they do exist. First of all, it is a fact that almost all the figurative art of Oceania is emphatically non-naturalistic. In general there is a prevailing tendency to reduce forms, or to modify them by exaggerated and 'fantastic' treatment, and thus to stress certain emotional values. The art of the South Seas is expressive in the widest sense of the word. One hardly ever has the impression that subjects found in nature are copied, although the artists were no doubt capable of doing so; this has been sufficiently well illustrated by the outstanding 'portrait' heads and 'naturalistic' animal figures from the Sepik district, the Solomons, Tahiti and other places. The fact is that naturalistic treatment is not the main object of Oceanic art. The artists are not concerned to portray human beings or animals but to represent non-human supernatural powers, to create tangible embodiments of the creative force. It is for this very reason that Oceanic art is not only so expressive but also possesses such pronounced vitality. But this vitality is not of a dynamic character, since (apart from some very isolated exceptions in western Micronesia) Oceanic art does not portray action at all. Yet this is what one might have expected; for the myths from which very many of the subjects in Oceanic art are derived describe the creation of the world in imagery expressing action, and this is acted out in the rites largely based upon these myths. In the same way ancestor worship is based upon the important achievements

— i.e., the acts — of deceased persons, which they were enabled to carry out by means of the creative or vital force contained within them. All this is only vaguely suggested, at the most, in sculptured and painted figures: in characteristic features relating to their form, or perhaps in attributes, which may for example be related to certain acts performed by some mythological figure, and so serve to make them recognizable. It is very rare for figures and motifs to be combined; they are almost always represented individually. Even if some of them do appear together, they do not form scenic compositions, but simply supplement or duplicate one another. In such cases it is usually quite possible to subtract one figure without any loss of meaning or value. Each individual motif in a work of art represents a supernatural force through its very existence, not in the action it depicts. This very idea may also have an effect upon the manner of representing human figures. All these works are static in character, devoid of any movement. The figures are mainly depicted in a resting, squatting or standing posture. Even where other attitudes occur, such as men striding along or raising their arms, for example, no impression of movement is conveyed; indeed, such attempts very often seem rather clumsy. But these figures always give an impression of strength and power, which is often enhanced by formal devices such as over-accentuation of the head, squat bodies, stout legs (often slightly bent), and block-shaped shoulders, hips and feet.

Art of early planters

As has already been noted, Oceanic sculpture is chiefly related to the round adze people, the southern Austronesians and the hybrid Austromelanid peoples. In any case it played a key part in the round adze culture. Now this was an archaic planter culture. But in the cultures subject to Austronesian influences, and particularly in their Polynesian and Micronesian forms, a very important role, and indeed an all-important one, is played by fishing in addition to agriculture. Accordingly the importance of sculpture here recedes into the background. Evidently then figurative art is related to the archaic form of planter culture. This relationship does not occur only in the South Seas: it can also be substantiated in archaic tropical planter cultures in Indonesia, Indochina and Africa. In all these areas the art forms correspond in essentials, evidently because the spiritual background and ideas of all these cultures, connected as they are with agriculture, are by and large the same. They are basically different from the religious beliefs of primitive hunters and food-gatherers, as well as Austronesian fishers and agriculturalists. The art of these people is accordingly completely different in character. If we call to mind Palaeolithic cave paintings or African rock engravings, we see that these too consist of figurative representations; but in these cases it is not the figure itself that is prominent but the action it performs. These works are dynamic; they represent the actions of a force and not merely its existence. Thus they correspond to a mental outlook based on magic, which seeks to obtain results through action rather than through a religious attitude, where the aim is to partake in the supernatural creative force. This is why in the works of hunters and food-gatherers even individual representations of animals and human beings give an impression of dynamism, and not only of vigour and strength. There are real scenic compositions here, not merely arrangements of individual motifs. For cultural reasons this form of art is not to be found in Oceania, but on the other hand it is much in evidence in Australia – e.g., in rock engravings and bark paintings. The fact that it is often only recognizable through parallels is probably due to influences from the planter culture, which in part is also very evident in the spiritual aspects of Australian culture. On the other hand, Austronesian, and particularly Polynesian and Micronesian, cultures have already become too far divorced from the archaic form of agriculture, both economically and spiritually, for the art typical of this culture to play any important part here. In most of them we are dealing with cultures that are distinguished by social stratification and other features characteristic of early advanced cultures. The divine powers are already conceived in abstract terms; religious speculation has developed into a veritable theology, and especially in connection wih the rank system a genealogical relationship has been established between men and their gods. Therefore the principle of representing divine force or the force of deified men no longer finds direct expression, but is much more closely linked to formal doctrines and the social structure generally. It is for this reason that figurative art is lacking in many Polynesian and Micronesian cultures. Wherever cult figures appear which correspond completely to the archaic form of planter culture, they have already been taken over by the inferior social groups, who have to some extent attached a different meaning to them, regarding them as the abodes of deities rather than as actual representations of them.

Oceanic styles

This survey of the characteristic features of art in the three major regions of Oceania and the attempt to outline the general characteristics of Oceanic art have shown very clearly how greatly certain styles and stylistic tendencies reflect historical facts. Students of Oceanic cultural history have taken some account of data relating to art styles, but they have made the mistake of seeing particular styles in isolation, endeavouring to follow the way in which they spread and to link them with certain groups of immigrants. Such comparative investigations were, however, for a long time limited mainly to two-dimensional surface delineation, and particularly ornamentation, and pursued evolutionistic aims rather than the study of cultural history proper: that is to say, students were more concerned with attempting to trace certain regular basic patterns of evolution than to analyse actual historical relationships. Only later was consideration also given to figurative, and particularly to three-dimensional, art; only then were its motifs examined, and related to the religious and mythological background in an attempt to draw conclusions with regard to history. The principal representatives of this school of thought are Heine-Geldern, Speiser and Schmitz.

In his investigations Speiser sets out from the contention that art styles can only disseminate in association with the cultures in which they have evolved. In his view extraneous stimuli have in part been responsible for the development of Oceanic styles, but their roots are nevertheless to be found mainly in Oceania itself. The curvilinear style, for example, he regards as evidence of Papuan culture; and the Tami style, wherever it is to be found, he traces to Tami Island and the area of the Huon Gulf. But other forms, such as the beak style of northern New Guinea or the *malanggan* style of New Ireland are according to Speiser strictly localized forms which were not disseminated to any significant extent. The deductions he makes with regard to cultural movements on the basis of his study of the art styles associated with these cultures are borne out to an astonishing degree by the findings of recent research in this field.

In contrast to Speiser, Heine-Geldern derives the origin of all Oceanic styles from areas outside the South Seas, and traces the further history of their development even as far as America. In a fascinating and impressive way he reconstructs the connections that existed between the early cultures of Europe and those of eastern and south-eastern Asia, and sketches those world-wide links which we have touched on above, when discussing the history of Oceanic settlement.

Schmitz has followed a completely different course. His starting-point is the spiritual, and especially the mythological, background of art. As has already been stated in Chapter III, he succeeded in assigning certain myths on the Huon peninsula to certain basic types of culture and in correlating their principal figures with corresponding art styles. Thus he was able to assign to the round adze culture the round figures shown holding the abdomen, and to the southern Austronesian culture the angular forms with arms hanging down and block-shaped shoulders, hips and feet. Furthermore, curvilinear two-dimensional surface delineations belong to the round adze culture, whereas purely geometrical ornamentation is the work of Austronesian immigrants. Very probably these assignations hold good not only for the limited area of the Huon peninsula, but also for New Guinea as a whole and for other parts of Oceania.

In our study the views of Heine-Geldern and Speiser as well as the findings of Schmitz have been extensively used, and in part even expanded upon. But we must not lose sight of the fact that in all three cases we are dealing with hypotheses which require corroboration, and that especially the new points made here should be regarded only as probable, not proven. As fascinating and convincing as many of Heine-Geldern's and Speiser's findings may be, and as much as we should like to accept them, they nevertheless often lack a precise factual foundation. They need to be checked on the basis of the most painstaking detailed studies, carried out with the aid of the most modern scientific techniques. On the other hand, there is no reason to doubt the findings obtained by Schmitz in north-eastern New Guinea. It is an absolute necessity, however, to check in other areas as well the relationship between the basic principles of mythology and the two basic types of style between which he distinguishes. Both approaches are important: that which sets out from external forms as well as that which takes as its starting-point the spiritual postulates of art. One day the findings arrived at by both methods may be discovered to coincide, and further conclusions will then become possible. For the first approach the rich treasures that have been collected, especially in museums, offer an inexhaustible reservoir of material, much of which has not yet been studied in this way. The collections of myths that are already available, and field-work in so far as this is still feasible nowadays, may be expected to yield material with which to pursue the second line of approach. It is thus evident that the study of Oceanic art is still only in its infancy. The groundwork has been laid, both in the form of working hypotheses and in methodology. But we cannot as yet speak of firmly established facts. In this connection one thing is certain: ethnological studies of art are essential for an understanding of the cultural history of Oceania, and future work in this field will have to rely to a considerable extent on such studies.

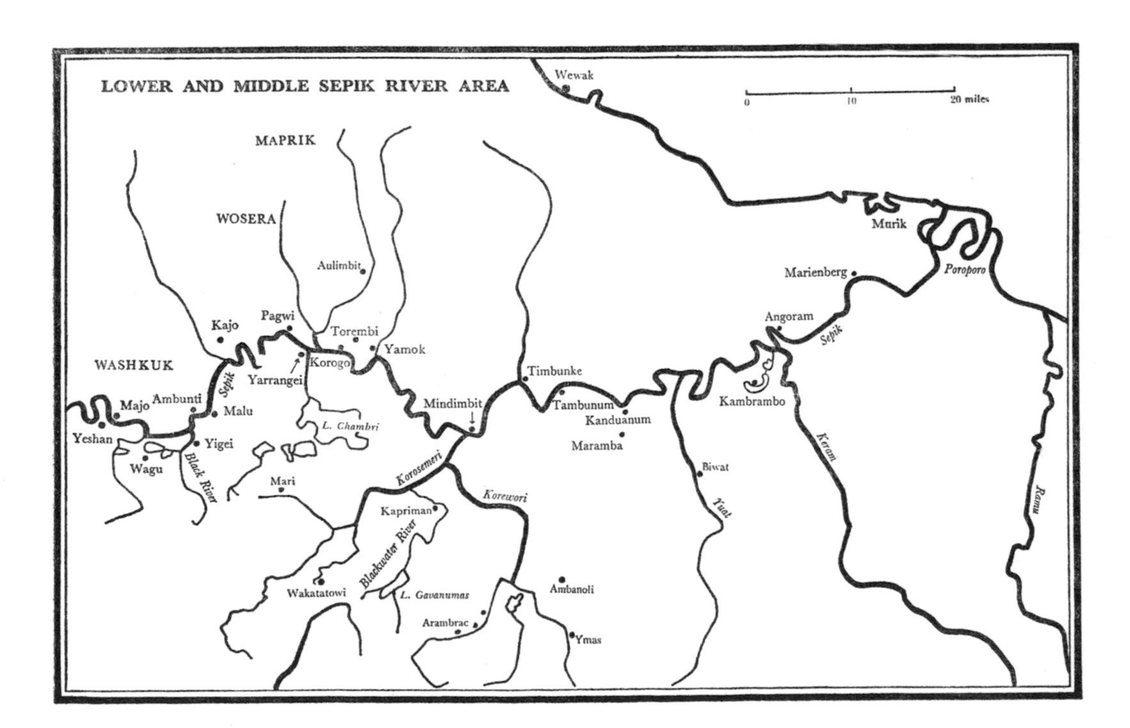

Whalebone weapon of a type known as *patu paraoa. Oldman Collection, Dominion Museum, Wellington. Length 16 in.* *Cf. p. 191.*

ART OF THE NEW ZEALAND MAORI

T. BARROW

New Zealand lies within temperate latitudes in the south-western corner of the great Polynesian triangle. The land area of New Zealand is so extensive that one could easily place within its boundaries all the other islands of Polynesia. Maori art as it was found by European explorers of the late 18th century is the product of a tropical island culture of the Neolithic eastern Polynesian type adapted to meet the needs of a comparatively cold climate, and developed over centuries of isolation in an environment which offered an unusual wealth of materials in the form of wood, stone, and bone. Stimulated by the needs of a cool climate, the ancestors of the Maori adapted their tropical culture to the new environment by ingeniously evolving warm dwellings, garments, food stores, and canoes suitable for transportation on inland and coastal waters.

Adaptation to environment

The techniques applied to the new materials of New Zealand, and the resulting artistic styles are usually traceable to the Cook or Society Islands, which supports the Maori claim that the immediate homeland, or Hawaiki, of their ancestors was the island of Tahiti or thereabouts. Local invention and the adaptation of traditional techniques developed in isolation over centuries resulted in the evolution of one of the most distinctive cultures in the Pacific. Almost every activity developed a decorative art of one type or another; for example, the perennial engagement in warfare produced fine weapons in stone, wood, and whalebone, while preoccupation with lineage and belief in the continuing power of the ancestor resulted in accomplished image-making.

PLATE P. 190

The pattern of human settlement in New Zealand is reasonably well understood, particularly as recent work in archaeology is yielding positive results. For a general study of Maori art it is necessary to keep in mind the presence of two cultural strata, both of Polynesian type. The first is the Archaic, pre-Fleet, or Moa-hunter period, which is thought to commence in the 10th century with the arrival of migrants from the central area of eastern Polynesia. Recent methods of dating are likely to press back the time scale by some centuries, but this need not concern us here. The early Maori found in New Zealand the flightless *moa* and other birds now extinct; the *moa* being of special importance as it provided, for a time at least, abundant supplies of flesh and bone. Archaeologically speaking, it conditioned the culture of the first settlers.

Settlement of New Zealand

The second period of Maori culture is labelled post-Fleet or Classic Maori. It appears to have reached a mature flowering about the arrival of Europeans in New Zealand in the late 18th and early 19th centuries.

Border of flax cloak with decorative *taniko* patterns. *Dominion Museum, Wellington. Cf. p. 194.*

According to Maori tradition a great *heke* or migration (placed by genealogical record about the mid-14th century) carried the ancestors of the existing tribes from the Society Islands to New Zealand, a distance of over 2000 miles. It is from many of the canoes of this great sea migration, for example the Arawa, Aotea, Matatua, Horouta, Tainui, Takitimu and Tokomaru, that present-day Maoris trace their lineage, derive tribal names, and establish claims to their land. Thus a Maori lament says:

Seafaring tradition

> The fame of your canoes can never be dimmed!
> The canoes which crossed the ocean depths,
> The purple sea, the Great-Ocean-of Kiwa,
> Which lay stretched before them.

Naturally enough modern Maoris are shocked to find a few European scholars telling them that there never was a fleet, and that their ancestors were castaways blown from other islands. However, it appears certain that there was some deliberate voyaging from the Society and Cook Islands to New Zealand; but it was probably less orderly than tradition suggests and the survival rate would have been low.

Where archaic Maori culture ends and classic culture begins is merely a theoretical datum point, for it is clear from archaeological investigation that there is a considerable chronological overlap and cultural merging. Because of the perishable nature of wood most of the surviving artifacts from the archaic period are of stone or bone, whereas the classic phase is roundly represented by collections made on the voyages of Capt. James Cook, by other European navigators, by missionaries, adventurers, and early settlers. Excellent collections of Maori art may bc seen in the museums of New Zealand, and in representative collections in England, Scotland, the countries of continental Europe, and North America.

MEDIA OF THE MAORI CRAFTSMEN

The Maori craftsman is primarily concerned with making articles for everyday use, and these are decorated with appropriate designs. Human images representing ancestors are found on artifacts of almost every type with the intention of increasing both the beauty and *mana* or power of the object.

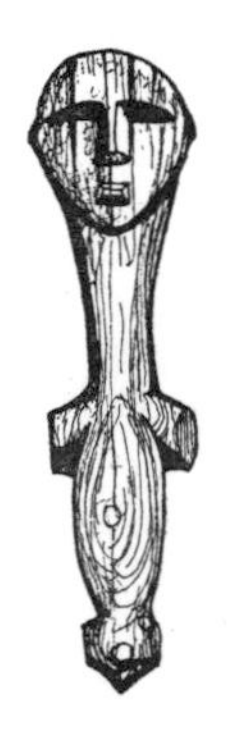

FIG. 74 — *God image, archaic style. Wood. From a cave on Okia Flat, Wickliffe Bay, Otago. Height 8¼ in. Cf. p. 199.*

Broadly speaking, the magical power of design appears to be of less importance than in Melanesia, and unlike his kinsmen in other Polynesian islands the Maori craftsman was little concerned with the manufacture of god symbols or the paraphernalia of ritual. Although godsticks are to be seen, Maori art is more secular than that of most other parts of Polynesia. Maori wood sculpture is notably an art of the ancestral image, adapted to the architectural requirements of ceremonial houses and food stores.

Classification of arts

In New Zealand the decorative arts may be classified under plaiting, weaving, lattice-work, painting, tattoo, and carving in stone, bone, and wood. The spectacular development of wood-carving and the interesting nature of its symbolism calls for special attention. Carving in hard materials, the painting of house rafters, and tattooing is the work of men; the manipulation of soft materials is assigned to women. Women are considered the destroyers of *tapu* and therefore should not be about when the sacred business of house-building, canoe-making or other ritualistic work is in progress. The women who do fine craftwork are esteemed and vie with one another in their work,

Craftsman priest

but the man of rank who qualifies as a skilled carver or tattooer is given the high social status of a *tohunga*. The skilled craftsman is a priest whose art is a dangerous field where personal behaviour is important, for any infringement of the laws of the craft could bring loss of knowledge or worse. Even inadvertent infringement such as an omission in a ritual chant or some unlucky act would have dangerous consequences. Chips from the carver's chisel are a potent cause of trouble if misused. For example, it would be disastrous to put them on a cooking fire or to blow them with one's breath from the surface of a carving.

Garment manufacture

Bark-cloth manufacture was attempted in New Zealand with little success because of the failure to establish fully the paper mulberry plant; also, the material is unsuitable in the New Zealand climate. A substitute for *tapa* was found in the indigenous flax *(Phormium tenax*), which provided long tough fibres for garment manufacture and plaiting of baskets and mats. Designs in weaving are obtained by the use of dyed elements and by changing the number of wefts crossed. Cloaks are decorated with feathers, coloured cords,

PLATE P. 192

strips of dog-skin, or with more elaborate bands of rectilinear designs worked in dyed fibres (*taniko*). As loom weaving was unknown in Polynesia the Maori used his unfailing ingenuity by developing a form of 'finger-weaving' based on a technique used throughout the Polynesian islands in the manufacture of fish traps. The story of the evolution of Maori clothing is an example of the use of a simple traditional technique as the basis for the evolution of a new artistic form.

Rafter painting

Decorative painting on the rafters in Maori ceremonial houses consists of predominantly curvilinear patterns of great variety rendered in red, black and white. The red pigment is obtained from burned ochrous, clay, black from soot, and white or bluish-white from natural clays. All colours are first powdered, then mixed with oil obtained from shark liver. The designs

Ancestral pendant of the *hei tiki* type. Nephrite. *Oldman Collection, Dominion Museum, Wellington. Height 5½ in.* *Cf. p. 196.*

on rafters do not appear to have been inspired by any natural form, although plant forms are suggested in some patterns. All designs are named. Scrolls, crescents, and occasionally rectilinear elements are combined in patterns running up the broad rafters.

Decorated lattice-work

We find associated with rafter patterns in the superior type Maori houses lattice-work panels called *tukutuku,* set between ancestral panels. *Tukutuku* are composed of light horizontal laths lashed from behind to vertical reeds with a great variety of stitches. As the laths are usually painted red with dyed flax or orange-coloured grass used in the lashing, the face of the panel is highly decorative. The resulting designs, although abstract, are assigned names suggested by the general pattern. Zigzag lines are termed *kaokao* (ribs), lozenges are referred to as *patiki* (flounder), and certain triangles as the teeth of monsters *(niho taniwha)*. These *tukutuku* panels were developed locally in New Zealand but relate to the Polynesian practice of employing lashings for ornamental effects.

Rock paintings

An aesthetically pleasing range of paintings on the walls of caves and limestone rock shelters is found in the South Island, but these await systematic collection and study. The subject matter of these drawings includes the human form, fabulous monsters (*taniwha*), dogs, fish, lizards, and birds (including the *moa*). This expressive aspect of Maori art is usually associated with the archaic culture, but as renderings of European sailing ships and colonial buildings also appear, the art was practised until a late period.

Petroglyphs

Rock engravings or petroglyphs occur in both the North and South Island. Although a considerable number of them have been recorded in the 'Journal of the Polynesian Society' and in other publications, their actual significance is largely a matter of conjecture. Like the wall paintings they may be associated either with magic ritual or with the human impulse to doodle. Each possibility is equally interesting.

Jade ornaments

A notable achievement of Maori art is found in the various ornaments of greenish nephrites and jade-like stones called *pounamu*. The material is found in Teramakau and Arahura rivers on the West coast of the South Island and in the Otago district. *Pounamu* is of such a hard texture that it is worked by laborious processes of abrasion. Because of this, and its rarity and beauty, ornaments in this material are highly valued. Fine examples of this beautiful art may be seen in the museums of the world, especially examples of the relatively common human-form *hei tiki* neck ornament. European collectors have usually sought *hei tiki* for their size and beauty, but by the Maori they are valued as symbols of ancestors and

PLATE P. 195

FIG. 75 — *Manaia creature from a feather-box* (waka-huia). *Cf. p. 202.*

FIG. 76 — *A* marakihau *on an ancestral panel from the Whakatane district. Wood painted with red ochre. Height 7 ft. 3 in. Cf. p. 204.*

gain value through their association with previous owners. Some of these ancestral pendants possess great *mana,* a word denoting prestige and magical power, and such specimens frequently possess a personal name.

Tattoo

Maori tattoo on face, thighs, and buttocks is characterized by curvilinear patterns which are directly related to surface decoration in wood-carving and painted rafter design. Ethnologists have an excellent opportunity to observe facial tattoo because of the Maori custom of preserving the heads of both friends and enemies. If a chief died on a distant field of battle, his head was carried home in lieu of his body to comfort his widow and relatives; but the head of an enemy was preserved so that all members of the tribe might have the opportunity to revile and insult it. Thus, feelings of love and hate inspired the skilful technique of preserving heads. The method of mummification was to break in the base of the cranium in order to remove the brain; the loose skin at the neck was stitched to a vine hoop; then the head was subjected to steaming in the earth oven, smoking, and oiling. As the skull was left in position the finished product was both life-sized and life-like. The head of the male chief is adorned with sweeping lines extending across the brow and from nose to chin, with spirals on cheeks and nose. Women of rank are tattooed on chin and lips. Skilled tattooers enjoyed social rank and their services were frequently in demand far from their own territory. Because of tattooers' itinerant habits there appears to be little local difference in tattooing style. Each pattern differs in detail from one individual to another, and in the case of portrait sculpture the identity is more a matter of tattoo than the modelling of features. The distinctive character of Maori tattoo is derived from its relationship with wood-carving, for it appears that the deeply grooved lines cut on the human face imitate carving technique. Buttocks and thighs were also tattooed by the milder method of merely puncturing the skin, then applying bluish or black pigment.

Origin of wood-carving

According to Maori tradition the origin of wood-carving (*whakairo rakau*) is assigned to Rua of divine origin who personifies many of the arts. Legend has it that Rua once paid a visit to Tangaroa, commander of the oceans and off-spring of the primeval parents Rangi (Sky) and Papa (Earth), to inspect a house Tangaroa had just completed. Rua was surprised to find that it was decorated only with painted designs, so he invited Tangaroa to visit his house to see a superior method of adornment. When Tangaroa arrived he was so deceived by the carved images on Rua's house that he walked up to them and pressed noses in the Maori manner of greeting. Rua was so delighted with this piece of deception that he shouted, "Now you see what wood-carving

Finial mask. East coast district. Painted wood with shell inlay. *Dominion Museum. Wellington. Height 15½ in.* *Cf. p. 199.*

FIG. 77 – *Crayon impression from the lid of a feather-box* (waka-huia). *Wood. Length 11½ in. Cf. p. 204.*

is. You thought that my wooden images were men." Myths dealing with the origin of carving differ from district to district, but the art is usually attributed to the gods. According to the East Coast Maori it was acquired by one Rua-i-te-pukenga in the realm of Rangi-tamaku, which is second in ascent of the twelve heavens of Maori cosmogony. The Matatua folk say that Rauru introduced the art to mankind, another that one Hura-waikato was the first wood-carver, and so on. One legend of special interest explains how images acquired their large staring eyes. Rongo who acquired his knowledge of carving from the carved house named Wharekura in the celestial realm used Koururu – the personified form of the owl – as a sacred offering which he buried beneath the rear wall. From that day many carvings were rendered with the staring eyes of the owl. Finial masks frequently exhibit this owl-like character.

PLATE P. 198

Symbols of wood-carving

Because of the limited fauna in New Zealand and the apparent lack of artistic interest in botanical forms or landscape, the Maori wood-carver used a very limited range of symbols. As the ancestor was of primary importance the art of image-making became highly developed, especially in relation to architectural adornment. One of the most outstanding skills of the Maori carver is his ability to adapt the human form to post or panel. Following the human form in order of importance is the polymorphic *manaia* creature which is abundant in Arawa, Bay of Plenty, and East Coast carving. The lizard, whale, and fabulous *marakihau* are also symbols of importance. Birds of both land and sea were abundant in former times, but their naturalistic treatment in carving art is rare. The Polynesian dog which was carried into New Zealand by the first settlers makes at least one appearance in archaic wood-carving, but is overlooked by craftsmen of the classic period. Dogs, canoes, pictorial compositions and other innovations made their appearance in carving under European influence.

Ancestral and god images

The art of image-making is wide-spread in Polynesia, particularly for the purpose of manufacturing material symbols of the gods. The Maori wood-carver is an active image-maker, but his art took a more secular turn as his subject is usually a non-deified ancestor, rarely a god. A number of 'godsticks' some ten to fifteen inches in length have been preserved in museum collections, but they are few in number and restricted to certain districts. The stick god form is very old for it occurs in the archaic style of New Zealand art, and has a close relationship with the stick gods of Hawaii.

FIG. 74

PLATE P. 203

A fine series of Maori godsticks was collected by the Rev. Richard Taylor in the Wanganui district of the North Island, about the middle of the 19th century. The head of one of these, the god Hukere, appears as an illustration. The peg form of these images is explained by their function, for the priest thrust the godstick into the earth before calling on a deity to enter this material vehicle. However the mere carved stick was not ritually effective until it was bound with braided cord, decorated with feathers, and smeared with red ochre.

Small human images of the ancestral type occur on numerous artifacts used by fishermen, fowlers, warriors, as well as on utensils of domestic life. Burial boxes in human form are found concealed in caves in the northern districts of the North Island, but we must look to the carved ceremonial house, food store, and war canoe for the most abundant and varied range of ancestral images. The ranks of honoured ancestors lining the interior of the ceremonial meeting-house serve as memorials to the great chiefs of the

Ceremonial house carvings

Manaia creatures grasping a central human image. Detail from the facade of a food store (*pataka*) named Te Oha. From Waerenga Village, Lake Rotorua. Wood, painted with ochre. *Auckland Museum. Size of detail 34 in. x 18 in. Cf. p. 202.*

past, keeping before the eyes of living members of a tribe their lineage and history. As it is believed that the power of the ancestor is still a force in tribal affairs it is appropriate that the great ones of the past should be represented in this manner. The out-thrust tongue, tattoo marks, and contorted posture of the war dance, stress the war-like character of the ancestor, thus providing an ever-present example to the young warrior. Eye inlay of shell (*Haliotis iris*) accentuates the fierce aspect of these images, especially in the night, when the people gather to hear the tales of the past and to discuss the affairs of the day. Exterior carvings of the ceremonial meeting-house are limited to the facade. Massive barge boards are carved or painted, and surmounted with a mask.

PLATE P. 198

Food store carvings

PLATE P. 205

Raised food stores are decorated with exterior carvings on four sides, and such carvings were so highly prized by members of the tribe that in times of threatened attack from powerful neighbours, they were quickly detached to be hidden by immersion in swamp mud or concealed in a cave. The symbols of food store carvings appear to be associated with ideas of abundance, preservation, or fertility. Thus the whale, an animal bringing plenty, appears on the barge boards of the facade. In some cases ancestral images in sexual embrace are seen on the upright panels on either side of the entrance porch. Sexual intercourse, and both male and female sexual organs, are frequently depicted in Maori wood-carving. This symbolism is difficult to interpret in general terms, but is associated with the usual ideas of generation, and in the case of the phallus, with belief in its protective and preservative power.

The manaia

FIG. 75

PLATE P. 201

Food store carvings also exhibit *manaia,* which usually appear in association with the human image. Attempts to interpret this symbol have caused more contention among experts than all the other problems of Maori art put together. The widely accepted view that the *manaia* is merely a rendering of the human image in profile is challenged here as being inconsistent with the observable facts, and not for taking into account the essentially mystical and non-rational atmosphere of Maori belief. It would seem reasonable to interpret the *manaia* as a hybrid creature possessing human and avian characteristics in varying proportions, and representing an inferior god, ghost, or supernatural spirit. Maori accounts of the *manaia* are vague yet significant – one has it that the creature is the personal *atua* (spirit) of the image it accompanies, another account from the Urewera is that it represents a great bird that attacked mankind in ancient times. As the *manaia* usually possess a beak with spur, claw hand, and (occasionally) feet webbed like those of a water bird, it is not difficult to associate the creature with the bird-man idea so wide-spread in Oceania. The malicious behaviour of the *manaia* in its relation to the human image suggests it may be a spirit of the *atua ngau tangata* or 'man-biting god' group. Bird-man images appear to have a marginal distribution in Polynesia, and the *manaia*-human image relationship in Maori carving finds its parallel in the bird and human image combinations seen in Melanesian carving.

Avian hypothesis

To return to the human image, the same process of hybridization of human and avian elements appears to occur, mainly by the imposition of bird-like characteristics on the basically human form. The legend of Rongo sacrificing Koururu (the personified form of the owl) is significant, and one type of mask design is referred to by carvers as 'an owl'. Naturalistic memorial portraiture occurs in Maori carving, but most figures are stylized: the eyes are slanting and staring, the hand claw-like, and in certain northern images the feet are webbed. This idea of avian elements in Maori carving is most likely to yield positive results in the study of stylization of human images, and in explaining the physical characteristics of the mysterious *manaia.*

The only reptiles found in New Zealand are the harmless skink, gecko, and

Image on a godstick representing the deity Hukere. Wanganui district. Wood painted with ochre. *University Museum of Archaeology and Ethnology, Cambridge. Height of image 15 in.* *Cf. p. 200.*

The lizard symbol

lizard-like *tuatara* (*Sphenodon*). In discussions concerning Maori carving these are all usually referred to rather loosely as "lizards". As an art symbol the lizard is not common but appears regularly on various house posts, panels, canoe thwarts, and other artifacts of nephrite, stone, and bone. The nature of this symbol is comparatively well understood, for in Maori belief the lizard is the visible manifestation of Whiro, who personifies the evil forces of the supernatural world. Thus when the gods wish to destroy a man they introduce a lizard into his body to eat away his vital organs. Huge lizard-like monsters termed *taniwha* are commonly associated with particular places, and are dangerous to travellers who venture near their lairs.

The marakihau

Fig. 76

The last symbol of Maori carving we need consider is a hybrid marine creature termed a *marakihau*. Half-man, half-fish, the *marakihau* possess a tube-like tongue which is said to be strong enough to suck down both men and canoes to a terrible fate. The appearance of *marakihau* on panels in ceremonial houses is explained by the belief that some ancestors are so transformed at death. The actual origin of the fabulous *marakihau* symbol is unknown, but the ideas concerning it, and indeed its material form, suggest some distant relationship with the *naga* serpent of India and Indonesia.

Surface decorations

Fig. 77

The abundant surface decoration occurring on most carved objects, especially on the small treasure boxes called *waka-huia*, gives an impression of being haphazard; but this is not so, for the practised eye will see that patterns are applied in an orderly manner. Most surface designs and their details are named. In human images spirals normally mark joints, or more broadly, points of movement, while other surface patterns are associated with food stores and other objects. Although curvilinear elements predominate, the rectilinear patterns characteristic of Polynesia are also found in certain styles of Maori surface decoration. Local style in carving is an important aspect of the subject, for there are about twelve or more distinctive regions, the most important being centered on North Auckland, Rotorua–Bay of Plenty, Taupo, Wanganui, and Taranaki. Wood carving from the South Island is very rare.

CONCLUDING REMARKS

Probability of diffusion

Archaeological evidence has affirmed the purely Polynesian character of both archaic and classic Maori cultures, and supports the thesis that marginal eastern Polynesian culture radiated outwards from the central area of the Society Islands. The so-called Melanesian elements present in the marginal islands appear to have survived to a marked degree in New Zealand, where the large land mass and abundant material resources offered the conditions likely to favour the retention of any Melanesian cultural characteristics present in the imported culture. Melanesian elements in western Polynesia (Samoa, Tonga) are readily explained, but the presence of motifs in New Zealand art which find their nearest parallel in northern Melanesia is an

Ancestral images depicted in sexual embrace. Detail from a food store named Te Puawai-o-te-Arawa (The Flower of the Arawa), from Maketu, Bay of Plenty. Wood, painted with ochre and black pigment. *Auckland Museum. Height of panel 40 in.* *Cf. p. 202.*

unsolved problem. The argument for local development of these motifs is unconvincing when one examines comparative evidence and keeps in mind the limits of coincidence. It appears certain that a better understanding of the symbols of Maori carving will come through viewing Oceanic culture as a related whole; accepting the importance of extensive local development, but not regarding it as the whole truth. The spectacular development of wood-carving in New Zealand is largely the result of abundant resources of wood (especially *totara*), and presence of various rocks suitable for the manufacture of stone tools. The migrants to New Zealand shores carried with them an ancient culture, and in many respects Maori art appears to have its ultimate sources in Indonesia and the Asian region. There is no evidence in Maori art to support the theory that Polynesia was settled from Peru and the north-west coast of America.

Maori art today

The arts of the ancient Maori began to decline with the arrival of European settlers early in the 19th century. Ceremonial houses are still being erected and dozens of carved houses stand today, but modern Maoris live and work in the Western manner, use telephones, own cars, and secure university degrees. Preserved heads and godsticks have been relegated to museums. As steel tools replaced the stone adze, so new ways of thinking have deposed the gods and ancestral spirits which inspired the craftsmen of former times.

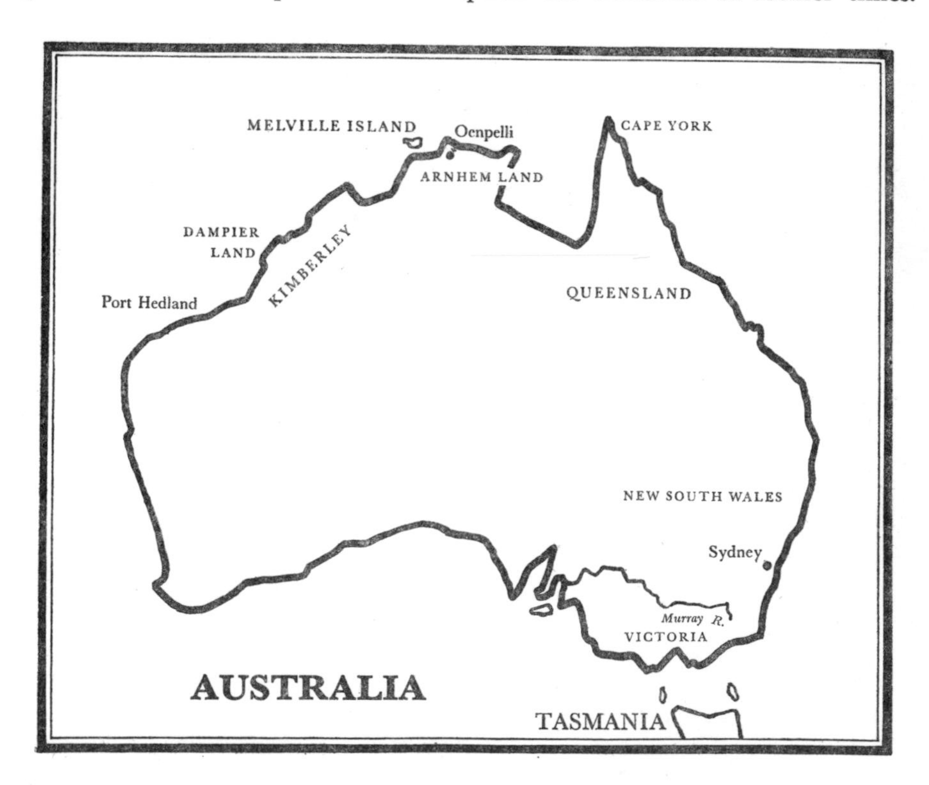

THE ABORIGINAL ART OF AUSTRALIA

BY

CHARLES P. MOUNTFORD

INTRODUCTION

The aesthetics of the Australian aborigines are of more than ordinary interest to students of the history and development of art, for in no other country is it possible to study the art of a living Stone Age people, to watch them at work, to observe the techniques they use, or to learn from the artists themselves the meaning of the motifs they employ.
This interest increases when it is realized that all Australian aboriginal people are of the same physical stock; that they all live as simple hunters and food-gatherers who use a particularly limited number of tools to gain their livelihood and who, because of their isolation in Australia for an unknown but lengthy period, have developed a way of life, a code of beliefs, and an art that are almost completely free from external influence.
The route by which the aborigines travelled, and the time they arrived in Australia have not, as yet, been established, but it is safe to postulate that they came from the Asiatic mainland and, moving along the Indonesian and Melanesian islands, entered Australia at Cape York in the extreme north-east, although other migrations may have reached the north-western shores of the continent. From these points the newcomers slowly spread outwards, until, when the Europeans arrived, the whole of the continent was populated, even its most inhospitable deserts. This migration into Australia must have taken place many thousands of years ago, there being little or no resemblance between the art of the Australian aborigines and that of the inhabitants of the adjoining Melanesian and Indonesian islands.
Australia is, in general, an arid land, for while the fertile edge of the continent has an adequate rainfall, the desert country, which occupies more than a third of the continent, receives less than ten, and much of it as little as five inches of rain in a year. In these areas the gaining of a livelihood is a strenuous and uncertain task.
The living conditions of these primitive artists could hardly be simpler, nor their material possessions more limited. Following the way of life common to all hunters and food-gatherers the aborigines are entirely nomadic, spending the days within their tribal country gathering at each time and place what Nature provides. If she is bountiful the people feast, but if she withholds from her store everyone starves philosophically until the tide of fortune turns.
The tools of these primitive hunters are remarkably simple and limited in number, those of the men being confined almost entirely to spears, spear-throwers, boomerangs and shields, and those of the women to bark and

FIG. 78 — *Aboriginal ground painting, associated with mythical emu. Kalaia, northern central Australia.*

wooden carrying dishes, grinding-stones, and digging-sticks. Except along the southern coasts, where everyone wore skin cloaks, the aborigines use no clothing whatever, both sexes going entirely naked.

Yet, in contrast to this poverty of material goods, the aborigines enjoy a rich philosophical and cultural life based on their conception of the creation of the world. They believe that before the time of creation, that is, before there was any life on the world, the earth was a level, featureless plain, extending to the horizon which, to them, was the edge of the universe. There was no light, no heat, nor did any living thing move on its desolate surface. Then, at some remote period which the aborigines poetically refer to as the "Dream Time", giant mythical beings, half-human, half-creature, rose miraculously out of the ground and, travelling from place to place, not only created the topography, the mountain ranges, the watercourses and the wide-spreading plains, but all the life that moves on its surface. At the completion of these earthly tasks these mythical people transformed themselves into the rocks and natural features which now make up the landscape.

These creation beliefs are perpetuated in a wide range of myths; myths that have not only provided the aborigines with a reasonable explanation of how the world was made, but have established their rules of good living, their behaviour one to another, and the pattern of their daily and ritualistic life. Indeed, so important are these beliefs to the aborigines, that they are reflected

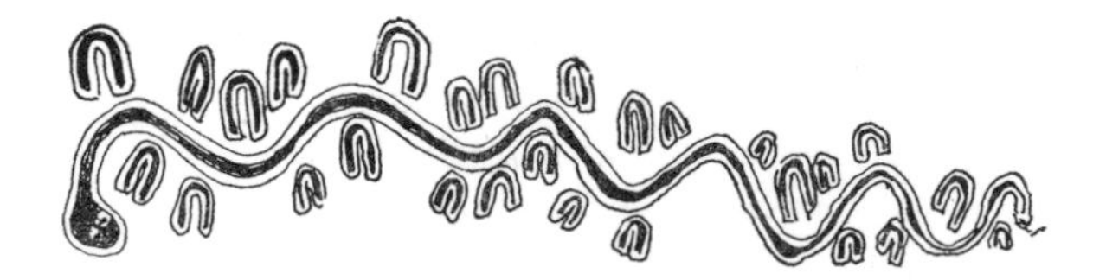

FIG. 79 — *The mythical snake Yarapi. The horseshoe-shaped designs are thought to be the camps of mythical wild dogs (malatji). Nama, central Australia.*

FIG. 80 — *Cave painting of a running spearman, carrying in one hand a bundle of spears and in the other a spear and spear-thrower. Inagurdurwil, western Arnhem Land, Northern Australia. Height 10 in.*

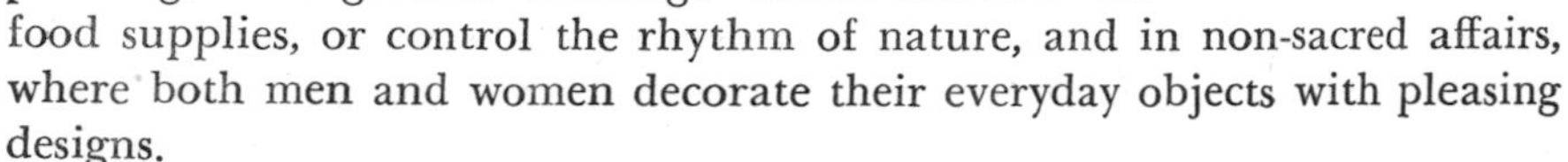

continuously in their graphic arts, their music, their drama and their dancing.

The graphic arts permeate all aspects of ceremonial and secular activities; in the decoration of the performers taking part in the rituals which commemorate the exploits of the great creators, and those which admit the youths into the secret life of the tribe; in the cave paintings and ground drawings which increase the food supplies, or control the rhythm of nature, and in non-sacred affairs, where both men and women decorate their everyday objects with pleasing designs.

Although the aborigines did not acquire the arts of the weaver or the potter, by means of which many civilizations have produced objects of beauty, they use a wide range of mediums in their desire for artistic expression: their own bodies, the surfaces of their weapons and implements, the trunks of trees, the walls of caves, the level rock faces, the ground, and the inside of their bark shelters.

The art of the aborigines can be grouped under two main headings: the immovable and the movable.

The immovable art includes paintings in the caves and shallow rock-shelters, on the ground, and inside of their bark huts; carvings or markings on the rocky outcrops, the trunks of trees and in the hard ground; and scratching or sculpturing in the sands of the watercourses and the sea-shore.

The movable art, which is much the more varied and decorative, enters into all aspects of secular and esoteric life. It is used in the decorating of shields, spear-throwers, boomerangs, throwing sticks, carrying bags, log coffins, burial poles and numerous small possessions. It also occupies a predominant place in the secret activities of the fully initiated men, not only in the painted decorations of the performers and objects of the ceremonial ground, but in the intricate engravings on the sacred stone and wooden objects. The highly decorative designs on these sacred objects vary widely, according to the locality to which they belong.

Techniques ana materials

Before dealing with the types of aboriginal art, the associated motifs and their meanings, it would be advantageous to examine the materials and tools employed in producing that art.

Painting

Painting is by far the most common technique. The colours employed are limited to black, white, yellow, red and, occasionally, greenish-blue pigments.

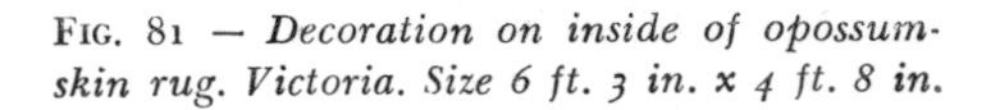

FIG. 81 — *Decoration on inside of opossum-skin rug. Victoria. Size 6 ft. 3 in. x 4 ft. 8 in.*

For black the aborigines prefer either a manganese oxide or one of the ferruginous ores. If these pigments are not available either crushed charcoal or, in the desert areas, the charred, cork-like bark of one of the hakea trees is used.

White, generally procured from pipe-clay or kaolin deposits, may be collected locally or acquired by trade. If this material is in short supply burnt gypsum or selenite takes its place.

Yellow ochre, possibly because of its rarity, is not used extensively. However, when available, it is either mined direct, as at Gurunga in eastern Arnhem Land, and Imilu, Melville Island, or obtained by barter from neighbouring tribes.

Red ochre is the most important and widely used pigment. It is secured by mining and trade or, as on Melville Island, by burning a yellow limonite pebble until it changes to a clear red. Because of mythological associations, some ochres are so important that groups of men will travel a hundred miles or more to collect these ochres from special localities. Those from Wilgamia, in Western Australia, Tempe Downs in central Australia and Blinman, in the northern Flinders Ranges of South Australia, are especially valuable.

A greenish-blue pigment, glauconite, appears to be available only in north and north-western Australia.

The aborigines, using a rough flat stone as a palette, grind pebbles or blocks of one or another of the ochres until the mixture is of a creamy-like consistency. If the ochres are friable they are crushed between stones to a fine powder, then mixed with water or one of the fixatives.

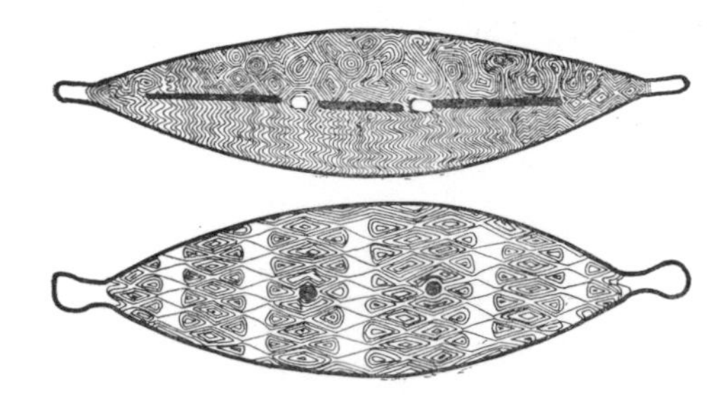

FIG. 82 — *Engraved bark shields.* Top: *south-eastern Australia. Length 36 in.* Bottom: *South Australia. Length 35 in.*

Carved wooden head of mythical figure. Banaitja, north-eastern Arnhem Land, Northern Australia. *National Gallery of South Australia, Adelaide. Length of face 6½ in.* *Cf. p. 223.*

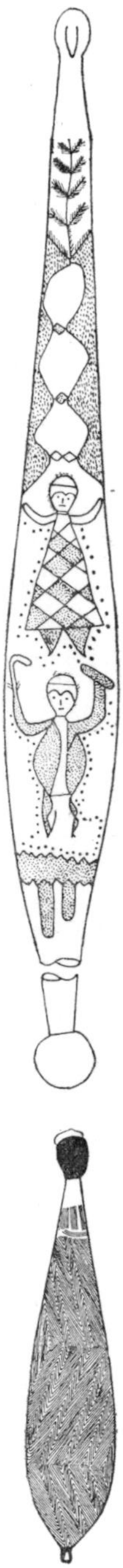

FIG. 83 — *Engraved spear-throwers.* Top: *south-eastern Australia. Length 30 in.* Bottom: *north-western Australia. Length 30 in.*

In general, fixatives are not used for work of a temporary nature such as body or ground paintings, but for the more permanent decorations on burial poles, log coffins, bark paintings or designs on ceremonial objects. Fixatives may be the whites of eggs, usually those of the sea-going turtle, the gelatinous sap of one of the tree orchids, or the wax and honey of the wild bee well mixed together. The fixatives may be combined with the pigments on the stone palette, or rubbed directly on the painting surface.

When the paintings are large the aborigines use their forefinger, or even the palm of their hand; otherwise there is the choice of several kinds of simple brushes. One is the twig of a tree with a slightly burred end, its diameter depending on the size of the dot required. To load this brush with colour it is tapped lightly on the palette. A narrow strip of eucalyptus bark chewed at one end is used for the broader lines. A third brush, made from a few fibres of palm leaf or a small feather, requires considerable skill. This brush, held delicately between the fingers, and drawn away from the body, is used for the fine cross-hatching of some of the Arnhem Land bark paintings.

There are three main types of rock markings in Australia. The wide-spread simple pocked markings, the large outline rock engravings, confined to the Hawkesbury River basin of New South Wales, and rock pounding, a living art in central Australia.

The simple pocked markings are undoubtedly an extinct art, the aborigines claiming them to be the work of some mythical hero of creation times. Consequently, there is no first-hand information about the tools used or the method employed, but as it is possible to make identical markings with a sharp-edged boulder held in the hand, it is likely that those who made these pocked markings used a similar tool.

The large outline engravings in the soft sandstones of the Hawkesbury River basin were probably cut with a tool similar to that used in the pocked markings. Again, this operation has not been seen by any white man.

Rock pounding is a living art in central Australia, where the aboriginal produces his pictures by pounding the rock face until the dark brown patina is destroyed.

Engraving is the most common technique in the decoration of spear-throwers, shields, and the smaller objects of every-day life, as well as the wooden and stone objects of the sacred rituals.

The only engraving tool I have seen in use was the incisor tooth of an opossum or some other small marsupial, still in the skull. This tool, held

FIG. 84 — *Engraved wooden sacred object. Port Keats, Northern Australia. Length 35 in.*

between the fingers, was used in somewhat the same manner as that employed by modern engravers in metals. Other engraving tools may have been constructed by mounting a small stone flake on the end of a stick, but I have neither seen them in the field, nor in any museum collection. Much larger tools, probably ground stone axes or large mounted stone flakes, would have been necessary to carve the designs in the large initiation and burial trees of eastern Australia.

Sculpture

The aborigine sculptures representations of both men and the creatures in wood and stone. There is no first-hand knowledge about the tools employed in the earlier wooden examples, but it is reasonable to suppose that these sculptures were carved by mounted stone tools or sea-shells, held in the hand. All modern examples of wooden sculptures, however, have been cut with steel tools. The stone objects were probably shaped by the hammer-dressing technique.

Skin rugs

The aborigines who lived along the southern coasts of Australia, using a sharp flake of stone or a shell, engraved complicated and intricate designs on the insides of their skin rugs, then darkened those designs by rubbing a mixture of fat and pigment into them. These markings not only made the rugs more flexible but they satisfied the owner's aesthetic desire for ornamentation.

Cave Paintings

Cave paintings are found almost exclusively on the walls and ceilings of shallow caves and rock shelters, for the aborigines of Australia, unlike Palaeolithic man of Europe, do not paint designs far removed from the light of day. Most of the cave paintings are non-sacred, and refer, in primitive symbolism, to current events, or to myths well-known to both men and women. There are, however, many cave paintings forbidden to all but the fully initiated men which belong only to the esoteric ceremonies.

The renovation of these paintings at the correct season, coupled with the relevant ceremonies, not only keep alive the memory of some secret myth but, in some localities, according to the aborigines, also control the rhythm of nature.

Throughout Australia cave paintings are somewhat unevenly distributed, depending on the existence of rock surfaces sufficiently smooth and protected from the weather, and an adequate water supply to make camping at these places possible.

Motifs employed along the south-western and parts of the eastern fringes of the continent are particularly simple, hand stencils predominating. The method of producing these hand stencils is simple. The aboriginal, taking

Bark painting of aboriginal spearing wallaby. Oenpelli, Northern Australia. *Charles P. Mountford Collection. Size 29 in. x 12 in.* *Cf. p. 221.*

a mouthful of water and some pigment, usually white, chews them until they are thoroughly mixed. Then placing the hand, foot, or some object against the cave wall, he sprays the mixture over it. When the object is removed a negative stencil remains.

In the central desert regions the rock stencils become less common, their place being taken by highly formalized designs, consisting almost entirely of circles, spirals, and groups of straight and meandering lines. In this art representations of men and women are rare, but not entirely absent. Although many of the central Australian cave paintings have little or no ceremonial meaning, I have recently visited two groups in remote localities, which are so sacred that no man under middle age is allowed even to go near the place, much less to see the paintings.

One of these cave paintings, a panel over a hundred feet long, deals with the journey of a mythical snake, Yarapi, and his companions. The designs are almost exclusively abstract symbols that could not be understood until explained by one of the old aborigines. Motifs in the other group of cave paintings – different, though equally abstract – deal with the meeting of two groups of mythical emus. Associated with both of these cave paintings are rituals, coupled with ground paintings or decorated objects which, if properly carried out, will increase the numbers of snakes or of emus.

North-western Australia is a particularly interesting art area. Both at the

FIG. 85 — *Engraved smoking-pipe. It is wrapped in bark so that women cannot see the sacred designs. North-eastern Arnhem Land, Northern Australia. Length 30 in.*

Forrest River in the east, and the Dampier Peninsula in the west, are simple paintings of men and the creatures that bear a close resemblance to each other. This resemblance is all the more surprising when it is realized that these two areas are separated, not only by a distance of over four hundred miles, but by two remarkable but totally different art forms, the large Wandjina paintings and the small Giro-giro figures.

The cave paintings of the Wandjinas — tall mouthless figures, with a halo-like design around their faces — are the largest examples of cave art in Australia. They have been found only in the Kimberley region, an area of rugged country between the King River and the Drysdale Ranges of north-western Australia.

The Wandjina paintings are remarkable both for their size, one being eighteen feet high, and the fact that the face is always in white and surrounded by one, sometimes two, horseshoe-shaped bows which, in some examples, have lines radiating from them. The aborigines believe that the paintings are filled with the essence of both water and blood; the water, so necessary for all living things, is symbolized by the white face and the blood, which makes men and the animals strong by the red ochre bows. The nose and eyes, surrounded by long lashes, are usually in one unit, but the figures are mouthless, a characteristic on which some investigators have placed considerable stress. Nevertheless, mouthless figures are common in the cave paintings of both northern and central Australia.

The creation stories tell how, during the early days of the world, mythical human beings called Wandjinas created the homeland of the aborigines. At the completion of their earthly tasks each Wandjina, after leaving his painting on the wall of some cave, entered a nearby water-hole which today is his home. But before doing so the Wandjina decreed that, just before the onset of the wet season, the ceremonial leader of the tribe must renovate

FIG. 86 — *Engraved smoking-pipe. Milingimbi, Northern Australia. Length 28 in.*

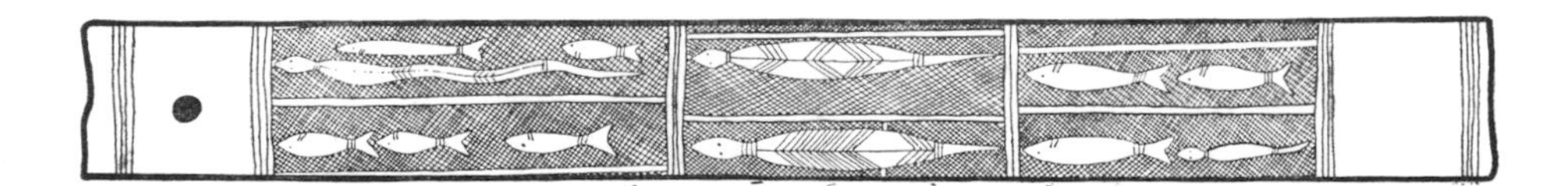

FIG. 87 — *Engravings on smoking-pipes. Milingimbi, Northern Australia.* Left: *length 27 in.* Right: *length 25 in.*

his painting. This act, which causes the thunder-storms and the monsoon rains to start, ensures the increase and thriving of the animals and plants. Disregard of this law of renovation brings drought and hunger in its train. When the painting on the wall becomes dim the Wandjina vanishes, and with him rain and fertility.

Immediately east of the Wandjina paintings are the small vital Dimi or Giro-giro figures. These figures, according to the aborigines, are the work of a small spirit-people called the Dimis or Giro-giros, who live in the surrounding forests. The paintings, small and always in red, depict human beings in strong action; in the Wandjina art the figures are large and at rest.

The most complex art area in the continent is Northern Australia, having within its boundaries five different art forms; the large Wandjina-like figures, similar to those in the Kimberley regions of north-western Australia, the curious polychrome X-ray art, the monochromatic Mimi art, the long-bodied figures, and the art of secular life. The only cave painting of the Wandjina-like figures yet investigated in Northern Australia is that of the Lightning Brothers at Delamere Station, several hundred miles south-east of the true Wandjina paintings in the Kimberley region.

The aborigines believe that, like the Wandjinas, the Lightning Brothers were painted by mythical beings during the creation period. They are associated with lightning and rain and their renovation at the beginning of the monsoon season causes the Rain-man and Lightning Brothers, who live in the west, to travel to the site of the paintings, bringing with them the monsoon rain and thunder-storms.

The polychrome X-ray cave paintings of eastern Arnhem Land are without parallel in the world. In this curious art the aboriginal not only portrays what he sees, but also the internal details which he cannot see but knows to be there; the skeleton, the heart, the lungs and other organs. Some of these X-ray paintings — up to eight feet long, and made up of thousands of fine multi-coloured lines — are among the most beautiful examples of

FIG. 88 — *Engraved wooden sacred object. Northern Australia. Length 9 in.*

cave art in Australia. In the movable art the X-ray motif has a much wider distribution than it has in the art of the caves.

In the same caves as the X-ray paintings are many small, monochromatic drawings of human beings in action. The aborigines claim that these drawings are self-portraits of a thin-bodied, fairy-like people called the Mimis (compare with the Dimis of Western Australia), whose homes are under the great rocks of the Arnhem Land plateau.

The Mimis have remarkably keen sight and hearing. If, when hunting, they detect the approach of the aborigines, these little fairy-like people will run quickly to a cleft in the rocks of the plateau and blow upon it. The cleft will open, admit the Mimis, then close behind them to keep out all intruders. This is the reason, the aborigines explain, why no one has ever seen a Mimi. This myth has obviously grown up to explain the art of an earlier unknown people.

The small, vital art of the Mimis differs widely from the colourful, but static, X-ray motifs of the aborigines. The Mimis depict only man in action — fighting, running, or throwing spears — the X-ray artists picture the creatures at rest, the human figure being almost entirely absent. This Mimi art bears more than a passing resemblance to some of the cave paintings of southern Spain, the Sahara, and those of the Bushmen of South Africa.

Within, and extending beyond the boundaries of the X-ray art, is another curious form which I have called the art of the long-bodied people — tall attenuated figures, sometimes only a few inches in width, but in one example, twelve feet in length. In general, these figures depict the subjects at rest, few of them having the vitality of the Mimi drawings.

Apart from these four unusual art forms there are cave paintings which might be classed as secular, a simple art that shows men and women, creatures, and episodes of daily life.

The cave paintings over the rest of Australia, allowing for small regional differences, are similar to the secular art of the north. They picture every-day activities, often in primitive symbolism. On the sea coasts the artists are concerned with their canoes, the fishing exploits, and the creatures of the sea while away from the coasts, hunting scenes, camps and the representation of some ceremony form the bulk of the designs.

Rock markings

There are three distinct forms of rock markings in Australia: the simple pocked markings, the large outline rock engravings, and the rock poundings.

Pocked markings

Simple markings in the first technique are sparsely distributed over most of Queensland, the Northern Territory, north-western New South Wales,

FIG. 89 — *Engraved wooden ceremonial object. Western Australia. Length 6 in.*

Tasmania, and South Australia; in the latter area they appear to be more numerous than elsewhere. With the exception of animal tracks, however, few of the South Australian designs have any apparent meaning.

At Port Hedland and Depuch Island on the western coast of Australia, large numbers of complex and naturalistic pocked markings have been cut into the soft rocks of the sea coast. The present-day aborigines, who do not know the significance of the majority of these markings, assert that they were made by the mythical people of creation times.

There is in South Australia an isolated pocked marking that bears an unmistakable resemblance to the head of a sea-going crocodile. Although fossil remains of this creature have been found in the Lake Eyre basin, less than two hundred miles to the north, the nearest habitat of the living crocodile is over a thousand miles away. It is hardly likely that the artist would have cut a design having so many points of resemblance to the living crocodile, had he not known the creature intimately. This unusual marking suggests that man and the crocodile were contemporary in Australia during late geological times.

Outline rock engravings

On the horizontally bedded sandstones of the Hawkesbury basin of eastern Australia there are innumerable outline rock engravings of men, fish and the creatures, some of the engravings being up to sixty feet in length. As no white man has seen these engravings being made, the manner of their production can only be speculated upon, but the fine proportions of some of the larger figures suggest that a preliminary design was first drawn on the rock to guide the artist, who with a sharp-edged boulder outlined the design with a series of punctures.

These outline engravings are highly stylized representations of human beings, animals, birds, reptiles and fish. There are also circles, weapons, ornaments, utensils and baskets. Unfortunately, the aborigines who produced these remarkable rock pictures, and those who knew their meanings, died many years before the white man became sufficiently interested to inquire about their art.

Although, at the present time, the aborigines do not use the pocking technique, I have seen the aborigines of central Australia use a simple, but related method to make their rock pictures. In these arid parts the exposed

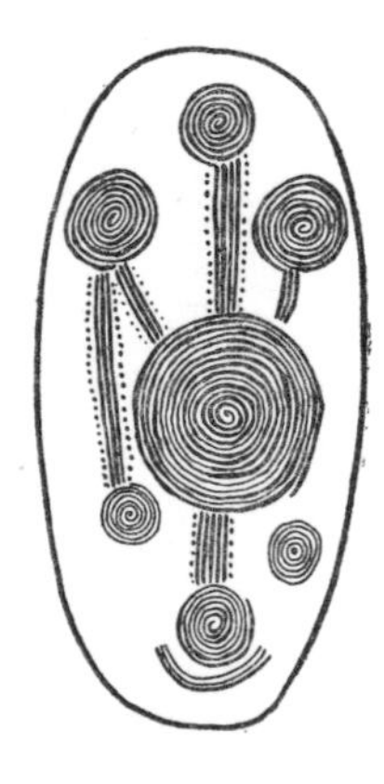

FIG. 90 — *Engraved stone ceremonial object, honey-ant totem. Central Australia. Length 10 in.*

rock surfaces are coated with a dark brown patina which, when struck with a hard object, leaves a white-coloured mark. The aborigines, taking advantage of this characteristic, make their rock pictures by pounding the rock surface with a small pebble. These rock pictures, in the symbolism of the art of central Australia, depict everyday incidents and non-secret myths.

On the west coast of Australia, however, the rock pounding designs, like those of the pocked markings, become increasingly complex. A group of boulders on the upper Yule River is covered with a maze of rock poundings depicting men and women in action, snakes, kangaroos and other creatures. Though we have no direct evidence that these markings were made in recent times, the freshness of many of the designs suggests that this might be so.

Other distinct types of rock markings have been found in Australia: the rock scratchings on the River Murray, probably cut into the soft cliffs with a piece of hardwood; the straight-line marks, a series of parallel incisions in the flat surfaces; and the cup and ring markings in South and central Australia, a motif found in widely separated localities throughout the world.

Bark painting of fr[illegible]hwat[illegible] Gr[illegible] Ey[illegible] Gu[illegible] [illegible]thern [illegible] P.
Mountford Collectio[illegible] [illegible] Cf. [illegible]

Ground paintings

In northern central Australia the aborigines paint elaborate, highly formalized designs on the surface of the ground during the performance of some of their totemic rituals. Recently I witnessed a ceremony for the increase of emus, which included a number of ground paintings referring both to incidents in the myth as well as to the internal organs of the emu of creation times. In some of the ceremonies of the Warramunga tribe of central Australia elaborate ground paintings are a prominent feature.

About 1900, Spencer and Gillen were present at the rituals of a mythical snake, Wollunqua, in which eight different ground paintings were made on eight consecutive days. The method of painting the designs on the ground was similar to that of the emu ceremony I saw, except that the motifs of the snake paintings were much larger and more elaborate, some of them being eighteen feet long.

Ground carvings

During the long and complicated rituals of the Bora initiation ceremony of eastern Australia, the participants carved designs in the hard ground in the form of grooves, several inches wide and deep. These carvings, in large numbers, extended throughout the ceremonial ground for a distance of a hundred yards or more. Many of these consisted of concentric squares, diamonds, meandering lines, and other abstract patterns; others were naturalistic, depicting kangaroos, emus, snakes and men. In the same ceremonies the participants moulded earthen figures representing one or another of the creators. These were of considerable size, one recorded example being over twenty feet long.

Unfortunately the aborigines of the eastern coast were destroyed by our civilization before investigators became sufficiently interested to inquire about the meanings of these remarkable ground carvings.

Initiation and burial trees

While some of the participants of the Bora ceremony were making the ground carvings others were cutting similar designs in the trunks of nearby eucalyptus trees. Attractive abstract patterns in diamonds, spirals, concentric circles and rhomboids formed the bulk of the tree carvings; the human figure was seldom used. There are still eighty carved trees in the initiation ground at Bannaway on the Barwon River, New South Wales. The amount of labour involved in making the ground carvings, the earthen figures, and the carved trees for a Bora initiation must have been greater by far than that involved in any other Australian aboriginal ceremony.

Trees were carved with similar designs at the graves of important tribesmen. Though again the meanings of these designs were not ascertained, evidence suggests that they were related to the totem of the dead man.

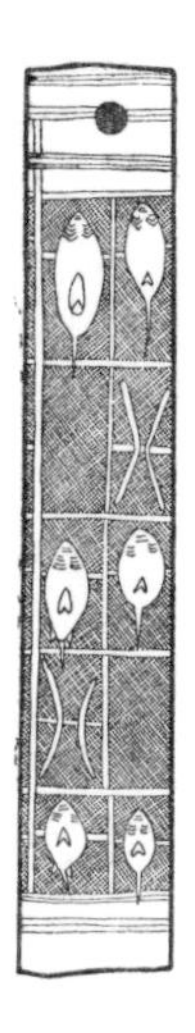

FIG. 91 — *Engravings on smoking-pipe. Milingimbi, Northern Australia. Length 26 in.*

FIG. 92 – *Engraved stone ceremonial object woman's totem. Central Australia. Length 6 in.*

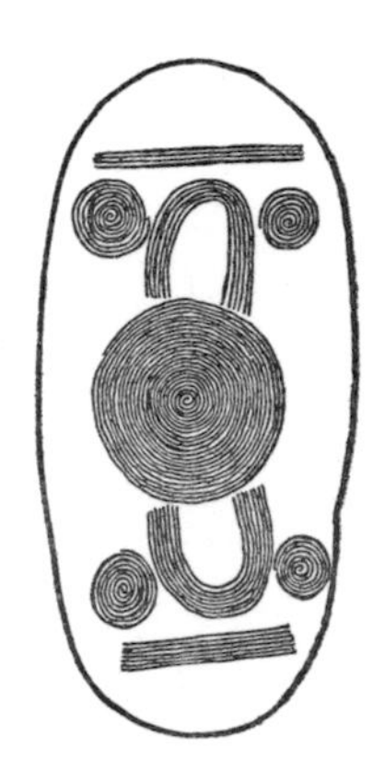

The aborigines of Melville Island, Northern Australia, carve and decorate elaborate burial poles. A grave in Melville Island, encircled by as many as twenty decorated poles from eight to twenty-five feet in height, is one of the most colourful sights in the aboriginal culture.

The painted log coffins of northern Arnhem Land are also effective works of art. Up to eighteen feet in length, they are covered in abstract and naturalistic motifs belonging to the totem of the dead man.

Bark paintings

Wherever the aborigines use sheets of bark to construct their wet-weather shelters, it appears certain that they paint or scratch designs on the inside surface during the enforced idleness of the wet season. Although few of the decorated sheets of bark from southern Australia have survived – and none from Tasmania – a large number have been collected in recent years from northern and north-eastern Australia. These bark paintings are particularly attractive both in colour and design, the motifs varying with the locality in which they are made; for example, the aborigines of Groote Eylandt, in the Gulf of Carpentaria, paint simple but naturalistic representations of men, animals, and sea creatures. In north-eastern Arnhem Land the subjects are highly decorative and stylized pictures of mythical human beings and creatures, while in western Arnhem Land, the home of the X-ray art, the tribesmen depict both mythical men and women of creation times, and the spirit people who, the aborigines believe, still live in the hollow trees, rocks and water-holes of the rugged Arnhem Land plateau.

Melville Island is separated from the X-ray art of western Arnhem Land by only fourteen miles of turbulent water, a natural barrier which has been responsible for a complete change in the art forms. Whereas the art of the mainland is totally naturalistic, that of Melville Island is so highly formalized that its subjects cannot be deciphered without the aid of the artists who produce them.

PLATE P. 3

As might be expected some of the bark paintings of north-western Australia picture the rain-making Wandjinas, others the plants and animals of the country-side.

Most of the bark paintings in Australia are secular, having been made within sight of the women and children. There are others, however, which are painted during the initiation rituals to instruct the youths in the secret myths, but they are destroyed at the conclusion of the rituals.

Movable art

The art of the movable objects, which is more complex, and covers a much wider field than that of the immovable art, enters all aspects of the aborigines' ceremonial and secular life: the secret rituals, forbidden to all but the fully initiated; the complex rites of death and burial; and the decoration of the tools, weapons, and personal objects of both men and women.

Tools and weapons

Few of the tools and weapons are large enough for extensive decoration, only the soft-wood and bark shields, and the spear-throwers offering much scope for the artist to express himself. Some of the shields from Queensland and central Australia, painted as they are with interesting designs in the soft harmonious colours of red, yellow, black and white ochres, are particularly attractive. The smooth surfaces of the bark shields of southern Australia too, have provided the aboriginal craftsmen with a medium for many complex and beautiful patterns. When the engravings on the bark shields were finished they were filled with white paint, which made the designs stand out in strong contrast to the body of the shield. In north-western Australia, concentric squares and interlocking key-patterns decorated both the shields and the sacred objects.

Throughout Australia many of the boomerangs and spear-throwers are engraved with pleasing patterns.

Sacred objects

Over most of southern, central, western, and northern Australia the aborigines use oval slabs, of wood or soft stone, in their sacred rituals. On these slabs are engraved motifs which describe, in primitive symbolism, incidents in their creation myths. In central Australia these motifs consist of little more than circles, spirals, loops and straight lines. Towards the north-west their designs change, first to concentric squares and diamonds, then to

Shield. Northern Queensland. *South Australian Museum, Adelaide. Length 40 in.* *Cf. p. 222.*

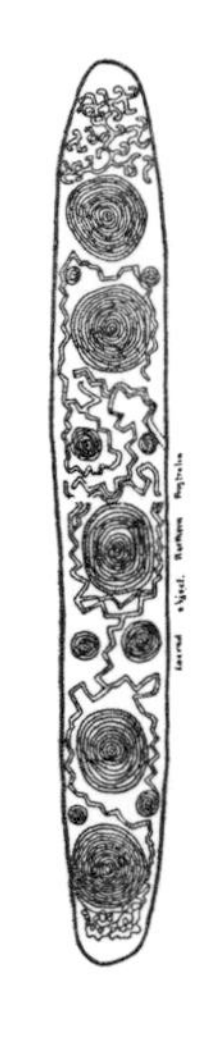

FIG. 93 — *Engraved wooden sacred object. Port Keats, Northern Australia. Length 27 in.*

interlocking key-patterns of various combinations. On the other hand, the sacred objects along the northern coasts are covered with an arrangement of intertwined circular designs, interspersed with primitive human figures. On the Dampier Peninsula, in the extreme north-west of the continent, the aborigines engrave large pearl-shells with both the interlocking key-pattern and naturalistic representations of plants and animals. These shells, worn as pubic ornaments by the young men during their initiation, later become articles of barter which find their way to the south coast of Australia, over two thousand miles from their source.

Until comparatively recently it was thought that the aborigines did not carve the human figure in the round. Research within the last decade, however, has shown that this art is practised in both northern, western and southern Australia. These human figures are made in several mediums: stone, wood, clay, and the soft wax of the stingless bee.

In north-eastern Arnhem Land the aborigines carve full-length figures in wood and wax, which represent one or another of the mythical creators of the world, while on the western side of Arnhem Land the aborigines are most skilful in modelling small heads in clay.

Examples of sculpturing from Western Australia include small carved figures and heads in wood, some most skilfully executed, and one in stone, produced by the hammer-dressing technique. In the same area are a number of representations of the male sex organ in wood, wax and stone. These stone phallic objects are an ethnological problem in a country where the working of stone has never reached a high level of efficiency.

Although these stone phallic objects may be of considerable age, evidence suggests that most, if not all of the present wooden sculptures of men and the creatures have been carved with steel tools. Nevertheless the fact remains that the art of sculpturing in the round, whether with stone or steel tools, is an indigenous activity which the aborigines have developed without the stimulus and, in most cases, without even the knowledge of the white man.

There is no special artist class in an aboriginal community. Every member, young or old, will sometimes be an artist. The children illustrate their simple stories by drawing in the sand, or decorate their own bodies or those of their companions, in childish ceremonies. The women depict, by sand

FIG. 94 — *Engraved sacred wooden object. North-western Australia. Length 13 in.*

Carved human head, used during initiation rituals. North-western Australia. *Prof. Helmut Petri Collection, Cologne. Length of face 6 in.* *Cf. p. 223.*

drawing, the incidents of food-gathering and camp activities, while the men use their art for a wide range of purposes in both ceremonial and secular life. Nor does the artist achieve higher social status for his work. It may be his duty at one time to decorate the performers for a ceremony, or a burial pole for a distant relative. On another occasion he may be the person who is decorated or, because of his relationship to the dead, he may not even be allowed to see the pole before the final burial rituals.

All aborigines are natural artists. I have yet to meet one who could not, or did not, paint. Of course, some are more skilled than others, and take more care. Yet anyone watching these people at work, totally absorbed in their task and oblivious to the world about them, will be convinced that these artists are experiencing the same pleasure as do artists in any community. In the ceremonial life every adult man will at some time be called to occupy the position of the tribal artist. He may carve simple wooden figures, engrave designs on wood or stone, depict mythical stories on sheets of bark, on cave walls, or on the ground. Or, he may instruct the initiates in the myths and folkways of the tribe, by means of sand drawings or cave paintings.

The art of the ceremonial ground is almost completely fossilized, and the designs which each individual can use strictly governed by the laws of the secret rituals and the dictates of the old men. But even though the art forms, the songs, and the rituals are rigidly controlled by age-old customs, they are the most vital part in the aborigines' lives, for it is by the employment of these mediums that the philosophies, the creation myths, and the laws of behaviour are perpetuated.

There is a difference however, between the ceremonial art restricted by tribal law and the secular art, where the tribesman is free to choose any subject or design that pleases his fancy. The secular artist not only tends to keep his subjects up to date, but to borrow new ideas and cultural traits from invading or adjacent people. For example, in the caves of western central Australia, side by side with paintings in the simple abstract art of the desert, are pictures of white men riding camels, or shooting emus, kangaroos or bullocks.

Australia offers a unique opportunity for the study of the art and the position of the artists in one of the world's most primitive living societies. The motifs of the aborigines are few and simple, their mediums and colours limited, and their tools most primitive. Yet each decorated object in their culture possesses that sense of balance and design that characterizes all good art primitive, ancient, or modern.

APPENDICES

GLOSSARY

ancestor worship (manism)
Belief in the supernatural power of one's ancestors, which the believer frequently seeks to maintain and realize by preserving the bodies (in mummified form), skulls, bones, hair, etc., of deceased persons, or using them for certain purposes (such as daggers, parts of spears, amulets of hair or teeth, etc.). Ancestor figures serve the same function.

animatism
Belief that all natural phenomena, and everything in man's environment, are alive or possess souls.

animism
Belief in souls, which are thought to determine the existence and spiritual qualities of men and animals, to detach themselves from the body temporarily in dreams and illness, and at death permanently, whereupon they become spirits.

antagonism between the sexes
An antithesis which finds expression in myths and ceremonies of a religious or social kind, as well as in a dualistic social organization (cf. *dualism*).

anthropomorphic
Fashioned after a human prototype.

archaic culture, art
Culture and art of the early settlers in New Zealand (*moa* hunters).

Austromelanids
People who developed from an intermingling of pre-Austronesians (especially the round adze people) and southern Austronesians, and whose culture consequently has a hybrid character.

Austronesians
Light-skinned people who speak one of the Austronesian or Malayo-Polynesian languages, which are closely related to each other. In Oceania they are disseminated above all in Polynesia, Micronesia and the eastern part of Melanesia.
The southern Austronesian branch is mainly to be found on the northern coast of New Guinea, and as a constituent part of the Austromelanid peoples and cultures. The northern Austronesians were responsible for the earliest cultures in Polynesia, but are also to be found in Micronesia.

Baining
Tribe in New Britain (on the Gazelle peninsula).

bark-cloth
A paper-like material of felted fibres, often termed *tapa*. It is obtained by scraping the inner bark of certain kinds of tree, esp. the paper mulberry, which is then beaten out and soaked. Frequently, above all in Polynesia, it bears gay designs. It is used for various purposes: clothing, ornaments, masks, plastic representations, etc.

basic type of culture
Cf. culture.

basketry masks
Masks made of strips of rattan and bamboo, or fine withes, by a method also used for making baskets, etc.

beak style
Style of carved figure characterized above all by the elongated beak-like nose. Found on the lower Sepik and the coastlands on either side of the Sepik estuary, probably also on the lower Ramu (northern New Guinea) as well as in kindred form in the New Hebrides and New Caledonia.

betel
A slightly intoxicating stimulant chewed by people in Melanesia and parts of Micronesia. It is made from seeds of the areca palm, leaves and fruit of the betel-pepper, and burnt lime in pulverized form.

Bronze Age
Cultural epoch following the Stone Age and preceding the Iron Age, characterized by the use of bronze (an alloy of copper and tin) for weapons, implements and ornaments. In Oceania it is properly speaking found only in western New Guinea (Vogelkop peninsula, Lake Sentani), but it may have had a far-reaching indirect effect upon ornamental designs.

bull-roarer
Thin board, often decorated, which, when

held by a cord and whirled around, produces a roaring sound.

cannibalism
The practice of eating one's kind. In Oceania it is connected with the belief that by consuming part of a human being one thereby can absorb some of his vital force. Alternatively it may be a ceremonial re-enactment of the killing and devouring of a mythological primeval monster, believed to have been an important event in the creation of the world.

cassowary
An ostrich-like bird, standing about 5 ft. high, with wings useless for flight. It is native to Australia and eastern Indonesia (particularly New Guinea).

Caucasoid
Group of races with common hereditary physical characteristics, especially relatively light skin and wavy or curly hair. In Oceania Caucasoids are found in Polynesia and (to a lesser extent) Micronesia, as well as along the north coast of New Guinea and in the Bismarck Archipelago.

ceremonial stool
Important cult object of the middle Sepik area, in the shape of a stool and decorated with a large number of carved figures. It plays a significant in councils and rites.

clan
A group of families who trace their descent back to a common mythological ancestor — often a totem, but in Polynesia frequently a god. Membership of the clan is determined by descent through the father (patrilineal organization) or through the mother (matrilineal organization). Marriage within the clan is forbidden (exogamy). The term sib (actually a group of kindred families with the same common ancestors) is frequently used instead of clan. Especially in Melanesia, clans perform the chief economic, social, political and religious functions.

classes
Groups in stratified societies (e.g., slaves, free men, nobles, etc.), typical of Austronesian, and more particularly Polynesian and Micronesian, cultures.

classic epoch of art
Term generally used in New Zealand for the art of the second group of immigrants, who had a style of their own. This classic art was flourishing when the first Europeans arrived in New Zealand.

concept of the world
Totality of knowledge about the world and the order or regularity existing in it. The outlook of the Oceanic peoples is preponderantly pre-scientific and is based in the main on religious beliefs.

conical mask
Ancient type of mask, worn over the head.

cosmogony
Theory of the generation of the universe.

creative force
The force responsible for the origin of the world and mankind. Personified in myths of creation and thought to be possessed by all living creatures, especially by human beings.

culture heroes
(Also 'donors of culture', 'donors of salvation'): Mythological figures who according to tradition introduced new cultural achievements, or who have been of assistance to the community in some other way.

cultures
In the history of settlement in Oceania a distinction is made between cultures of a basic type (introduced by the earliest immigrants), hybrid cultures (which developed from the fusing of various cultures of a basic type), and the present-day local cultures (in which one or more cultures of a basic type are fused and modified by the influence of local historical factors).

curvilinear style
Style found in two-dimensional art, and particularly in ornamentation, which is characterized by swirling curved design elements (spirals, arcs, circles, wavy lines). It is especially widely disseminated in New Guinea and other parts of Melanesia, but is also found in eastern Polynesia. From a historical point of view it is apparently related to the round adze and Papuan cultures.

decorative art
A form of art which predominantly serves ornamental purposes, without any value or significance in itself, on two- and three-

dimensional objects. Frequently a special decorative style is found in such ornamentation which follows formal principles distinct from those applied in plastic art and painting.

Dimi figures
Small figures, painted red, which according to the beliefs of the aborigines of the wooded areas of north-western Australia represent spirits who live in this area.

division of labour
Performance by certain elements of the community of particular functions. In Oceania there is usually a strict division of labour between the sexes in the arts and crafts, as well as in the economic, social and ritual sphere. Specialization also occurs within each sex, but specialized professions developed only in Polynesia, Micronesia, and the Austronesian areas of Melanesia.

Dongson period
Bronze Age cultural epoch, named after a site in northern Annam (Indochina). Outside Indochina it has been authenticated in western New Guinea (Vogelkop peninsula, Lake Sentani). The curvilinear styles found in Melanesia and New Zealand may be derived from forms of this period.

'donors of salvation', 'donors of culture'
Cf. culture heroes.

drums
In Oceania two types of drum are known:
(i) Skin or hour-glass drums. These are made of wood and are cylindrical. They are frequently narrower in the middle than at the ends and have a handle in the middle and a skin (usually a lizard skin) stretched across one end. They serve as musical instruments and are beaten with the hand.
(ii) Slit-drums. These are made of wood or bamboo, and are more or less cylindrical, with a longitudinal slit. They are placed horizontally and are beaten with the front of sticks or with heavy pieces of wood. They serve as musical instruments as well as for the transmission of messages, and often measure several feet in length.

dualism
Myths, religious beliefs and ritual practices based upon antitheses or pairs, such as heaven and earth, man and woman, etc. Such dualism is also frequently reflected in a division of the community into two complementary parts.

dynamic art
Art in which the principle of movement or action is especially pronounced.

dynamism
Belief in the existence of forces that created the universe and determine its entire course.

emu
A large ostrich-like bird, native to Australia, with wings useless for flight.

evolution
Theory that human culture developed gradually according to certain laws.

fertility ceremonies
Rites performed during planting and harvesting to ensure abundant crops, and similarly to bring about the propagation of animals.

food-gatherers
People who obtain their means of livelihood by collecting wild plants, roots, small animals, etc. They have as yet no knowledge of plant cultivation or the raising of live-stock, and are usually hunters. People at this stage of cultural development are characteristic of Australia, but elsewhere in Oceania only traces of this culture are to be found — above all in New Guinea.

gecko
Kind of lizard (adhesive lizard).

Giro-giro figures
Cf. *Dimi* figures.

ground paintings, drawings
Form of two-dimensional art, particularly common in Australia. The painting or drawing is done at a spot where the earth is hard and smooth.

harvest ceremonies
Cf. fertility ceremonies.

head-hunting
Ritual practice of capturing human heads with the object of obtaining for oneself the vital force of the person killed. Alternatively, this may be the re-enactment of a mythological event thought to be of importance in the creation of the world, serving to confirm the latter in its effect.

hour-glass drums
Cf. drums.

hybrid cultures
Cf. cultures.

initiation rites
Passage rites performed when young men and women are accepted into adult society. These rites are particularly elaborate for men in Melanesia, with lavish use of cult figures and masks; those for women are simpler.

kava
In Polynesia and some areas of Melanesia, an intoxicating beverage prepared from the roots of the *kava* shrub, which are chewed and then spat out into a bowl, or grated and mixed with water.

korwar style
Style of sculpture characterized especially by large heads of cubist shape, rectangular faces (and angular forms generally), and often by squatting figures. It is above all typical of north-western New Guinea. *Korwar* in the narrower sense of the word: a skull-container in the shape of a human figure. Closely related to Indonesian styles.

lime spatula
Implement used for placing pulverized lime into one's mouth when chewing betel.

local cultures
Cf. cultures.

magic
Belief in irrational forces, which the believer seeks to control in order to bring about good or evil results through the performance of symbolic acts. A person in a magical frame of mind does not take account of notions of time and space, or perceive rational causal connections. Cf. dynamism.

malanggan
Wooden cult object (three-dimensional figure, also mask), or rite in which this object is used. *Malanggan* style: a style characterized by fantastic motifs and combinations of motifs, with lavish use of colour. A local style in north-western New Ireland.

Malayo-Polynesians
Cf. Austronesians.

mana
The original Melanesian term for an irrational force or quality possessed to a varying degree by men, animals or inanimate objects, with the aid of which attempts can be made to explain unusual achievements, events or phenomena (cf. *dynamism*).

manism
Cf. ancestor worship.

mask
Disguise in which the wearer is rendered unrecognizable, mostly for the purpose of personifying a supernatural being (deceased person, ancestor, spirit).
Frequently a distinction is made between a masked costume, worn over the body, and a mask in the narrower sense of the word, covering the upper part of the body, head or face. 'Mask' is also a term commonly used for a face modelled plastically on buildings, canoes or as amulets.

Megalithic cultures
Neolithic and Bronze Age culture, still extant in some parts of southern Asia and Indonesia, characterized by the existence of monuments and buildings consisting of large stones: *menhirs* (upright stones), *dolmens* or *dysse* (small chambers with cap-stones), burial-places, terraces, platforms, etc. Sites of this kind have also been found in Oceania.

men's house
Meeting-house for men. Frequently men spend the night in such houses as well, and the building may also serve as a cult-house ('spirit house' in New Guinea). Adolescents' house (in Micronesia): assembly and dwelling-house of young men who are still bachelors.

Mimi
Magical creature in human guise, represented in dynamic style in the petroglyphs of Arnhem Land.

moa
In New Zealand, a bird, now extinct, that stood as much as 11 ft. 6 in. in height and had wings that were useless for flight.

Mongoloid
Term used to denote members of the Mongoloid race, one of the world's main ethnic groups, embracing the Chinese, Japanese, and many peoples of South-east Asia. In Oceania they appear in particularly large numbers in Micronesia, less frequently in Polynesia; there are only few traces of them in Melanesia.

myths
Oral traditions of legendary prehistoric times

which came to an end with the creation of the present-day world. The supernatural beings and events featured in myths are of the greatest importance in Oceanic art.

head-rest
Object similar to a stool, upon which the head is placed when sleeping or resting.

Negroid
Term used to designate one of the main racial groups of mankind, which embraces the dark-skinned and frizzly-haired peoples of Africa, southern Asia and Oceania. In Oceania they are to be found above all in Melanesia, and in particular in New Guinea.

nomads
Unsettled peoples or tribes that are obliged to roam from place in search of food: they are mainly hunters, but in some parts of the world also stock-breeders. Although there are no true nomads left in Oceania, there are some in Australia. Cf. semi-nomads.

northern Austronesians
Those Austronesian immigrants who reached Polynesia by way of Micronesia.

opossum
Kind of marsupial mammal native to Australia and many parts of Melanesia.

ornaments
Two-dimensional decorations composed of designs and design elements which are repeated over and over again; they are in most cases markedly conventional, and either abstract or representational in character. They often possess a symbolic significance.

outrigger canoe
Craft cut out of a single tree-trunk or plank boat (i.e., craft of which the sides are heightened by boards, the wash-strakes), the stability of which is increased by one or two floats, which are held by transverse booms affixed to the hull.

Papuans
People whose language and culture have been authenticated only in parts of New Guinea and some other Melanesian islands. They can be traced back to immigrants from Asia, or in New Guinea may have developed from an intermingling of Australians and Tasmanians.

passage rites
Ceremonies to mark important events in men's lives (birth, name-giving, puberty, marriage, death) which are performed in order to emphasize the importance of such occasions, the transition of man from one stage of existence to another, and at the same time to protect the community from dangerous influences of a supernatural character — for such unusual occasions could disturb the cosmic order, and are therefore regarded as dangerous.

plastic work of art
Three-dimensional work modelled in clay or other malleable material.

Pluvial epoch
Cf. Stone Age.

pointed mask
Cf. conical mask.

poker-work
Burning designs on wood, bamboo, reeds and calabashes.

Pre-Austronesians (non-Austronesians)
Collective term used to designate the peoples of Tasmania, Australia, large areas of New Guinea and other Melanesian islands; only vestiges of them are to be found in Polynesia and Micronesia. They immigrated into Oceania before the Austronesians. Although they are all dark-skinned, they are heterogeneous; from a linguistic and cultural point of view they are extremely diversified. Their most important representatives in Melanesia are the Papuans and the round adze people. They intermingled with Austronesians to form Austromelanids.

primeval monotheism
Hypothesis that in primeval times men believed in one single god, and that this belief was then superseded later by other forms of religion. Concepts of a Supreme Being are held to be vestiges of this original belief.

primitive peoples
Peoples who have made little technical, economic and political progress, and who have to adapt themselves more to their natural environment than do civilized peoples. But they also possess a culture, for there are no human societies devoid of culture.

race
An ethnic division, members of which are connected by common hereditary physical features. In Oceania the three main races,

Negroids, Mongoloids and Caucasoids (*qq.v.*), have intermingled almost everywhere and formed local groups (hybrid and local races).

radio-carbon dating
Method by which the antiquity of organic substances can be dated on the basis of the radio-activity of the carbon found in them.

round adze culture
Basic type of culture of dark-skinned pre-Austronesian immigrants. It is disseminated primarily in northern New Guinea and other Melanesian islands, and possibly in Polynesia as well — but in the latter case it may only have penetrated later, in the hybrid form of Austromelanid culture. The name is derived from the round adze (polished blade, oval or pointed oval in cross-section).

sago
Starchy food obtained from wild or cultivated sago-palms. The pith of the hewn trunk is pounded into small pieces, cleaned and strained. It is a staple article of diet in the swampy areas of New Guinea and other Melanesian islands.

sculpture
Three-dimensional work produced by chiselling or carving stone, bone or wood.

semi-nomads
Groups of people who live in the main by food-gathering and hunting, but who nevertheless occasionally remain in certain places for a certain length of time to obtain vegetable or animal foodstuffs (e.g., in south-western New Guinea and the upper Sepik area).

secret societies
Organizations composed of men who have to undergo an initiation ceremony in order to gain admission. Such societies may originally have been designed to maintain a divinely-sanctioned order, or at least to serve the advantage of the community; but later they frequently became corrupted into terrorist organizations which exploited the community. Masks were extensively worn by members of such societies, whose secret rites were attended only by initiates.

shield mask
Mask in the shape of a shield, which appears in association with animal heads or human faces. It is found in the coastlands of the Gulf of Papua.

sib
Cf. clan.

skink
Burrowing lizard.

skeleton figures
Sculptures which are carved in skeleton form, or which evoke this impression by reason of the very slender treatment of the torso and limbs. They are to be found on Easter Island and in Asmat, south-western New Guinea.

slit-drum
Cf. drums.

southern Austronesians
Those Austronesian immigrants who reached Melanesia by way of the north coast of New Guinea.

spear-throwers
Staff- or board-shaped implements, more rarely cord slings, used for throwing spears.

squatting figures
Squatting human figures frequently depicted with elbows supported on the knees and the head resting in the hands.

Stone Age
Era of the most ancient prehistoric human cultures, characterized by extensive use of stone for weapons and tools and by the absence of metal.
Palaeolithic Age (Old Stone Age): a term often applied to that period of the Stone Age which coincides with the Glacial and Pluvial period (Pleistocene) in geological reckoning. From a cultural point of view it is characterized by extensive nomadic hunting. Weapons and implements are made of hewn stone.
Mesolithic Age (Middle Stone Age): post-Glacial period, likewise characterized by nomadic hunter cultures and hewn (but more delicately worked) stone implements and weapons (microliths).
Neolithic Age (New Stone Age): most recent period. The beginning of settlement with a primitive form of agriculture, domesticated animals, pottery and weaving; use of polished stone implements.
All Oceanic peoples have Stone Age, and especially Neolithic, cultures; the Tasmanians were a Palaeolithic people; the Australians

belong to the Palaeolithic and Mesolithic period, with only vestiges of Neolithic elements; in the present-day cultures of Melanesia, on the other hand, only vestiges of these two more ancient stages of culture have survived.

style
Manner of rendering works of art in accordance with certain typical basic repetitive design elements, mostly traditional, which are selected and combined in an identical way.

Sulka
Tribe in New Britain.

Supreme Being
A vaguely-conceived supernatural being, often only occurring in mythological tradition and disregarded in rites. Such a Supreme Being is usually thought of as far removed from the affairs of this world. On this concept was based the theory of primeval monotheism (*q.v.*).

suspension hooks
Wooden hooks (often anchor-shaped), affixed to cross-beams of a house by cords so that they hang freely. They are used for suspending nets, bags of food and clothing, etc.

Suque
Men's society in the northern New Hebrides and the Banks Is., pursuing religious and social ends. Membership is bought for money; so too is higher rank in the society, which brings with it a correspondingly high degree of prestige. Members are entitled to have rank statues (particularly huge figures of tree-fern wood) erected which correspond to the rank they themselves hold.

taboo (tabu)
A prohibition i.e., an order to abstain from or avoid something, violation of which leads to punishment (in the form of illness and death) by supernatural powers.

Tami style
Style characterized by voluminous forms, in which preference is given to right angles and straight lines. Such figures are usually rendered with arms hanging down or resting on the hips. Lavishly painted carvings are popular. This style is characteristic of the coastal areas on the Huon Gulf (northern New Guinea), the islands of Tami, Umboi and Siassi, and western New Britain. Related forms are also to be found in other parts of Melanesia.

tapa
Cf. bark-cloth.

tendril-like designs
Designs consisting of elements that break off sharply, and are frequently in the shape of hooks. They are disseminated particularly widely in north-western New Guinea.

totemism
Belief in the existence of a mystical relationship between certain groups of men (clans, classes, etc.), and possibly also between individual persons on one hand and a totem (animals, plants, inanimate objects and natural phenomena) on the other. In an extreme form totemism may mean belief in the existence of a kin relationship between groups of men or individuals and the totem (descent from the totem).

two-dimensional style
In two-dimensional art (painting, decoration), a style that follows certain laws applicable only to two-dimensional art.

uli
Wooden cult figures from central New Ireland. Commemorative images of mythological figures, and possibly also of ancestors.

vitalistic art
Concept of art in which vital or creative force is expressed and represented in a latent state, not in action.

Wandjina
Mythological figure associated with the creation of the world, representing a human being and depicted in a characteristic style. Wandjinas are found in the petroglyphs of the Kimberley district, in north-western Australia.

X-ray style
Characteristic style of petroglyphs and bark paintings in Arnhem Land, in which animals are rendered in such a way that the bones and inner organs are visible.

BIBLIOGRAPHY

GENERAL

Adam, L., Primitive Art. Penguin (Pelican) Books. Harmondsworth, 1949.

Balfour, H., The Evolution of Decorative Art. London, 1893.

Basler, A., L'art chez les peuples primitifs. Paris, 1929.

Bossert, H. Th., Geschichte des Kunstgewerbes, Vol. I. Berlin, 1928.

Burland, C. A., Man and Art. London, 1959.

Christensen, E. O., Primitive Art. New York, 1955.

Danzel, Th. W., Kultur und Religion des primitiven Menschen. Stuttgart, 1924.

Forman, W. and B., L'art des pays lointains. Prague, 1956.

Haddon, A. C., Evolution in Art: as illustrated by the life-histories of design. London, 1902.

Hooper, J. T. and Burland, C. A., The Art of Primitive Peoples. London, 1953.

Kühn, H., Die Kunst der Primitiven. Munich, 1923.

Lützeler, H., Führer zur Kunst. Freiburg, 1956.

Schmalenbach, W., Grundsätzliches zur primitiven Kunst, in: Acta Tropica, Vol. 15. Basle, 1958.

Sierksma, F., Götter, Götzen und Dämonen. Vienna, 1959.

Springer, A., Die aussereuropäische Kunst. Handbuch der Kunstgeschichte, Vol. 6. Leipzig, 1920.

Sydow, E. von, Die Kunst der Naturvölker und der Vorzeit. Berlin, 1923.

Sydow, E. von, Kunst und Religion der Naturvölker. Oldenburg, 1926.

Vatter, E., Religiöse Plastik der Naturvölker. Frankfort-on-Main, 1926.

OCEANIA

Archey, G., South Sea Folk: Handbook of Maori and Oceanic Ethnology. Auckland, 1937.

Bodrogi, Th., Die Kunst Ozeaniens. Würzburg-Vienna, 1960.

Brown, J. M., Melanesians and Polynesians. London, 1910.

Buschan, G., Illustrierte Völkerkunde. Stuttgart, 1923.

Finsch, O., Südseearbeiten. Hamburg, 1914.

Heine-Geldern, R., Urheimat und früheste Wanderungen der Austronesier, in: Anthropos, Vol. XXVII, Vienna, 1932.

Heine-Geldern, R., Vorgeschichtliche Grundlagen der kolonial-indischen Kunst, in: Wiener Beiträge zur Kunst und Kulturgeschichte Asiens, Vol. 8, Vienna, 1934.

Heine-Geldern, R., L'art prébouddhique de la Chine et de l'Asie du Sud-Est et son influence en Océanie, in: Revue des Arts Asiatiques, Vol. 11, 1937.

Koch, G., Die Kunst der Südsee, in: *H. Weigert,* Kleine Kunstgeschichte der Welt, Vol. I, Zurich, 1956.

Krämer, A., Die malaiisch-pazifische Kunst, in: Springer, Handbuch der Kunstgeschichte, Vol. VI, Leipzig, 1929.

Leenhardt, M., Art de l'Océanie. Arts du Monde. Paris, 1947.

Linton, R. and Wingert, P. S., Arts of the South Seas. The Museum of Modern Art, New York, 1946.

Nevermann, H., Südseekunst. Staatliches Museum für Völkerkunde, Berlin, 1933.

Parkinson, R., Dreissig Jahre in der Südsee. Stuttgart, 1907.

Plischke, H., Der Stille Ozean. Entdeckung und Erschliessung. Janus-Bücher, Vol. 14. Munich-Vienna, 1959.

Portier, A. and Ponceton, F., Les arts sauvages: Océanie. Paris, 1930.

Schmalenbach, W., Plastik der Südsee. Stuttgart, 1956.

Sharp, A., Ancient Voyagers in the Pacific. Penguin (Pelican) Books. Harmondsworth, 1957.

Speiser, F., Über Kunststile in Melanesien, in: Zeitschrift für Ethnologie, Vol. 68, 1936.

Speiser, F., Versuch einer Siedlungsgeschichte der Südsee. Denkschriften der Schweiz. Naturforschenden Gesellschaft, Vol. LXXVII, Part 1. Zurich, 1946.

Tischner, H., Kulturen der Südsee. Hamburg, 1958.

Tischner, H. and Hewicker, F., Oceanic Art. London, 1954.

Wingert, P. S., Art of the South Pacific Islands. London, 1953.

MELANESIA

Codrington, R. H., The Melanesians. Oxford, 1891.

Lewis, A. B., Ethnology of Melanesia. Chicago, 1945.

Lewis, A. B., The Melanesians: People of the South Pacific. Chicago, 1951.

Nevermann, H., Masken und Geheimbünde in Melanesien. Berlin, 1933.

Reichard, G. A., Melanesian Design. New York, 1933.

Rivers, W. H. R., The History of Melanesian Society. Cambridge, 1914.

Stephan, E., Südseekunst. Berlin, 1907.

NEW GUINEA

Bateson, G., Naven. Cambridge, 1936.

Behrmann, W., Im Stromgebiet des Sepik. Berlin, 1922.

Bodrogi, T., Some Notes on the Ethnography of New Guinea, in: Acta Ethnographica, Vol. II, Budapest, 1953.

Bodrogi, T., New Guinean Style Provinces: The Style Province 'Astrolabe Bay', in: Opuscula Ethnologica Memoriae Ludovici Biro sacra. Budapest, 1959.

Bühler, A., Heilige Bildwerke aus Neuguinea. Führer durch das Museum für Völkerkunde Basel. Basle, 1957.

Bühler, A., Kunststile am Sepik. Führer durch das Museum für Völkerkunde Basel. Basle, 1960.

Chauvet, St., Les arts indigènes en Nouvelle Guinée. Paris, 1950.

Firth, R., Art and Life in New Guinea. London, 1936.

Fischer, H. W., Ethnographica aus Süd- und Südwest-Neuguinea, in: Nova Guinea, Part VII, Leyden, 1923.

Fraser, D., Mundugumor Sculpture: Comments on the Art of a New Guinea Tribe, in: Man, Vol. 55, London, 1955.

Fuhrmann, E., Neuguinea. Kulturen der Erde, Vol 14. Hagen, 1922.

Gardi, R., Sepik: Land der sterbenden Geister. Bilddokumente aus Neuguinea. Introductory text and captions by A. Bühler, Berne, 1958.

Gerbrands, A. A., Kunststijlen in West-Nieuw-Guinea: een voorlopig onderzoek, in: Indonesië, 4e Jaargang.

Girard, M. B. F., Les peintures rupestres Buang, District de Morobé, Nouvelle Guinée, in: Journal de la Société des Océanistes, Vol. XIII, Paris, 1957.

Haddon, A. C., The Decorative Art of British New Guinea. Dublin, 1894.

Haddon, A. C., Reports of the Cambridge Anthropological Expedition to Torres Straits. Vols. I, IV, V, VI, Cambridge, 1904–35.

Kaberry, Ph. M., The Abelam Tribe, Sepik District, New Guinea, in: Oceania, Vol. 11, 1940-1.

Kooijman, S., De Kunst van Nieuw-Guinea. The Hague, 1955.

Kooijman, S., Art of South-western New Guinea: a preliminary Survey, in: Antiquity and Survival, No. 5. The Hague, 1956.

Kooijman, S., The Art of Lake Sentani. The Museum of Primitive Art, New York, 1959.

Landtman, G., The Kiwai Papuans of British New Guinea. London, 1927.

Laumann, K., Geisterfiguren am mittleren Yuat-River in Neuguinea, in: Anthropos, Vol. 49, Posieux (Fribourg), 1954.

Lewis, A. B., Decorative Art of New Guinea: Incised Designs. Field Museum of Natural History, Anthropology, Design Series, No. 4. Chicago, 1925.

Malinowsky, B., Argonauts of the Western Pacific. London, 1922.

Neuhauss, R., Deutsch-Neuguinea. Berlin, 1911.

Nuoffer, O., Ahnenfiguren von der Geelvinkbai, Holländisch-Neuguinea. Abhandlungen und Berichte des Königl. Zoologischen und Anthropologisch-Ethnographischen Museums zu Dresden, Vol. 12. Leipzig, 1908.

Reche, O., Der Kaiserin-Augusta-Fluss. Ergebnisse der Südsee-Expedition 1908-10. Hamburg, 1913.

Röder, J., Felsbilder und Vorgeschichte des MacCluer-Golfes, West-Neuguinea. Ergebnisse der Frobenius-Expedition 1937-8 in die Molukken und nach Holländisch-Neuguinea, Vol. IV, Darmstadt, 1959.

Sande, G. A. J. van der, Ethnography and Anthropology, in: Nova Guinea, Part III. Leyden, 1907.

Schmitz, C. A., Zwei Telum-Figuren aus der Astrolabe-Bai in Nordost-Neuguinea, in: Tribus, Vol. 8, 1959.

Schmitz, C. A., Die Jawik-Figuren der Pasum in Nordost-Neuguinea. Jahrbuch des Museums für Völkerkunde zu Leipzig, Vol. XVII (1958), Berlin, 1960.

Schmitz, C. A., Historische Probleme in Nordost-Neuguinea, Huon-Halbinsel. Studien zur Kulturkunde, Vol. 16. Wiesbaden, 1960.

Seligmann, C. G., The Melanesians of British New Guinea. Cambridge, 1910.

Serrurier, L., Die Korware oder Ahnenbilder von Neuguinea, in: Tijdschrift Indische Taal-, Land- en Volkenkunde, Vol. 40, 1898.

Thurnwald, R., Die Gemeinde der Banaro. Stuttgart, 1921.

Williams, F. E., Orokaiva Society. Oxford, 1928.

Williams, F. E., Drama of Orokolo. Oxford, 1940.

Wirz, P., Die Ornamentik und insbesondere die Darstellung menschlicher Formen in der Kunst von Holländisch-Süd-Neuguinea, in: Tijdschrift van het Bataviaasch Genootschap van Kunsten en Wetenschappen, Part LX. Weltevreden, 1921.

Wirz, P., Die Marind-anim von Holländisch- Süd-Neuguinea. Hamburg, 1922-5.

Wirz, P., Beitrag zur Ethnologie der Sentanier (Holländisch-Neuguinea), in: Nova Guinea, Part XVI, Leyden, 1934.

Wirz, P., Beiträge zur Ethnographie des Papua-Golfes, Britisch-Neuguinea. Abhandlungen und Berichte der Museen für Tierkunde und Völkerkunde zu Dresden, Vol. 19. Leipzig, 1934.

Wirz, P., Kunstwerke vom Sepik. Führer durch das Museum für Völkerkunde Basel. Basle, 1954.

Wirz, P., Kunst und Kult des Sepik-Gebietes, Neuguinea. Amsterdam, 1959.

ADMIRALTY ISLANDS

Bühler, A., Versuch einer Bevölkerungs- und Kulturanalyse auf den Admiralitätsinseln, in: Zeitschrift für Ethnologie, Vol. 67, 1935.

Mead, M., Growing up in New Guinea. New York, 1930.

Nevermann, H., Admiralitäts-Inseln. Ergebnisse der Südsee-Expedition 1908-10. Hamburg, 1934.

ST. MATTHIAS

Nevermann, H., St.-Matthias-Gruppe. Ergebnisse der Südsee-Expedition 1908-10. Hamburg, 1933.

NEW IRELAND

Bühler, A., Totenfeste in Neu-Irland. Verhandlungen der Schweiz. Naturforschenden Gesellschaft. Altdorf, 1933.

Bühler, A., Neuirland und Nachbarinseln. Führer durch das Museum für Völkerkunde Basel. Basle, 1948.

Krämer, A., Die Malanggane von Tombára. Munich, 1925.

Peekel, G., Die Ahnenbilder von Nord-Neumecklenburg, in: Anthropos, Vol. 22, 1927.

Powdermaker, H., Life in Lesu. New York, 1933.

Stephan, E. and Gräbner, F., Neu-Mecklenburg. Berlin, 1907.

NEW BRITAIN

Meyer, A. B. and Parkinson, R., Schnitzereien und Masken vom Bismarck-Archipel und Neu-Guinea. Königl. Ethnographisches Museum zu Dresden, Vol. 10. Dresden, 1895.

Speiser, F., Neubritannien. Führer durch das Museum für Völkerkunde Basel. Basle, 1945.

SOLOMONS

Bernatzik, H. A., Owa Raha. Vienna, 1936.

Blackwood, B., Both Sides of the Buka Passage. Oxford, 1935.

Fox, C. E., The Threshold of the Pacific. London, 1924.

Frizzi, E., Ein Beitrag zur Ethnologie von Bougainville und Buka. Baessler-Archiv, Berlin, 1914.

Ivens, W. G., Melanesians of the South-east Solomon Islands. New York, 1924.

Paravicini, E., Reisen in den britischen Salomonen. Frauenfeld-Leipzig, 1931.

Paravicini, E., Salomonen. Führer durch das Museum für Völkerkunde Basel. Basle, 1933.

SANTA CRUZ

Speiser, F., Völkerkundliches von den Santa-Cruz-Inseln, in: Ethnologica, Vol. II, 1916.

Speiser, F., Die Neuen Hebriden und Santa-Cruz-Inseln. Führer durch das Museum für Völkerkunde Basel. Basle, 1929.

NEW HEBRIDES AND BANKS ISLANDS

Deacon, A. B., Malekula. London, 1934.

Layard, J., Stone Men of Malekula. London, 1942.

Speiser, F., Ethnographische Materialien aus den Neuen Hebriden und Banks-Inseln. Berlin, 1923.

Speiser, F., Die Neuen Hebriden und Santa-Cruz-Inseln. Führer durch das Museum für Völkerkunde Basel. Basle, 1929.

NEW CALEDONIA

Guiart, J., L'art autochtone de Nouvelle-Calédonie. Editions des Etudes Mélanésiennes, Nouméa, 1953.

Luquet, G. H., L'art néo-calédonien. Institut d'Ethnologie, Paris, 1929.

Sarasin, F., Ethnologie der Neu-Caledonier und Loyalty-Insulaner. Munich, 1929.

Sarasin, F., Neu-Caledonien und Loyalty-Inseln. Führer durch das Museum für Völkerkunde Basel. Basle, 1931.

OUTLYING ISLANDS OF NORTH-WESTERN POLYNESIA

Damm, H., Luangiua und Nukumanu. Ergebnisse der Südsee-Expedition 1908-10. Hamburg, 1931.

Damm, H., Sakrale Figuren von den nordwestpolynesischen Randinseln, in: Jahrbuch des Museums für Völkerkunde zu Leipzig, Vol. X, 1926/51. Leipzig, 1952.

POLYNESIA

Buck, P. H., Vikings of the Pacific. Chicago, 1959.

Christian, F. W., Eastern Pacific Islands. London, 1910.

Damm, H., Polynesien: Die Schatzkammer, Vol. I. Leipzig, 1959.

Greiner, R. H., Polynesian Decorative Designs, in: Bulletin of the Bernice P. Bishop Museum, No. 7, Honolulu, 1923.

Hambruch, P., Ozeanische Rindenstoffe. Oldenburg, 1926.

Handy, E. S. C., Polynesian Religion, in: Bulletin of the Bernice P. Bishop Museum, No. 34, Honolulu, 1927.

Hiroa, Te Rangi (P. H. Buck), An Introduction to Polynesian Anthropology. Honolulu, 1945.

Linton, R., Ethnology of Polynesia and Micronesia. Mentor Books. New York, 1960.

Nevermann, H., Götter der Südsee: die Religion der Polynesier. Stuttgart, 1947.

Oldman, O., The Oldman Collection of Polynesian Artifacts. Wellington, N.Z., 1943.

Suggs, R. C., The Island Civilizations of Polynesia. Mentor Books, New York, 1960.

FIJI

Thompson, L., Southern Lau, Fiji: an Ethnography, in: Bulletin of the Bernice P. Bishop Museum, No. 162. Honolulu, 1940.

Thomson, B., The Fijians. London, 1908.

TONGA, SAMOA

Hiroa, Te Rangi (P. H. Buck), Material Representatives of Tongan and Samoan Gods, in: Journal of the Polynesian Society, Vol. 44, New Plymouth, N.Z., 1935.

Hiroa, Te Rangi (P. H. Buck), Additional Wooden Images from Tonga, in: Journal of the Polynesian Society, Vol. 46, 1937. Wellington, N.Z., 1937.

Krämer, A., Die Samoa-Inseln. Stuttgart, 1903.

Stair, E. B., Old Samoa. St. Pauls, 1897.

Turner, G., Samoa. London, 1884.

TAHITI

Handy, E. S. C. History and Culture of the Society Islands, in: Bulletin of the Bernice P. Bishop Museum, No. 74. Honolulu, 1930.

Henry, T., Ancient Tahiti, in: Bulletin of the Bernice P. Bishop Museum, No. 48. Honolulu, 1928.

COOK AND AUSTRAL ISLANDS

Aitken, R. T., Ethnology of Tabuai, in: Bulletin of the Bernice P. Bishop Museum, No. 70. Honolulu, 1930.

Hall, H. V., Wood carvings of the Austral Islands, in: Journal of the University of Pennsylvania Museum, Vol. 12, 1921.

Hiroa, Te Rangi (P. H. Buck), Arts and Crafts of the Cook Islands, in: Bulletin of the Bernice P. Bishop Museum, No. 179. Honolulu, 1944.

MARQUESAS ISLANDS

Handy, W. C., L'art des Iles Marquises. Paris, 1938.

Linton, R., The Native Culture of the Marquesas Islands, in: Memoirs of the Bernice P. Bishop Museum, Vol. 8, No. 5, Honolulu, 1923.

Steinen, K. v. d., Die Marquesaner und ihre Kunst. Berlin, 1925-8.

HAWAIIAN ISLANDS

Dodge, E. S., The Hawaiian Portion of the Polynesian Collection of the Peabody Museum of Salem. Salem, 1937.

Emory, K. P., Hawaii: Notes on Wooden Images, in: Ethnologia Cranmorensis, No. 2, 1938.

Handy, E. S. C. and Buck, P. H., Ancient Hawaiian Civilization. Honolulu, 1933.

Krämer, A., Hawaii, Ostmikronesien und Samoa. Stuttgart, 1906.

Luquiens, H. M., Hawaiian Art. Honolulu, 1931.

Malo, D., Hawaiian Antiquities. Honolulu, 1951.

EASTER ISLAND

Barthel, Th., Grundlagen zur Entzifferung der Osterinselschrift, in: Abhandlungen aus dem Gebiet der Auslandskunde, Vol. 64, Hamburg, 1958.

Heyerdahl, Th., Aku-Aku: The Secret of Easter Island. London, 1958.

Métraux, A., Ethnology of Easter Island. Honolulu, 1940.

Métraux, A., Easter Island. London, 1957.

MICRONESIA

Linton, R., Ethnology of Polynesia and Micronesia. Chicago, 1926.

PALAU AND YAP

Furness, W. H., The Island of Stone Money. London, 1910.

Krämer, A., Palau: Ergebnisse der Südsee-Expedition 1908-10. Hamburg, 1919-26.

Müller-Wismar, W., Yap: Ergebnisse der Südsee-Expedition 1907-10. Hamburg, 1917-8.

CAROLINES

Christian, F. W., The Caroline Islands. London, 1899.

Eilers, A., Inseln um Ponape: Ergebnisse der Südsee-Expedition 1908-10. Hamburg, 1934.

Hambruch, P., Ponape: Ergebnisse der Südsee-Expedition 1908-10. Hamburg, 1932.

Krämer, A., Truk: Ergebnisse der Südsee-Expedition 1908-10. Hamburg, 1932.

Sarfert, E., Kusae: Ergebnisse der Südsee-Expedition 1908-10. Hamburg, 1919.

NEW ZEALAND

Archey, G., Sculpture and Design: an Outline of Maori Art. Handbook of the Auckland War Memorial Museum. Auckland, 1955.

Barrow, T., Maori Decorative Carving: an Outline, in: Journal of the Polynesian Society, Vol. 65, New Plymouth, 1956.

Barrow, T., Human Figures in Wood and Ivory from Western Polynesia, in: Man, Vol. 56, London, 1956.

Barrow, T., Maori Godsticks collected by the Rev. Richard Taylor. Dominion Museum Records in: Ethnology, Vol. 1, No. 5, Wellington, 1959.

Barrow, T., Maori Free Standing Images, in: Anthropology in the South Seas, New Plymouth, 1959.

Best, E., The Maori. Wellington, 1924.

Best, E., Notes on the Occurrence of the Lizard in Maori Carvings, in: New Zealand Journal of Science and Technology, Vol. 5, Wellington, 1923.

Buck, P. H., The Coming of the Maori. Maori Purposes Fund Board. Wellington, 1949.

Dodge, E. S., The New Zealand Maori Collection in the Peabody Museum of Salem. Salem, 1941.

Duff, R., The Moa-Hunter Period of Maori Culture, 2nd ed., Wellington, 1956.

Firth, R. W., The Maori Carver, in: Journal of the Polynesian Society, Vol. 34, New Plymouth, 1925.

Hamilton, A., Maori Art: the Art Workmanship of the Maori Race in New Zealand. Wellington, 1896-1901.

Hiroa, Te Rangi (P. H. Buck), The Coming of the Maori. Wellington, 1950.

Oldman, W. O., Oldman Collection of Maori

Artifacts. Polynesian Society Memoir No. 14, Wellington, 1938 (2nd ed., 1946).

Phillipps, W. J., Maori Art. Wellington, 1946.

Skinner, H. D., Evolution in Maori Art, in: Journal of the Royal Anthropological Institute, Vol. 46, 1916.

Skinner, H. D., The Maori Hei-Tiki. Otago Museum Booklet No. 1. Dunedin, 1946.

Taylor, C. R. H., A Pacific Bibliography. Polynesian Society Memoir No. 24. Wellington, 1951.

Webster, K. A., The Armytage Collection of Maori Jade. London, 1948.

AUSTRALIA

Basedow, H., The Australian Aboriginal. Adelaide, 1925.

Elkin, A. P., Rock Painting of North-West Australia, in: Oceania, Vol. 1, 1930-1.

Elkin, A. P. and Berndt, C. and R., Art in Arnhem Land. London, 1950.

Kupka, K., Kunst der Uraustralier. Führer durch das Museum für Völkerkunde Basel. Basle, 1958.

Lommel, A. and K., Die Kunst des fünften Erdteils: Australien. Staatliches Museum für Völkerkunde, Munich, 1959.

McCarthy, F. D., Australian Aboriginal Decorative Art. Sydney, 1956.

Mountford, Ch. P., Aboriginal Decorative Art from Arnhem Land, Northern Territory of Australia, in: Transactions of the Royal Society of South Australia, Vol. 63, 1939.

Mountford, Ch. P., Art, Myth and Symbolism. Records of the American – Australian Scientific Expedition to Arnhem Land, 1948. Melbourne, 1956.

Mountford, Ch. P., Art, Myth and Symbolism of Melville Island. Melbourne, 1958.

Read, H. E., Australia: Aboriginal Painting, Arnhem Land. Paris, 1954.

Speiser, F., Australien. Führer durch das Museum für Völkerkunde Basel. Basle, 1929.

Spencer, B. and Gillen, F. J., The Native Tribes of Central Australia. London, 1899.

Spencer, B. and Gillen, F. J., The Northern Tribes of Central Australia. London, 1904.

Spencer, B., Native Tribes of the Northern Territory of Australia. London, 1914.

INDEX

The numerals in italics refer to the plates and figures. The letter (G) indicates Glossary.

Admiralty Is. 22, *43*, 86, *103*, *108*, *109*, *121*, 137, 139, 140, 142, *151*, 152, 157, 175, 184
adze (G), 32, 91-2, *162*, 172, 206; quadrangular 26, 28, 29; rectangular *23*; round *20*, 21, 22, 23, 26, 28, 29, 30, 72, 76, 77, 82-3, 183-6, 188; shouldered 26, *27*; tanged 27
Africa 50, 51, 186, 217
agriculture 21, 26, 33, 34, 70, 76, 79, 95, 186-7
Aibom *38*, *76*, 86
Amanggabi *61*, *84*
Ambanoli *75*
Ambrym *137*, *140*, 157, 159
Ambunti 109-110, 111, 112
America 17, 23, 28, 60, 91, 188
ancestor figures 62, *66*, *79*, *86*, *102*, 110, *120*, *121*, 127, 128, 136, 137, *137*, 140, 147-9, 153, 159, 160, 161, 163, *167*, 176, 193, 194, 199, 200; houses *135*, 159; panel *197*; pendant *195*, 197; poles 125; skull *51*; worship (G), *56*, 60, *65*, 71-2, 77, 79, 80, 83, 88, 106, *117*, *122-3*, *141*, 142, 146, 160, 162, 172, 186, 191, 204, *205*, 206; cf. manism
animals 129; figures 60, 99, 100-3, 114, 131, 140, 152, 153, 160, 223; motifs *44*, 48, 50, 61, 76, 77, 88, 103, 106, 117, 119, 120, 132, 136, 139, 145, 155, 159, 160, 168-9, 176, 178, 180, 185, 196, 218, 221; cf. also individual animals
animatism (G), 60
animism (G), 60; cf. manism
annatto tree 91
anthropomorphic motifs (G): cf. motifs
Antifuogo *70*
Aotea 193
appliqué work 131
Arahura R. 196
Arawa 193, 199, *205*
Arawe Is. 149
archaic culture (G): cf. *moa* hunters
architecture 77, 94, 106, 112, 137; architectural parts *38*, 72, 160, 161, 172, *178*, 180; decoration on buildings *44*, *58*, *91*, 119, 131, 137, 142, *142*, 161, *169*, *171*, 179, 194-6, 197, 199, 200, 201, 206; cf. houses, posts, roof decorations
areca 33, 91
Arnhem Land *209*, 210, *211*, 212, *215*, 221, 223
art, content of 40, 42, 43, 45; conventional 45; decorative 39-40, 42-3, 52, 55, 69; function of 42-3, 57, 85-6; immovable 209; modern 53; movable 209, 221; nature of 37-9, 43-5, 55; and environment 48-51; and technique 51-4
artifacts 193, 200, 204
artist 39, 40, 42, 43, 45, 47, 91, 94-5, 109, 207, 223-5
Asia 17, 26, 27, 28, 35, 79, 206-7; eastern 22, 26, 28, 188; north-eastern 22; southern 21; south-eastern 17, 20, 28, 188
Asia Minor 50
Asmat *102*, *110*, 112, 124, 128
Assam 27
Astrolabe Bay *79*, 86, 88, 115-7, 119, 175, 183-4
atua 202
atua ngau tangata 202
Auckland 204
Austral Is. 169-172, 184-5
Australia, geography of 15, 16; languages of 19; peoples of 19, 20, 21, 30, 31; settlement of 21, 28; religious beliefs in 129; cultures of 29, 30, 125, 187; cultural influences elsewhere 28, 183; central *208*, 210, 212, *218*, 218-9, 220, *221*, 222, 225; Northern *209*, 210, *211*, *213*, *214*, *215*, 216, *216*, 217, *219*, *220*, 221, 222; north-eastern 221; north-western 210, *212*, 214, *223*, *224*; South 210, *210*, 218, 219, 220; south-eastern *210*, 212; Western 210; cf. Arnhem Land, New South Wales, Queensland, Tasmania, Victoria
Austromelanid culture 23, 26, 28, 29, 30, 77, 99, 120, 183-6
Austronesian culture 72, 76, 77, 83, 124, 184-5, 187-8; influences 77; language 19, 22, 31, 32; religion 80; social structure 35; Austronesians 22, 23, 26, 31, 76, 183, 186, 188; pre-Austronesians 22, 23, 26; pre-Austronesian culture 23, 28, 72, 82; language 31, 32; religion 80
Awar *66*
axes 213; bronze 27
Ayajo *41*

Baining (G), *125*, 149-150, 183
balsa 89
Baluan 137; Baluan Is. 137
bamboo *76*, *78*, 89, 92, 100, 112, *116*, 117, *122-3*, *125*, 128, 142, *146*, 162
Banaitja 211
bananas 33
Bannaway 220
Banks Is. 86, *141*, 157-160
bark 91; bark-cloth (G), 32-3, *36*, *44*, 73, 91, 103, *115*, *116*, 117, *118*, 119, 120, 142, 145, 146, 150, 160, *164*, 165, 166, 168-9, 173, 176, 178, 183; bark belt *100*; bark painting 187, 212, 214, *219*, 221; bark shield *210*, 222

Barwon R. 220
basket-work *68*, 175, 180; cf. masks
bast 16
batata 17, 33
Bay of Plenty 199, 204, *205*
beads *36*, *108*, 173
beak style (G): cf. styles
bee 212, 223
Beechey Cape *133*
belt *100*, 115, *168*
betel-chewing (G), 137; betel-pepper 33; betel-palm: cf. areca
beverage 33, 160, 165
Biak *36*
Bipi Is. *103*
birds 16, 76, *77*, *79*, *83*, 86, 88, 89, 103, 106, 108-9, 111, 114, 117, 119, 120, *122-3*, 128, *129*, *132*, 139, 141, 145, *147*, *149*, 155, 157, 159, 160, 176, 178, 180, 191, 199, 202, 218; cf. frigate-bird, *moa*, dove
bis poles *107*
Bismarck Archipelago 16, 33, 69, 73, 96, 97, 149, 163
bivalve shells 88, 157
Black R. 112
Blackwater R. *84*, 112
Blinman 210
boar *47*, *52*, *67*, 76, 86, *138*, 160
board *81*, *141*
boats 20, 21, 55, 106, 128, 176, 180, 201-2; boat-building 76; boat-houses 179; cf. canoes
bone 20, 32, 88, 92, 103, 157, 172, 173, 191, 193, 194, 204
boomerang 207, 209
Bopope *144*
Bora 220
Bougainville *135*, 153
bows 32
boxes *196*, *199*, 200, 204
bread-fruit 16, 33, *166*, 173
Bronze Age (G), 26, 27; Late Bronze Age 28
bronze axe 27
brushes 212
Buka I. *127*, 153
bull-roarers (G), *85*, 106, 117, 128, 132
burial 70, 136, 155, 157, 160, 176; boxes 200; coffins 209, 221; poles 209, 221, 225; trees 213, 220
Burra *126*
Bushmen 217

camel 225
cannibalism (G), *52*, 70
canoes 69, 127, *128*, 153, 191, 193-4, 199-200, 204, 217; canoe ornaments 77, 100, 103, 109, *110*, 111, 119, 120, 125, 128, 134-6, 137, 149, 152, 180, *182*; canoe prow 155, 160; cf. outrigger canoe
capes: cf. feather
caps 115, 142
Carpenteria, Gulf of *219*, 221
carver 95; carving 47-8, 69, 73, 86, *86*, 88, 89, 94, 103, 111, 128, 131, 132, 134, 136, 142, 160, *163*, 173, 179-180, 183-4, 194, 202, 204, 213, *224*; in relief 86, *92*, *112*, 114, 119, *127*, 127, 131, *133*, 139, 142, 153, 157, 165, *165*, 173, 179, 180; cf. sculpture
Carolines 23, 32, 140, *168*, *174*, *177*, 179, 180, *182*
cassowary (G), *68*, *70*, *72*, 88, *102*, 103, *118*
Caucasoid (G), 22
caves 200, 202; cave painting 50, 186, 196, *209*, 209, 213-5
Celebes 21, 155
ceremonies 106, 108, 114, 129, 131, *135*, 139, 142, 175, 209, 213, 217, 220, 225; ceremonial adze *162*, 172; architecture 179, 194, 200-1, 204, 206; fly-whisk 169; objects 212, *218*, *221*; paddle *163*; poles (*bis*) *106*, 127; shields 127, 132, 134; staff 178; stool 111; cf. initiation
chalk figures 86, 146
Chambri, Lake *38*, *76*, 86
charcoal 91
charms 59-60, 112, *140*, 160
China 21, 27
chisel 92
Choiseul Is. *39*, *60*, 88, *131*, 155
Christianity 67, *121*
church 67, 71
clam-shells *50*, *52*, 91, 140, 155
clan (G), *44*, *64*, *68*, 83, 85, 86, *87*, *90*, 103, 106, *116*
classes (G), 34-5, 39, 159
classic epoch of Maori art (G), 193, 199, 204
clay *38*, *61*, 79, 86, 92, 109, *124*, 132, *138*, *152*, 159, 160, 165-6, 194, 210, 223
climate 15, 16
clothing 32, 39, 55, 91, 117, *135*, 140, 145, 175, 191, *192*, 194, 208
club 32, 89, *112*, 117, 120, *134*, 140, *149*, 153, *153*, *155*, *157*, *159*, 163, 165, 166-8, 170, 173, 178; club-heads 69
club-houses 137, 162, 179
coal 86
coconut 91, 136, *168*; coconut-palm 33, 176
combs *103*, *114*, 117, 134, 140, 155
concept of the world (G), 65
Cook, J. 193
Cook Is. *151*, *162*, *163*, 169-172, 184-5, 191, 193
cord *49*, *52*, *70*, 88, *102*, *103*, *114*, *117*, 124, *126*, 127, 145, *148*, 168, 170, 175, 200

cosmogony (G), 199
costume: cf. feather
cowrie-shells *38, 49, 72, 84*
crab 16, 145
crafts 34, 38, 45-6, 79, 173; craftsman 47, 193-4
Creation, the 66, 67, 69, 71, 72, 73, 76, 80-1, 185, 216, 222, 225; creative force (G), 71, 76
crocodile *75, 77,* 99, *103,* 106, *108, 109,* 109, 111, 119, 134, 136, 137, 139, 218
Croisilles, Cape 106, 115
cults 146, 172; figures 70, *75, 82, 84, 87,* 99, *110, 119,* 134, 145, 159, 161, 175
cult-house *56, 74, 75,* 77, *78, 90, 92,* 94, *95,* 106, 109, 114, *122-3, 141,* 155, 159, 160, 170, 179; cult objects 55, 59, 67, 69, 106, 119, 131, 132, 140, 160, 169, 173, 183; cf. rites
culture heroes 61, 79, 80
curcuma 91, 129
curvilinear style (G): cf. styles
cuttle-bone 88, 157

dagger 32, 88, 103, 139
Dampier Land 215, 223
dance *43, 47,* 67, 115, *115,* 139, 201, 209; dance club *134;* emblem 111, 114, 145, 160; mask *125, 144*; paddle 180; rattle 117; shield *101,* 120, *133,* 153; staff *88,* 89, *111,* 136, 140, 157, 180
Daudai 134
death 70; death cult 146
decorative art (G), 194
deities: cf. gods
Delamere 216
demi-gods 79
D'Entrecasteaux Is. 120
Depuch Is. 218
digging-stick 33, 208
Digul R. 33, 99, 112, 124, 127
Dimi figures 216
Djiginabu *87*
dogs 17, 34, 76, 77, *158,* 196, 199, *208*
dolphin *132,* 155
Dongson 27, 28
'donors of salvation' (G), 61
doors 112; door-jambs *121,* 134, 137, *143,* 161, 162
dove *128*
dragon 99
drama 67, 209
drums (G), 175; hour-glass drum 103, 106, 117, 136; pounding drum 76; slit-drum 76, 106, 160; stamping drum 76
Drysdale Ranges 215
dualism (G), 83
dugongs *171*
Dukduk *130,* 150
Duke of York Is. 149, 152
dye 91
dynamism (G), 57-9, 71, 187

eagle 76
Earth Mother 82
East Indies 51
Easter I. 22, *167,* 176-8, 184-5; geography of 15; script of 17; settlement of 23; raw materials on 51
coony 89, *111, 112*
Eilanden R. *110, 113,* 127
Ellice Is. 23
emblems *44,* 111, 114, *116,* 145, 153, 159, 160, 168
emu (G), *208,* 214, 220, 225
engraving *43, 53, 57,* 89, 91, 92, 131, 134, *146,* 209, *210, 212,* 212-3, *213, 215, 216, 218, 220, 221,* 222, *223,* 223
Etna Bay 124
Eurasia 26, 27
Europe 27, 35, 188, 191, 193, 196, 199, 206, 207; Western Europe 50; prehistoric 38; races of 31, 32, 35, 40
evolution (G)

fabrics 166, 179-180; cf. clothing
fan 173
fauna 16, 199
feather *67, 68, 70, 72,* 88, *102,* 109, *118,* 160, 168, 170, 173, 175-6, 200, 212; belt 85; box *196, 199;* cape 85, 89, *161*; costume 162; head-dress 89; helmet 89; mosaic 89
fertility (G), 59, 70, 76, *107,* 137, 176, 202, 216
Fessoa *129*
festivals 70, 103, 106, 114, 131, 142, 170; cf. rites
Fiji Is. *152, 153, 155,* 165-6, 184; geography of 29; pottery in 32, 86; implements in 51
Finschhafen *80*
fish 16, 21, *53,* 79, 80, *86,* 99, 103, *112,* 117, 119-120, *122-3,* 136, *136,* 137, 145, *150,* 155, 157, 160, 176, 180, 196, 218, *219,* 221; fishing 33-4, 79, 95, 186
fishermen 22, 72, 200
fixatives 212
flax *192,* 194, 196
Flinders Ranges 210
flutes 76, 106
Fly R. 131, 134, 137
fly-whisk *148,* 169
food-gatherers (G), 20, 61, 73, 82, 183, 186-7, 207, 225
food stores 191, 194, 200, *201,* 202, 204, *205*
foodstuffs 16, 17, 20, 21, 33, 34, 209
forest 79
Formosa 21, 26

Forrest R. 215
fowl 17, 34
France 51
frigate-bird 137, 155
fruit 91, *103*, 117, *117*, 131, 145
funerary figures *135*, 160
furniture 55, 137

game 20
gaming-boards 175
Gaua *141*
Gazelle peninsula *124*, *125*, *130*, *132*, 149, 150
gecko (G), 204
Geelvink Bay *36*, *62*, 99
Gilbert Is. 23, 179
Gillen, F. J. 220
Giro-giro figures (G), 215
glauconite 210
gods 35, 61, 73, 77, 79, 80, 83, 129, *151*, *154*, *156*, 165, 166, 168, 170, 172-3, 175, 176, 179, 199, 200, 202, 204, 206
godsticks 194, 199-200, *203*, 206
gourds *54*, 89, 91, 140, 157, 175
Green R. *80*, 112
Groote Eylandt *219*, 221
ground drawings (G), 209; paintings *208*, 212, 214, 220
Guadalcanal *131*
guardian figures 103, 153, *156*, 173
Gurunga 210
gypsum 210

hair-dress *103*, *108*, *126*, *157*, 175
hakea 210
haliotis iris 201
hand stencils 213-4
Hansa Bay *66*
harvest ceremonies (G): cf. ceremonies
Hawaii Is. 23, 85, 89, *156*, *158*, *164*, 173, 176, 181, 184-5, 191, 199
Hawkesbury R. 212 218
headband *52*, 88, 89, 173
head-dress 88, 89, 115, *115*, 120, 142, 178; cf. caps
head-hunting 70, 76, 88, *92*, 108, 128; head trophies *134*
head-rest *49*, *62*, 100, 119, 166
heads of money 161
Heine-Geldern, R. 187-8
hei tiki *195*, 196
heke 193
helmet 89, 175
Hervey I. *162*, *163*
Heyerdahl, Th. 17
Hienghene *142*

Horouta 193
hour-glass drum: cf. drums
houses 55, 69, *78*, 96, 103, *121*, 155, 172, 179, 191, 194, 196, 199, 200; cf. cult-houses
Hukere 200, *203*
human figures: cf. motifs
Humboldt Bay *44*, 100-3, 184
hunters, nomadic 20, 21, 48, 72, 73, 183, 186-7, 207; hunting 34, *52*, 59, 61, *75*, 82; cf. head-hunting
Huon peninsula 72, 76, 99, 115, 188; Gulf *80*, 117-120, 163, 175, 179, 183-4, 188
Hura-waitkata 199

Ice Age 19-20
idols *39*, *92*, *128*, *151*, *154*, *158*, 173, *174*, *193*, 199, 202, *203*
Imilu 210
implements 16, 17, 20, 28, 29, 32, 39, 51, 55, 67, 69, 89, 91-2, 106, 111-2, 119-120, 131, 140, 145, 155, 163, 165, 66, 168-9, 173, 175, 179-180, 209, 218
Inagurdurwil 209
India 27, 204
Indochina 20, 186
Indonesia 20, 22, 26, 28, 29, 32, 80, 100, 124-5, 166, 184-6, 204, 206, 207
Ingiet 152
initiation (G), *64*, *69*, 70, *75*, *87*, *90*, *93*, 114, 129, 142, 153, 213, 220; cf. Bora
inlay *128*, *132*, *136*, 152, 155, 157, 179, *198*, 201
insignia 85, 163
irrigation 33
Iron Age 27, 28
Iru *109*
Islam 124
ivory 88, 165, 172

jade: cf. nephrite
Japan 21, 26
Jerik *98*
jewellery 27, *36*, 88, 140, 173, 175, *195*, 197
jungle 50, 62

Kailua *156*
Kalaia *208*
Kambrambo *56*
Kampong R. 127
Kanabu *50*
kangaroo 214, 219, 220, 225
Kaniet *150*
kaokao 196
kapkap *50*, 88, 140, 142, 149, 155, 157, 173
Kapriman *84*

Kararau *68, 72*
kava (G), 33, 160, 165
Keram 89, 96, 109
Kerewa *100*
Kerker *67*
Kilimbit *53*
Kimberley 215, 216
King R. 215
Kiriwina *88, 89*
Kiwa 193
knotting 32
Kon-Tiki 17
Konos *119*
Korewori *61, 74, 75, 84,* 110-2
Korogo *72*
Korosemeri 112
korwar (G), 36, 99, 100; style 99, 120, 125, 139, 155, 184
Koururu 199, 202
Kupkei *77*
Kusaie 180

lamp *152,* 179
language of Oceanic peoples 17, 18, 19, 137; cf. Austronesian (pre-Austronesian), Melanesia, Micronesia, Polynesia
Lavongai: cf. New Hanover
legend 70, 197-9, 202
Lelet *115,* 146
lime (G), *51, 53, 54, 56, 63, 76, 83, 89, 92, 100, 103, 108, 111, 112, 114,* 117, 119, *119,* 120, 137, 140, *150, 177,* 180; cf. spatula
limonite 210
limestone 86, 91, *120, 131,* 196
lizard 80, 103, 106, *109,* 119, *137,* 176, 196, 199, 204
local cultures (G): cf. styles
Lorentz R. *102,* 112, *113,* 127
Lou 137
Louisiade Archipelago 22, 120
Loyalty Is. 160

Madagascar 22
magic (G), 59-60, 71, 95, 136, 152, *154,* 157, 160, 168-9, 172, 194, 196, 197
Maketu 205
malanggan (G): carvings 142-5; figures 89, *122-3, 126,* 145, 146, 149; frieze *129;* masks 142; style *122-3, 129,* 188
malatji *208*
Malaya 17
Malayo-Polynesian (language) 19; cf. Austronesian
Malekula *138,* 157, 159
Mamberamo R. 97, 99, 100
mana (G), 59, 61, 79-81, 83, 197
manaia *196,* 199, *201,* 202
Mangaia I. *163,* 172
manism (G), 60; cf. ancestor worship, animism
Manus 137, 139; Manus I. *103, 108, 109,* 137
Maori 86, 191-206; cf. classic Maori culture, 'pre-Fleet', 'post-Fleet' periods
Mapi R. 124
Maprik *47,* 69, *87,* 89, *90, 93,* 106, 108, 110, 112, 114-5, 142, 145
Maravo Lagoon *128*
marakihau *197,* 199, 204
Marianas 179; weaving on 32; rice-growing on 33
Marienberg *67*
Marind-anim 124, 128-9, 131
Marquesas Is. 23, 27, 88, *154, 165, 166,* 172-3, *173,* 184-5
Marshall Is. 23, 179
marsupials 16, *84,* 145, 212
Masanei *74*
masks 67, 70-1, 76, 86, 91, 99, 106, 108, 110, 111, 129, 131, 136-7, 142, 145-6, 149-150, 153, 157-160, 162, 180, 183-5, 201, 202; basketry *93,* 96, 114, 124, 127; clan mask *68*; cone-shaped mask *130,* 132; dance mask 144; face mask *67, 70, 72, 85*; finial mask *198,* 199; gable mask *58*; head mask *117, 118*; helmet mask *64,* 132, 153; pointed mask *130*; secret society mask *130, 138*; shield mask *116*; skull mask *124*; wooden mask 88, 109, *115,* 115, 119, *177*
Massim *88, 89, 101,* 120
Matankol 137
Matatua 193, 199
matrilineal clan structure 83
mats 179
May R. *80,* 111
Mbranda *52*
McCluer Gulf 124
Medina *50*
Mediterranean, eastern 28
Megalithic monuments (G), 27-8
Melanesia: agriculture in 33; carvings in 73, 76, 86, 88, 180, 181; culture of 20, 22, 27, 28, 29, 31, 32, 37, 73, 76, 83, 163-5; geography of 15, 29, 33; implements in 91-2; languages in 19; masks in 76, 86; Megalithic phenomena in 28; ornaments in 76, 88; ornamental style in 27, 97-100; painting in 76, 86, 91, 181; pottery in 32, 34; races in 19, 23, 30, 31; raw materials in 88, 91; religious beliefs in 35, 60, 61, 66, 69, 70, 72, 82; rites in 76; settlement of 22, 26, 27, 31, 97, 183; shrines in 86; social structure in 34-5, 82; weaving in 32
Melville I. 210, 221

Menge 150
men's house (G), *44*, 77, 94, *98*, 99, 103, 106, 137, 159, 160, *169*, *171*, *178*, *179*, 180
Mesolithic 20
metals 32; metal-working 26
Micronesia: agriculture in 33, 34; architecture in 94; culture of 22, 26, 29, 30, 32, 83, 179-180, 187; geography of 15, 19; implements in 91-2; influences exerted from 140; languages in 19, 32; objects in 157; pottery in 32; races in 19, 26, 31-2; raw materials in 51, 91; religion in 35, 61, 80; settlement of 23, 28; social structure of 35, 83; styles in 97, 185; weaving in 32; cf. Para-Micronesia
migrations: cf. settlement
Milingimbi *215*, *216*, *220*
Mimi figures (G), 216, 217
Mimika 124, 125-8
Minahassa peninsula 155
moa (G), 191, 196
moa-hunter period 191, 193, *193*, 199, 204
mollusc-shells 16, 88, 136, 172
Moluccas 21, 23
Mongoloid (G), 22, 26, 31, 32
monotheism (G), 61
moon 145
mortar 28, 69
Mortlock *177*, 180
mosaic: cf. feather
mother-of-pearl 88, *119*, *128*, *132*, 136, *136*, 152, 155, *158*, 175, 179
motifs 106; anthropomorphic *60*, *100*, *113*, 134, 136, 139, 152, 170, 172; human *47*, 97, 99-100, 103, 106, *106*, 108, 109, *110*, 112, *113*, 117, 119, 120, 125, 128, *128*, 134, 136, *137*, 139, 140, *141*, 145, *147*, 152, 153, 155, 157, 162, *163*, 165, 169, 170, 172-3 176, 178, 180, 185, 187, 196, 199, 200, *201*, 202, 215, 218, 220, 221, 223, *224*; cf. animal motifs, mythology
mummification 197
Mundugumor 109
Murray R. 219
musical and sound-making instruments 76, 106, 108, *209*, 225; cf. bull-roarers, drums, flutes, trumpets
Mussau I. cf. St. Matthias Is.
mussel-shells 168
myths 70, 72-3, 77, 129, 185, 199, 208, 212, 213, 215, 219, 221, 225; mythical figures *52*, 67, 69, 71, *93*, 99, 106, 110, *122-3*, *126*, 132, 136, 142, 145, 163, 186, *208*, *211*, 214, 220, 221, 223; mythology *56*, 76, 80, 82-3, 96, 146, 176, 179, 187, 188-9

naga 204
Nakanei *132*
Nama *208*
Namatanai 146, 149
neck-rest: cf. head-rest
Negroids (G), 20-1, 23, 31-2
Nemassalang *117*
Neolithic 22, 191
nephrite 86, *195*, 196, 204
net sinkers 86, 120, 155
New Britain 117, *132*, 149-150, 183; aboriginal culture in 35; Papuan culture in 21; masks in 88, 89, *124*, *125*, *130*, 149
New Caledonia 21, *142*, *143*, *144*, *146*, *149*, 160-3
New Georgia *128*, 155
New Guinea: agriculture in 17, 20, 21, 33; architecture in 77, 94; carving in 88, 109; culture of 20, 21, 23, 27, 28, 29, 30, 32, 73, 106; geography of 15, 16, 27, 48, 97-8; implements in 69; language in 31; masks in 88, 89, 145; Papuan culture in 21; races in 19, 20, 23, 30, 31, 33; religion in 59, 61, 69, 72, 73, 77, 82; settlement of 18, 20, 22, 77, 125, 183; social structure of 82, 83; style in 97, 115, 175, 188; external influences on 149; central 89, 108; eastern *89*, 120; northern *38*, *47*, *53*, *63*, *66*, 89, 99, 115, 142, 175, 180, 183 188; north-eastern 86, 188; north-western *36*, *62*, 89, 120, 125; southern 124, 183; south-western *107*, 112, *113*; western 99, 184; cf. individual regions
New Hanover 140, 142, 146
New Hebrides: aboriginal culture in 35; art in 157, 160, 184; carving in 88, 89, *137*, *140*; masks *138*; painting in 142; people of 31; religious beliefs in 69; social structure in 86
New Ireland 22, 69, 89, *115*, 140, 142, 149, 152, 184, 188; central *51*, 88, *115*, *119*, *120*, 142, 146; southern 86; north-western *50*, *117*, *122-3*, *126*, *129*, 142, 145
New South Wales 212, 217, 220
New Zealand 191-206; architecture in 94, 199; cultures of 191; geography of 15, 29, 191, 194; implements in 193; painting in 194-6; religious beliefs in 194, 199; settlement of 23, 27, 191, 193, 200-1; wood-carving in 197-9, 202; North Island 196, 200; South Island 196, 204; cf. Maori
niho taniwha 196
Nitendi *50*, *134*
nomads (G), 183, 207; semi-nomads 33, 149
notched decoration 88, 89, 180
Nuku Hiva *165*
Nukumanu 163
Nukuoro 29, *174*, 179, 180
Numbungai *93*
nut-shells *134*

obsidian 92, 139
ochre *197*, 200, *201*, *203*, *205*, 210, 215, 222
Oenpelli 214
Okia Flat *193*
Oleai *168*
Omo *115*
open-work *62*, 88, 100, 103, 111, 114-5, *115*, 125, *129*, 134, 137, 140, 145, 155, 160, *162*, 173, 184
opossum (G), 119, *210*, 212
oracle 114
ore 91, 210
ornaments (G), 16, 17, 32, 39, *47*, 55, 69, 76, 80, 86, 88, 91, 100, 115, 119, *121*, 140, 142, 155, 157, 160, 179, 180, *195*, 196, 197, 218, 223
Orokolo Bay 132
Otago *193*, 196
Ouebia *143*
Oubatche *146*
outrigger canoe (G), 21
owl 199, 202

paddle *163*; blades 127
painter 95-6
painting *44*, *47*, 47-8, *49*, 50, *51*, 53, *56*, *58*, *63*, *66*, *67*, 69, *70*, *75*, 76, *77*, *78*, *80*, *81*, *82*, *84*, 86, *90*, 91, 94, 96, 99-100, 103, 106, 109, 111-2, 114-5, 117, 119, 120, 125, 131, 139, 142, 146, 149-50, 155, 157, 159-161, 165, 176, 178, 179-180, 183-6, 194-5, 197, *197*, *201*, *203*, *205*, 209-210, 212, 215, 222, 225; cf. bark painting, cave painting, ground painting, Wandjina
Palaeolithic 20, 50, 51, 186
Palau Is. *178*, 179
palm 16, 17, 20, *56*, 89, *90*, 109, 112, 140; leaves *47*, *78*, *81*, *122*, 212
pandanus-palm 33
Papa 197
Papua, Gulf of 89, *92*, 94, *95*, *100*, 112, *116*, *117*, *118*, 124, 131, 183
Papuans (G), 21, 30, 183; Papuan culture 21, 29, 30, 72, 82, 120, 188; Papuan language 19
Para-Micronesia *150*, 163-4
passage rites (G), 69-70, *76*
pataka 201
patiki 196
patina 219
patrilineal clan structure 82
patu paraoa *190*
pestle 28, 69, 86, 173
Philippines 21
Phoenix Is. 23
phormium tenax: cf. flax
pigs 17, 21, 34, 76, *112*, 119, 136, *140*, 145, 155
pigments *44*, *64*, *80*, 91, 194, 197, *205*, 209-210, 212, 213
pipes (tobacco) 112, 134, *215*, *216*, *220*
Pitiliu I. 121
plaiting 32, 124, *133*, 194
plants 33, 34, 73, 129; tuberous 33; plant figures 131, 221, 223
planters 22, 77; planter culture 72, 73, 76, 82-3, 186-7
Pleistocene 19, 20, 21
pluvial period: cf. Pleistocene
pocked markings 217, 218, 219
poetry 50
poker-work (G), 89, 91, 139, 140, 180
Polynesia: agriculture in 33, 34; carving in 88, 157; culture of 22, 26, 29, 30, 31, 32, 37, 77, 80, 83, 172, 179, 187, 204; geography of 15; implements in 51, 91-2; languages in 19; pottery in 32; races in 19, 23, 26, 31, 79; raw materials in 88; religion in 35, 59, 61, 69, 77, 79, 80; settlement of 17, 23, 26, 28, 185; social structure of 80, 83, 85; styles of 80, 97, 185; central 172-3, 175, 178, 184; eastern 26, 172, 191, 204; north-western 163, 165, 184; western 172-3, 204
polytheism 61
Ponape 180
Port Hedland 218
Port Keats *213*, *223*
Port Moresby 124
Possession Cape 131
post-Fleet period 191, 193
posts *41*, *74*, *78*, 99, 115, 119, 140, 155, 157, 159, 160, 173, 179-180, 204
pottery 21, 26, 32, 34, 86, 92, 209
pounamu 196
pounder 127, *166*
pounding drum: cf. drums
pre-Austronesians (G): cf. Austronesians
pre-Fleet period 191
priests 77, 85, 95, 99, 165
Prince Alexander Range 114
puberty 69, 70
Purari *95*, *118*

Queensland 125, 217, 222, 222
quiver 100, 117

radio-carbon dating (G), 20, 21, 23, 28, 191
Ramu 99, 106, 108
Raiatea 79
Rangi 197
Rangi-tamaku 199

Rarotonga 172
rattan *64,* 89, *92, 93, 103, 116, 117, 118, 126,* 127, 131, *133,* 145, 146, 183
Rauru 199
raw materials 51, 92, 94, 165, 191
ray 92
religious beliefs 35, 38, 46, 55-85, *56,* 95, 96, 165, 173, 175, 176, 186-7, 208; religious ceremonies 66, 67, 142; religious works of art 95, 114, 117, 137, 149, 165, 170, 172, 184, 214, *215;* cf. rites, sacred objects
reptiles 218; cf. lizard, *naga,* snake
rhizome 91
rice 26, 33
rites *41,* 70, 71, 76, 80, 85-6, 96, 106, 108, 110, 129, 136-7, 146, 160, 172-3, 176, 180, 184, 209, 212, 214, 220, 221, 225
rites de passage: cf. passage rites
rock drawings and engravings 50, 186-7, 196, 209, 212, 217, 218; rock paintings 196; rock poundings 217, 218-9; rock-shelter 196, 209
Rongo 199, 202
roof decorations 103, 114, 120, 160
roots 71, 89, 145
Rotorua, Lake *201*
Rua 197-9
Rua-i-te-pukenga 199
Rurutu 172

sacred objects 222-3, *223*
sago (G), 33, 127; sago-palm *56*
Sahara 217
St. Matthias Is. 51, *54,* 111, *112, 114,* 157, 180
Samoa 23, 26, 166-170, 184-5
San Cristoval I. *132, 136*
sandstone 160, 212, 218
Sandwich Is. 23
Saipan culture 21
Santa Cruz Is. 32, *50,* 88, *134,* 157
sarcophagus *131,* 155
Saukorem *36*
Schmitz, C. A. 72, 187-8
Schouten Is. 99
script 17, 45
sculptor 95-6, 142-5, 176, 178
sculpture (G), *41, 47,* 50-4, *52,* 61-2, 67, 69, 73, 76, 86, *90,* 92, 94, 99-101, 106, *106,* 108, *108, 110-1,* 115, 117, 119, 120, *120, 122-3,* 128, 131, 134, *135,* 137, 140, 149, 152, 153, 155, 157-8, *159,* 160, 162-3, 164-5, 166, *167,* 168-9, 170, 175, 179-180, 183-7, 194, 197, 209, 213, 223
sea-cow 136, 180
sea-shells 34, 161
sea-snails 146
secret societies 70-1, *130, 138,* 149, 150, 152, 159, 160
seeds 91, *102,* 131
selenite 210
semi-nomads: cf. nomads
Sentani, Lake 27, *41, 63,* 100-3, 184
sepia 88
Sepik 21, 82, 86, 89, 97, 106, 131, 145; district *49,* 51, *52, 61,* 86, 88-9, 94, 96, 100, 103-114, 117, 124, 128, 183-5; lowlands 69, *75, 77, 84,* 108, 112, 128; lower *56, 67,* 106, 109; middle *38, 53, 58, 64, 68, 74, 76, 78,* 88, 106, 109-112, 114, 179; upper 33, *80,* 89, 106, 111-2, 125
settlement 17-29, 76, 77, 187-8, 191
shark 92
shells 16, 88, 92, 109, *126,* 145, 179, *198,* 201, 223; shell money *123;* cf. bivalve shells, clam-shells, cowrie-shells, mussel-shells, tridacna shells, trochus shells, turtle-shells, univalve shells
shields *58, 80,* 89, *95, 101,* 111-2. *113,* 119-20, 127-8, 132, *133,* 134, 152-3, 207, 209, 212, 222
shield masks (G): cf. masks
shrine 86
Siassi 117
sib (G): cf. clan
skink (G): cf. lizard
skulls *36, 60,* 88, *92,* 109, 111, 146, 150, 155, 159, 160, 172; skull-container 99; skull mask *124*
Slei *78*
sling 32
slit-drum: cf. drums
snails: opercula of 51, 117, 119, 129
snake 73, *86,* 89, 99, *101,* 103, 106, *112,* 114, 119, 120, *129,* 134, 145, 155, 160, *208,* 214, 219, 220
social structure 34-5, 38, 57, 80, 82, 83, 85, 86, 164-5, 170, 172, 173, 175, 176, 187; cf. matrilineal, patrilineal, secret societies
Society Is. 23, 79, 169, 184-5, 191; cf. Raiatea
Solomon Is. 22, *39, 60,* 86, 88, *127, 128, 131, 132,* 152-7, 184-5; central 153-5; eastern 155-7; western *135,* 153
Spain 51, 217
spatula *89, 103, 108,* 119-120, 137, 140, *150*
spear 32, 89, 120, 128, 140, 155, 207, *209;* spear-head *108;* spearman *209;* spear-thrower (G), 207, *209, 212,* 212, 217, 222
Speiser, F. 187-8
Spencer, B. 220
sperm-whale 88, 165
spirits *36, 64, 68, 75, 90,* 115, *118,* 132, 137, 144, 153, 159, 161, 180, 202; spirit boats 180; spirit figures *52,* 112, 168; spirit houses 106, 179
spoons 179

staffs *88*, 89, *111*, 136, *138*, 140, 157, 163, 172, 178, 179-180
stamping drum: cf. drums
sting-ray *108*, 139
stone 69, 71, 191; club-head 69; implements 20, 69, 86, 91-2, 155, 206, 213; platforms 170; object *140*, 155, 160, 169, 173, 191, 204, 210, 212, *221*; polishing of 21; sculpture 51, 86, 157, 168, 172, 175, 176, 178, 179, 194; stonemason 95; structures 94; stone-working 172
Stone Age 32, 207
stools 111, 127
style (G), 29, 48, 53, 181-9; abstract 111; archaic 193; 'beak style' *49*, *66*, 108-9, 160, 188; curvilinear *56*, *58*, *63*, *68*, *75*, *76*, *78*, *81*, *89*, 103, 106, *110*, 111, 112, 120, 128, 131, 134, 140, *150*, 152, 157, 173, 183-5, 188, 197, 204; figures holding the abdomen 100, 172, 183; figures with arms raised 183; local *70*, *72*, *74*, *75*, 99, 106, 108, 150, 152, 188; rectilinear style *87*, *141*, *143*, *147*, 157, *159*, 162, 163, 166, 168, 173, 180, 185, 196, 204; style provinces 97-180; X-ray 216, 221; cf. *korwar*, vitalistic (G)
Sulka (G), *133*, 150, 152, 183
sun 76, 145, 146
Supreme Being (G), 61-2
Suque (G), 159, 160
suspension hooks (G), 111, 119
sweet potato: cf. batata
Switzerland 15

Tabar Is. 140, 142, 146
taboo (G), 59, 194
Tahiti 85, *148*, *166*, 169, 185, 191
Tainui 193
Takitimu 193
Tambunum *58*, *64*
Tami (G), *80*, *82*, *83*, *85*, *86*, *98*, 117, 119, 139, 152, 163, 183, 188; cf. *korwar*
Tangaroa 197
taniko *192*, 194
taniwha 196, 204
tapa (G): cf. bark-cloth
tapu: cf. taboo
Taranaki 204
taro 21, 33
Tasmanians 19-21, 30; Tasmanian culture 29, 183
tattoo 173, 194, 197, 201
Taupo 204
Tauu I. 163-4
Taylor, R. 200
technology 38, 48, 51, 63, 86, 94, 112, 128-9, 140, 163, 166, 172, 176
Telefolmin 112
Tempe Downs 210
temple *156*
Te Oha 201
Te Puawai-o-te Arawa *205*
tern 131
textiles 32
Thailand 20
Tiki *154*
tobacco 33
tohunga 194
Tokomaru 193
Tonga *157*, 166-170, 184, 185, 204
Tonking 27
tools 33, 55, 91, 94, 173, 206, 207, 209, 212, 213, 222, 225
Torembi 72
Torres Straits 88 124, 134, 137
totemism (G), 60-1, *123*, 129, 220, 221
totara 206
trade 139
tree-fern 89, *137*, *138*, 159, 160
tridacna shells 155
Trobriand Is. *88*, *89*, *101*, 120
trochus shells 34
Truk 180, 182
trumpets 76, 106, 128, 173, 179
Tuamotu Archipelago 23
tuatara 204
tuberous plants 176; cf. taro
tukutuku 196
tumbuan *130*
turtle 16, 77, 88, 136, 165, 180, 212; turtle-shells *50*, 92, 117, 140, 172, 173
tusks *47* *52*, *67*, 92, *138*, 160, 165

Ukurawi *95*
uli (G), 142; figures 146, 149; rites 146
Ulupu *47*
Umboi I. *57*, *85*, *98*, 117
univalve shells *43*, *47*, *52*, *67*, *68*, *70*, *72*, 88
Ussiai 137

vessels *53*, *57*, *61*, *63*, *76*, *83*, *86*, 103, *109*, 112, 117, 128, 132, 139-140, *152*, 155, 160, 165, *165*, 166, 173, 175, 179, 208
Victoria *210*
vitalistic style (G): cf. styles
Viti Is. 165
Vitu Is. 150, 152
Vogelkop peninsula 27, *36*, 99
volcanic rock *39*, 86, *154*, 155, 157, *166*; tufa 176

Waerenga *201*
waka-huia *196*, 199, 204

walrus 165
Wandjina (G), 215, 216
Wanganui 200, *203*, 204
Wango *136*
Wapo *116*
Wapo-Gope *92*
warfare *43*, *47*, *52*, 59, *75*, 79, 108, 115, *128*, 132-3, *133*, 152, *157*, *159*, 166, 168, 170, 173, 175, 191; gods of war 80, *156*, *158*, 173
Warramunga 220
Washkuk 109-11
weapons 16, 17, 32, 55, 69, 106, *116*, 120, 145, 153, 155, 166, 173, 191, 207, 209, *210*, 212, 218, 222
weaving 26, 180, 194, 209; techniques 32, 96, 194
whakairo rakau 197
Whakatane *197*
whale 176, 191, 199, 202
Wharekura 199
Wickliffe Bay 193
Wilgamia 210
withes 89, *93*, *114*, *116*, 131, *144*, 175
Wollunqua 220
wood 16, 51, 73, 89, 92, 109, 176, 191; architecture 94, *122-3*, *201*, 202; boards 160, 162, 201, 202; carving *36*, *41*, *52*, *66*, 76, 79, *79*, *80*, *82*, *84*, *87*, 89, *98*, 100, *102*, 103, *110*, 119, *119*, 124, *126*, *128*, *129*, *131*, 145, *151*, 157, *158*, 159, 163, 165, 168, 170, 172-3, *174*, 175, 176, 178, 179, 180, *182*, 183, 193, 194, 197-8, 202, 204, *205*, *211*, 223; masks *65*, *70*, *72*, *85*, 88, 115, *115*, *117*, 119, 137, 145, 150, 152, *177*, 180; musical instruments 106; objects *49*, *63*, *83*, *85*, *88*, *89*, *103*, *108*, *109*, 117, 119, 120, 127, 128, *132*, 132, *134*, 139, *148*, *149*, *150*, 155, 160, *162*, *163*, 165, *165*, 169, *173*, 178-9, *199*, 209, 212, *213*, *218*, 223; weapons *58*, *95*, 191; wood-working 32, 92, 145, 166
Woodlark Is. 120

X-ray style (G): cf. styles

yam 33, 77, *86*, 120
Yap *171*, 179-180
Yarapi *208*, 214
Yellow R. 112
Yeshan 109-111
York, Cape 207
Yuat 52, *70*, 109, 117
Yule R. 219